*The Arizona Diary
of Lily Frémont,
1878–1881*

The Arizona Diary of Lily Frémont,

1878–1881

Edited by Mary Lee Spence

The University of Arizona Press
Tucson

The University of Arizona Press
© 1997
The Arizona Board of Regents
All Rights Reserved

⊗ This book is printed on acid-free, archival-quality paper
Manufactured in the United States of America
First printing

Library of Congress Cataloging-in-Publication Data

Frémont, Lily, b. 1842.
  The Arizona diary of Lily Frémont, 1878–1881 / edited by Mary Lee Spence.
    p. cm.
  Includes bibliographical references and index.
  ISBN 0-8165-1449-6 (cloth : acid-free paper)
  1. Frémont, Lily, b. 1842—Diaries.   2. Children of governors—Arizona—
Prescott—Diaries.   3. Silver mines and mining—Arizona—Prescott Region—
History.   4. Gold mines and mining—Arizona—Prescott Region—History.
5. Prescott (Ariz.)—Social life and customs.   6. Arizona—Politics and
government—To 1950.   I. Spence, Mary Lee.   II. Title.
F819.P9F74   1997
979.1/04/092—dc20
[B]   96-25304
                                                                            CIP

British Cataloguing-in-Publication Data
A catalogue record for this book is available
from the British Library.

Publication of this book is made possible in part by a grant from the J. W.
Kieckhefer Foundation of Prescott, Arizona.

For Clark

Contents

Illustrations

Acknowledgments

Many scholars, librarians, and institutions have assisted in the preparation of this volume. Although it is impossible to list them all by name, I am profoundly grateful to them. At the institutional level, I would like to single out several for special thanks: Columbia University (Allan Nevins Papers, Rare Book and Manuscript Library) for making the diary available to me and granting me permission to reproduce it; the Henry E. Huntington Library and the University of Illinois (both the Research Board and the History Department) for their financial support; the Sharlot Hall Museum for its archives on Prescott; and the University of Arizona Press, my publisher, for its sustained interest in the project.

At the personal level, I wish to thank University of Illinois professors Stanley Shinall for assistance with French translations and John Hoffmann for advice on knotty research problems. Robert Spude of the National Park Service answered questions about Arizona mining; Alice S. Creighton of the Nimitz Library and Constance W. Altshuler provided information about some of the naval and army officers. In person and by correspondence, James E. Officer of the University of Arizona explored with me the question of the Frémonts' Tucson residence or residences. On more than one occasion, Clark Spence extracted me from computer problems, and Dawn Dollard of Dewey, Arizona, responded to my pleas for information on nineteenth-century Prescottonians. Special thanks goes to Pamela Herr for encouragement and for insights into Elizabeth Benton Frémont's character.

Above all, I am grateful to Paula Frémont Cummings (the great-great-niece of Elizabeth Benton Frémont) of Boulder, Colorado, for granting the Frémont family's permission to publish the diary.

Editorial Procedures

The manuscript diary of Elizabeth Benton (Lily) Frémont is among the papers of John C. Frémont's biographer, Allan Nevins, in the Rare Book and Manuscript Library at Columbia University. The handwriting is small but quite legible; in editing the diary, I followed the text as closely as the demands of typography would permit. In the matter of capitalization I followed the original unless Lily's intention was not clear, in which case I resorted to modern practice. Often, in the interests of clarity, a long involved sentence has been broken into two sentences. Missing periods at the ends of sentences have been supplied, dashes terminating sentences have been supplanted by periods, and superfluous dashes after periods have been omitted. In abbreviations, raised letters have been brought down and a period supplied if modern usage calls for one. Words underscored in the manuscript have been italicized.

Procedures for dealing with missing or illegible words, conjectural readings, and other items are shown in the list of abbreviations and editorial aids that follows this section. Throughout the text, Lily Frémont spelled proper names, such as Willcox and Wollenberg, inconsistently. If I know the correct spelling, I show the correction at the first mention but continue thereafter with her rendition. The spellings of proper names in the census of 1880 and in the newspapers sometimes differ from each other as well as from hers.

Lily Frémont was also inconsistent in the use of the apostrophe to indicate the possessive case. Where she failed to supply it, I have done so unless it is not essential to the meaning.

The notes to the diary identify and explain people, places, and events. People are identified at their first mention with sufficient biographical information for understanding the text; these identifications are not comprehensive biographical sketches, and no source is cited if the information is to be found in standard directories, genealogies, and similar aids. Where it has been difficult to identify a person, however, the source is cited.

To avoid the constant repetition of names, I have freely used the initials JCF, JBF, EBF, and NHB for John Charles Frémont, Jessie Benton Frémont, Elizabeth Benton Frémont, and Ella (Nelly) Haskell Browne, respectively.

For the most part the diary was kept daily or written from notes shortly after the events occurred and is remarkably accurate. Indeed, Lily Frémont documented her writing activities: "I sat up late copying my 'notes'" (Jan. 3, 1879).

Routine entries recounting visits and visitors have been omitted from this book, as well as some information on eastern friends, which adds nothing to the Arizona story; these omissions constitute less than 5 percent of the diary. Such omissions are indicated by ellipses.

Abbreviations and Editorial Aids

EBF, Elizabeth Benton Frémont
FP, Frémont Papers
JBF, Jessie Benton Frémont
JCF, John Charles Frémont
MP, Morton Papers
NHB, Nelly Haskell Browne
RP, Rogers Papers
SHM, Sharlot Hall Museum
[ ] Word or phrase supplied or corrected. Editorial remarks within the text are italicized and enclosed in square brackets.
[?] Conjectural reading, or conjectural identification of an addressee.
[. . .] A word or two missing or illegible. Longer omissions are specified in notes.

*The Arizona Diary
of Lily Frémont,
1878–1881*

Introduction

On October 4, 1878, two days before she reached Prescott, Elizabeth Benton Frémont wrote in her diary, "Gov. Hoyt and Sec. Gosper arrived at about 3, having come out to meet Father. I suggested that as two emperors meet on barges in the middle of rivers so the two governors should stand on a broad plank in Date Creek & discuss the territorial affairs." With this simple entry, the thirty-six-year-old daughter of the famous explorer established her reason for being in the Territory of Arizona, her sense of humor, and her knowledge of history. Date Creek was not the Niemen River, nor were outgoing governor John Philo Hoyt and incoming governor John Charles Frémont the warring emperors Alexander I of Russia and Napoleon Bonaparte of France. Whereas in 1807 the two emperors had discussed peace and the fate of Europe, the two governors in 1878 discussed territorial elections. After taking tea with the Frémonts, Hoyt and Gosper hurried back to Prescott, the capital of the Territory of Arizona, to prepare for the formal entry of the new official family on October 6.

In addition to Elizabeth (or Lily, as she was known), Frémont was accompanied by his wife, Jessie Benton Frémont—the daughter of deceased senator Thomas Hart Benton—and his twenty-three-year-old son, Francis Preston Frémont (Frank), who had dropped out of West Point because of incipient tuberculosis but aspired to an army commission and received it while in Arizona. The family was accompanied by a maid, Mary McGrath; their dog, Thor; and a Chinese cook, Ah Chung, who had joined them in San Francisco. Left behind in New York were Lily's other brother, young naval officer John Charles Frémont, Jr. (Charley), and his wife, Sally Anderson. Sally's "unexpected & dangerous illness"—Lily's euphemism for the premature birth and death of the young Frémonts' child—was one of the reasons for the governor's three-month delay in departing for his post.

Although he had been the Republican Party's first presidential candidate in 1856, Frémont was out of political favor due largely to his checkered Civil War career and the bankruptcy of the Memphis, El Paso, and

Elizabeth Benton (Lily) Frémont, early 1860s.
(Courtesy of the Billings Mansion Archives, Woodstock, Vt.)

Pacific Railroad Company with the accompanying accusations of fraud on the Paris bond market. Because he had been the president and chief promoter of the company, not only his reputation but also his possessions were swept away. So desperate were his finances that the family was not always able to live together and Jessie began to write for a living. When Rutherford B. Hayes, an old admirer of his, became president, Frémont sought the support of Republican Party leaders, especially Zachariah Chandler and James G. Blaine, in obtaining the governorship of Arizona. He reminded them that he had saved the Republican Party and ensured the reelection of Abraham Lincoln in 1864 by withdrawing his own candidacy. His appointment as territorial governor came on June 8. The Frémonts were jubilant: it was a last chance to restore the power, wealth, and prestige they had lost. Mining and mine promotion, livestock raising, and railroading beckoned as rewarding enterprises. The family left for the west on September 2.

The capital of Arizona Territory had been returned to Prescott the year before they arrived, and nearby Fort Whipple[1] was the headquarters for the Department of Arizona. Since their founding, the town and the fort had been closely associated with each other and with gold. Eight months after President Lincoln signed the bill separating Arizona from New Mexico on February 24, 1863, the commander of the Department of New Mexico, Brigadier General James H. Carleton, had responded to pleas of miners, including Joseph R. Walker, in north-central Arizona along the Hassayampa River and Big Bug, Lynx, and Weaver Creeks for protection from Indians by sending a military force to the new gold area. The first Fort Whipple, named after Amiel Weeks Whipple, the explorer of northern Arizona in 1853–1854, was located shortly before Christmas on Del Rio Springs in Chino Valley. General Carleton likewise directed the new territorial government officials to northern Arizona, because he believed Tucson was sympathetic to the Confederacy and to the secessionists. Governor John N. Goodwin and his party arrived at Fort Whipple in January 1864.

Almost immediately Goodwin began seeking a suitable place for the meeting of the legislature. Del Rio Springs was not close enough for the gold-panning miners on Lynx and Granite Creeks and was also too far from timber for construction. By late spring Goodwin had decided on a location along Granite Creek. The little settlement that was beginning to spring up along the west bank was named Prescott (at the suggestion of Territorial Secretary Richard C. McCormick) in honor of William Hickling Prescott, author of *History of the Conquest of Mexico,* a best-seller of the times. Almost immediately, the new Fort Whipple was built on the east bank of Granite Creek, two miles northeast of Prescott; the old site of the fort, some twenty miles away, became known as Camp Clark.

The first legislative assembly made Prescott the capital of the territory, but in 1867 the fourth assembly transferred the capital to Tucson. This was a second blow to the struggling community, because the previous year the military headquarters for the territory had also gone to Tucson. Fort Whipple remained in existence, however, and was revitalized in 1869 when Arizona and southern California were formed into a military department with headquarters at Fort Whipple. The loss of the seat of government was temporary; the capital was returned to Prescott in 1877 and remained there for twelve years before being permanently moved to Phoenix in 1889.[2]

The placer gold that had brought the establishment of Fort Whipple and Prescott was quickly taken. With the introduction of more sophisticated mining and milling techniques, the "gold of the land" was augmented by silver and then copper in the Prescott area, thus broadening both the economic and the population base.

Being both territorial capital and military headquarters, Prescott had an enviable position for federal patronage and contracts. In addition, favorable territorial legislation in 1877 aided the Arizona community's quest to become the terminus for wagon roads in northern Arizona. One, heading south into Black Canyon and on to Phoenix, was often taken by Frémont and other Prescottonians. Prescott had also become the financial, supply, and manufacturing center for the expanding ranches and farms to the north, west, and east and for the mines.

New legislation of 1878 seemed to guarantee a continuing profitable sale of silver from such mines by reestablishing a bimetallic standard (after a lapse of five years): under the Bland-Allison Act the treasury was to purchase a limited amount of silver each month and have it coined into silver dollars at the existing legal ratio with gold. At the time, the act was considered a panacea for silver miners and farmers, but for many reasons the price of silver did not rise, nor did commodity prices increase for farmers and others who were interested in a cheaper currency.

However, by April 1879, according to one newspaper, more than 20,000 mines of gold and silver had been located and recorded in Arizona; another reported that between 1863 and February 20, 1880, 7,541 mines had been recorded in Yavapai County, of which Prescott was the county seat.[3] Capital was needed to develop the territory's mineral and scarce water resources, yet without better transportation, the richest of mines would have little value.

By the time the Frémonts reached Arizona, there was still not a mile of railroad within the territory, but that deficiency was quickly corrected. In November 1878, the Southern Pacific began building eastward from Yuma and reached Maricopa (about 150 miles from Prescott, to the south) on April 29, 1879, and Tucson on March 17, 1880. By September 1880, the Southern Pacific had completed rails to the eastern border of the territory. Prescott was not joined to the Atlantic and Pacific, which was building westward from Albuquerque, until the Prescott and Arizona Central was completed on January 1, 1887; this short rail line connected Prescott with Prescott Junction, now called Seligman. Until the rail lines removed some of the remoteness, Arizonans spoke of going "inside" when traveling to other areas of the United States and of going "outside" when returning to the territory. In his first report as governor to the secretary of the interior, Frémont emphasized the importance of rail communication not only within the borders of the United States, but also with Mexico. Rail communication with the seaport of Guaymas he considered a necessity if the rich products of Mexico were to be acquired and the wealth locked up in the mines of Arizona put to use. But for more than six months after the Frémonts' arrival in Arizona, every necessity for work and comfort—from a steam engine to a lemon—had to be hauled in wagons with mule teams over hot and almost waterless lands. There were telegraph connections, and the mail stage could make the distance from Yuma to Prescott in approximately forty-eight hours, but too often the passenger stages were "cheese boxes, drawn by wormy animals." The *Arizona Enterprise* hoped and prayed "for the bursting up of all 'cheap' and nasty mail contractors."[4]

Prescott was approximately 235 miles from Yuma and 245 from Tucson, as calculated by writers of that day. At an altitude of 5,354 feet, it nestled in an exquisite valley with mountains and forest on all sides. In 1878, there were still a great many quail, rabbits, and other small game in the nearby valleys and deer, elk, bear, and wild turkeys in the mountains. The streets were broad but rutted, and all ran with the cardinal points of the compass. In the center of town was a large plaza in which the courthouse had just been completed. Despite the presence of more than twenty saloons in Prescott, many of them on Montezuma Street (called Whiskey Row), the U.S. postal inspector, Benjamin C. Truman, pronounced it the "model frontier settlement of the United States." With some few exceptions, it reminded him of a quiet village in New England, having very little of the violent "man-before-breakfast style" characteristic of settlements in Wyoming or Montana.[5] It had a bank, two newspapers, more than twenty lawyers, sawmills, a foundry, brickyards, three breweries, two hotels, and a number of boardinghouses.[6] In June 1879, Mrs. Frémont noted a "fresh bloom" on Prescott. There were rich discoveries in mines near the town;

the plaza was being fenced in; the donkeys and goats were driven off the streets or impounded; the milliners and dressmakers were too busy to fill all their orders; and the gamblers were up all night.[7] By 1881, Prescott contained "the handsomest mercantile establishments in the Territory, many of which would be a credit to older and more prestigious communities."[8]

A fine school building, the Prescott Free Academy—to which the children from Fort Whipple went in a four-mule "school ambulance"—had been completed in 1876. Its 500-pound bell was a present from the principal, Moses H. Sherman. In the fall of 1878, the enrollment was 163, with the students divided among three departments: primary, intermediate, and high school. The ages of the male students ranged between six and twenty-one years, the females between six and seventeen.[9] It was but a block from the Wilson house occupied by the Frémonts; during the year she was in Prescott, Jessie went up the hill each Friday afternoon to give a history lesson to the older students.

Fraternal orders, popular everywhere in the nation, flourished in Prescott as well: the Knights of Pythias, the Masons, the Odd Fellows, and the Daughters of Rebekah. Churches were not very evident when the Frémonts arrived, and one local newspaper wondered if Arizona had been "given up to the devil."[10] The Roman Catholics were active, and a ball was given in October 1878 to raise funds to build the church,[11] but there were no Protestant Christmas services for Lily to attend in 1878. Mrs. Frémont wrote Bishop John Franklin Spalding that she missed the Episcopal church services but was afraid of overstating the ability of the town to support a clergyman on a permanent basis.[12] The earliest permanent Protestant church came to be the Methodist Episcopal church on Marina Street. The first church wedding occurred there on May 14, 1879. Both Baptist and Congregational churches were organized in the fall of 1880.[13]

On the lighter side, Prescottonians could join the Dramatic Association or attend its theatrical productions, which ranged from the popular minstrels to *H.M.S. Pinafore.* Horse racing attracted many, as did cockfighting, and a few even bought tickets for the short-lived lottery.[14] There were ice cream socials, balls, and dancing, and much visiting back and forth among townspeople and between civilians and fort personnel. Children rode horseback, raced burros, played marbles, flew kites, and gathered wildflowers. Newspapers informed the citizenry who was arriving and leaving town, who was ill, and whom the "angel visitor" had summoned to the "starry home"; they sometimes noted the death of such pets as six-year-old "Stockings," the well-known feline of W. M. Buffum, a prominent merchant. They described wedding gifts and named the givers. Territorial Secretary John J. Gosper presented a saddle pony to Eli P. Clark and

Lucy Sherman on the occasion of their marriage; the editor of the *Arizona Miner* and his wife gave a milch cow. The *Arizona Miner* noted that Mrs. W. N. Kelly had some beautiful goldfish and a nest of little white mice, "real beauties," which had been brought to her from San Francisco by her husband, a merchant. At the 1878 reception for General William Tecumseh Sherman, a newspaper reporter described in great detail the costumes and jewelry of the ladies, but after the reception for the Frémonts he wrote that he hoped "to be smothered in silks and choked to death with lace handkerchiefs" if he ever attempted detailed descriptions of ladies' dresses again.[15]

Society was both formal and informal. Lily implied that it was "bad manners" when acquaintances neglected to call to say goodbye on leaving Prescott. Society was also fractured into cliques; sometimes Lily found it difficult to sort out guest lists for her small dinner parties, with the whole process becoming "an egg-dance" before she was through with it.[16] For example, the Fitch women were unhappy that Clark Churchill, a former law partner of Tom Fitch's, was able to buy their residence, and during the later part of their stay in Prescott, "they made things as unpleasant as they could for" Margaretha Churchill.[17]

Politics in Arizona were becoming increasingly fractured, too, although initially Frémont was well received in Arizona (except perhaps in Democratic Tucson, which had recently lost the capital to Republican Prescott). As was usual in the territorial governmental apparatus that had evolved piecemeal in the United States since 1789, Frémont's appointment was a matter of patronage dictated by the party in power in Washington, which in this instance was Republican. Along with a chief executive, each territory had a secretary—a lieutenant governor of a sort, who also served as dispersing officer for federal funds—and three judges, all appointed by the president with the advice and consent of the U.S. Senate. In addition, the territory had an elected legislature and an elected delegate who sat in the lower house of Congress but did not vote.

No previous governor had had Frémont's early, stunning national reputation; many citizens hoped that he would be able to do something "good" with the territory—as Jessie had promised a friend he would do, perhaps even bring it to statehood.[18] Frémont seemed to look upon himself as governor of all the people and established a rapport with the Democratic members of the legislature when it convened in January 1879. Lily did note that some Democrats attempted to block his mission east to plead against the settlement of Pima Indians in the Salt River Valley and that insulting remarks were made about all federal officers and her father in particular, but party lines in the territory were really not drawn until the

November election of 1880. Entrepreneur-politicians saw in him the perfect liaison man to use to secure eastern capital. Unfortunately, Frémont's emphasis on his own economic pursuits, which involved extensive absenteeism, set down his name in Arizona history as a "part-time governor and carpetbagger par excellence."[19]

When compared to her remarks on her father's business activities, Lily's diary entries on his political affairs are relatively few and no doubt reflect his dominant interests at the time. His official messages to the legislature emphasized development of the territory's resources, spending for improved roads, federal assay and refining facilities in Prescott, water storage projects for irrigating desert lands, increasing trade with Mexico, enrolling volunteers to keep order along the border, and removing the tax on mining products (the only one of his suggestions to be adopted). Arizonans had a Democratic delegate to Congress during the entire decade following 1875 and enough Democrats in the territorial assembly to challenge the Republican federal officers. Thus, when the legislature voted its own members additional pay despite a federal law to the contrary, Frémont approved the bill in 1879 but rejected a similar measure two years later, only to have it passed over his veto.

Frémont was in Arizona to recoup his sagging fortune. His salary was modest—$2,600 a year set by Congress, from which he paid $90 a month for the Wilson house in Prescott, $40 for a cook, and an unspecified sum for a maid. The way to prosperity, he believed, was through the promotion of mines, connecting the discoverers of mineral property with entrepreneurs having access to capital and the technological expertise to develop mines. Such promoters were a dime a dozen throughout the west. Normally, the promoter did not purchase mining property outright but instead "bonded" it; that is, he took an option to buy at an agreed-upon price before some specified date, three or four months or perhaps as long as a year hence. During that time, he tried to attract capitalists at whatever profit the market would bear, taking his reward in cash or in a share of whatever business enterprise resulted.

Thus it was imperative for Frémont to spend time in the eastern centers seeking capital for the mines on which he and Judge Charles Silent had acquired options, as well as for those of Arizona mineral owners in general (as long as the interests of others did not conflict with his and Silent's). Lily reported her father's depressions over mining matters, especially when he thought he had lost the mines in the Tonto basin to competitors or when he and Judge Silent believed Curtis C. Bean had gone to intercept eastern investors and divert them to his own mines. And she records the anxiety with which they watched for money to arrive for the purchase of the bonded property.

After his first trip east, the *Arizona Miner* reported that Frémont had formed a syndicate in New York composed of wealthy men who were willing to invest several millions of dollars in Arizona should the reports of the experts being sent out to examine the properties prove satisfactory. Forty-six mines were reputed to be on the list for examination; by October 3, 1879, twelve had been examined.[20] Divisions developed quickly among the examiners, and the *Arizona Miner* reported that one of the experts, R. Einhorn, had joined with Secretary Gosper and the owner of the Lone Star mine in Mohave County, George Pinkham, to ruin the chance of purchases by the New York syndicate. The newspaper labeled Einhorn a "blackmailer" and speculated that Gosper and Pinkham had joined him "less from the hope of profit, than from a small spirit of revenge against those who might be apt to make money out of the transaction."[21]

With the departure of the experts, Frémont and Silent sent Jessie (who had much influence and many friends) east as their agent in the selling of mining properties and as their personal lobbyist in Washington. The president's private secretary, William King Rogers, was financially interested in some of Frémont's speculations and could be depended upon to protect him from the growing criticism his lengthy absences from the territory brought. Jessie stopped in San Francisco and sold the Silver Prince to the Shillabers, her hosts during the previous fall, and as her commission received a quarter-interest in the mine. On reaching New York, she wrote Rogers that capital was needed to work it as well as the several mines near it, "now bonded personally to the General and Judge Silent."[22] She had been promised that the capital would be furnished by a strong New York financial house that was placing English capital in Arizona mines. She asked for the replacement of Gosper, a "thwarting official" who worked underhandedly "and in all sorts of ways makes trouble and loss." She pleaded for another leave for her husband that he might return to the east "to give his own impress to new work which she had been so fortunate as to start." She admitted that it would best suit his interests "to be quite foot loose—but to resign now would give the power next winter when the Legislature meets again, to unknown people and interests." If he continued as governor, he could "prevent and veto any vexatious legislation regarding mines and railroads—both of which make openings for black mail work in mining country legislatures."[23] When it was made clear that leave could not be granted again so soon, Jessie understood, but she also knew that mine promotion was an active business: "no sitting on the nest and looking at the village [Prescott] can equal the work to be done by going to and fro."[24]

As the Frémonts and Judge Silent battled for fortune, they either filed claims to or bonded mines in Yavapai, Mohave, and Yuma Counties. The Silver Prince and nearby mines (Black Warrior, Tuscumbia, and Tuscarora—all in the Peck district of Yavapai County) became the most important of their investments. The Shillabers sold out the Silver Prince to a New York syndicate, which also purchased the three adjoining mines.[25]

As Frémont spent more and more time in the east, the good rapport that he had previously enjoyed with the Prescott press evaporated. Much had been expected of him, but he had turned out to be a governor in name only and "of no earthly use to the territory."[26] Judge Silent also came under attack. Arizona's congressional delegate, John G. Campbell, a Democrat, charged that Silent and Frémont had been buying, bonding, and selling mines that were within the jurisdiction of the judge's court and indeed in some instances involved in litigation before his court. Lily in Prescott fretted over these charges; she supported Silent and thereby risked her friendship with the widower General Orlando B. Willcox, commander of the Department of Arizona. Frémont and Jessie in Washington, D.C., intervened on the judge's behalf, with Jessie writing to President Hayes that Silent's exoneration would be "a case of justice for a man deserving it—for a personal friend—and for one whose mining interests are identified with ours."[27]

In addition to the fever of mining activity, with both triumphs and disappointments for the Frémonts and Silent, Lily's diary gives an excellent picture of her world in Prescott. It was predominately peopled by Anglos, of whom a remarkable number were first-generation Europeans. The 1880 census indicated a population of less than 2,000 in Prescott. Of these 114 were Mexicans, 8 were Blacks, and 99 were Chinese, many of whom, with the French, were market gardeners along Granite Creek.[28] Lily had a high regard for the Frémonts' cook, Ah Chung, a man about thirty years old, who did not live with them but "roosted" in Chinatown, which centered on Granite Street between Gurley and Goodwin Streets.[29] For the most part the Chinese in Arizona did not encounter the violent prejudices that greeted them in California, Colorado, Wyoming, and Montana, but occasionally the newspapers lashed out at them: "The Chinese are getting numerous and noisy in Prescott. Let them emigrate."[30] Unlike Tucsonans, Prescottonians were vehemently anti-Mexican; Mexicans, like the Chinese, were near the bottom of the occupational scale. A profession that finds no mention in Lily's diary is prostitution, but it flourished in Prescott, just as it did in every western center.

Lily was not a prude, nor had her experiences been narrow, but she was very much a product of Victorian culture. She had been born in 1842 at the Washington, D.C., home of her maternal grandfather, Senator Benton of Missouri. Before she was nine, she had made two trips to California by way of the Isthmus of Panama and then in 1852 had sailed with her parents from San Francisco to Europe, where a brief stay in London was followed by a more lengthy residence in Paris. She was fourteen when her father was nominated by the newly formed Republican Party for the presidency of the United States; fifteen when she had another brief residence in Paris; sixteen when she returned with her parents and two brothers to California (crossing the isthmus by rail this time), where the family resided first on their isolated estate of Las Mariposas, adjoining Yosemite, and then at Black Point, the Fort Mason area of San Francisco. After the beginning of the Civil War, eighteen-year-old Lily, her mother, and her two brothers sailed east to join Frémont (he had been in Europe trying to raise capital for the development of Las Mariposas), who had been appointed major general and given the command of the Western Department, with headquarters at St. Louis. After the war was over, the Frémonts purchased a beautiful home, which they named Pocaho, on the Hudson River, about twenty-five miles outside of New York City. Lily had two more trips to Europe, one resulting in a six-month stay with her brother Frank in Dresden, where she improved her German and learned to paint flowers on china while he was tutored in German, Latin, arithmetic, fencing, and music. The failure of Frémont's several railroad schemes—especially the Memphis, El Paso, and Pacific—and his trial and conviction in absentia in a Paris court for swindling French bondholders brought an end to their comfortable, even extravagant living.

Nearly all of Lily's education had been private and centered on history, literature, and languages, but she also received instruction in fencing, dancing, drawing, and horseback riding. She often rode with fine horsemen, such as the commander of the Frémont Bodyguard during the Civil War, the Hungarian Károly Zágonyi; in her mother's estimation she was worthy to ride with Kit Carson.[31] But the Frémonts were too poor to keep a horse in Prescott, and until Lily went to Tucson, she had not traveled more than five miles outside the town.

For most of her life, Lily had lacked nothing in the way of material benefits. Moreover, her parents' national prominence, activities, and friendships afforded many opportunities for her to meet interesting people and desirable men in every occupation: politicians, military officers, literary figures, artists, and businessmen. In the post–Civil War years, she was often a bridesmaid; doubtless, much of Jessie's socializing at this time was done so that her daughter could meet eligible young men. One wonders whether General Willcox's frequent visits to the Frémonts early in their stay in Prescott were "courting" visits to Lily. However, on Thanksgiving Day in 1881, in Tucson, he married Julia E. Wyeth of Chicago.[32]

Lily never married, but her diary and letters reveal a touching relationship with Judge Silent, a married man of her age. She wrote her intimate friend Ella (Nelly) Haskell Browne of the comfort she and her father had in Judge Silent, "each in our way." She went on to note that "there are some nice women in town so I have them for a resource but just the one [and] only human being who is sympathique to us is the Judge & we value him accordingly."[33] She related how he worked "thoroughly in accord" with her father "both in the government of the Territory & in regard to projects for" his and their future welfare. His was a fertile brain for conceiving feasible plans and meeting and vanquishing a tangled situation and for keeping "all the rough edges of business from reaching" her.[34] She was careful to decline invitations when she thought he would be coming to her house for dinner, and on Easter Sunday in 1880, she wrote Nelly, "All the family are gone now but Thor [the dog] & the house is uncommonly still. However, as long as Judge Silent is in town it isn't dreadfully lonely for he takes breakfast & dinner with me, & knowing what a still time I am having sometimes actually stays ten minutes & talks over things with me." The relationship between the two was all very proper, but eating meals with him daily must have suggested to her the psychological comforts of marriage. Lily went on to add to her letter, "I shall miss him when he goes to the mines, but eight days of Father's leave are out now so he will soon have to head this way."[35] When Silent became seriously ill, she did not telegraph his spouse but in a way played the role of a solicitous wife. When he also left Prescott, her loneliness overwhelmed her. By that time, too, fewer people were coming to the house on political and mining affairs.

Lily was a rather plain, practical woman with a tendency toward stoutness and, like her father, was reticent, with a slight stutter. She was an intelligent, compassionate, and good woman but not particularly religious or political. When the family had lived at Pocaho, she had belonged to a society of ladies for visiting the poorhouse and had gone there regularly every two weeks to talk to the old women.[36] Her Prescott diary indicates a concern for the poor and for the Indians, whom the settlers and the army were all against. In her diary she catches the pathos of a child's accidental death; the ceremonies of funerals, holidays, and school; tensions between town and fort; and the fear of fires in Prescott, which had an inadequate water system and supply.

In addition to the diary published here, short diaries survive for a part of the family's residence at Pocaho and for their brief stay in Nassau while Frank was recuperating from an illness. If there were other diaries, Lily may have destroyed them when she burned family letters and papers in 1907 before they could "get into [the] wrong hands."[37] Keeping diaries is often an indication of an interest in self-exploration, but Lily was not especially introspective. Her writings are largely descriptive accounts of activities and events, but they reveal an even temper, a delightful sense of humor, a quick perception of human nature, a loyalty to family and friends, and a love of horses and dogs. Her quiet occupations were reading, visiting, observing the landscape and weather, managing the household, and in general being of service to others, especially her family. On one occasion she wrote that she had sewed so much that she was "quite getting to feel a little lost" when the thimble was not on her finger in the daytime, and she regularly gave lessons in the French language to one of the young officers. Natural phenomena fired her imagination: "Sunset wonderfully beautiful soft canary yellow on dull grey brightening into burnished gold & fading away in softest Venus saffron—& Venus herself at one moment appearing with 'trailing robes' of shimmered saffron—then a baby crescent moon."

The Frémonts were generous with their hospitality, but the "pennies were not there for a real dinner." They simply served guests their "regular home dinner," and it pleased Lily when her father praised the smooth running of the house and the excellent food.[38] She resolutely looked away from all but the bright side of everything, and a French maid once remarked that "one will always live in peace with Miss Lily."[39] Lily kept a firm rein on her tongue when Mary, the Irish maid, took too many nips from the bottle in Prescott.

By the end of 1880, many Arizonans were convinced that their governor favored the removal of the capital to Tucson. In February 1881, the house passed a bill to do so, but the council did not concur. Regulations required the governor to live within the territory but not necessarily in the capital. Frémont was determined to move his residence to Tucson as soon as the eleventh legislative assembly adjourned, and shortly after it did, a wagon drove up to the dining room gate to take the boxes to the railroad station in Maricopa. The Frémonts' good friends in the town, the Buffums and the Lewises, had been told—but many Prescottonians were displeased as well as surprised, and the *Arizona Miner* editorialized that the move was made so that Frémont "could be 'cheek by jowl' with Judge Silent in manipulating mining claims."[40] Some furniture was kept, including the beds; other items were given away or sold. Private houses and restaurants competed for Ah Chung's services, offering as much as $60 to $100 per month, but he stayed with the Frémont family at $40 per month.[41]

Frémont's decision to shift his home to Tucson reflects his changing economic interests as well as the fact that Silent had gone to Tucson. Although he was still interested in promoting metal mines, other interests such as land, coal, and railroads had come to the fore. He hoped that he and his friends, including Silent, would be able to acquire the 18,000-acre San Rafael del Valle ranch in southeastern Arizona, in addition to large mineralized areas on both sides of the Mexican border. He negotiated to obtain half of Edward Conkling's nebulous ownership of the San Juan del Rio ranch along the Yaqui River in Sonora, and he attempted to secure a franchise for a railroad from Tucson to Point Lobos on the Gulf of California.[42] The help of the American consul at Guaymas was enlisted in obtaining coal property in Mexico.[43] The wife of the editor of the *Arizona Miner* reported from Washington, D.C., that Jessie had been lobbying for a year to get Frémont appointed minister to Mexico.[44]

Frémont and Lily reached Tucson on Sunday, March 20, 1881, and on March 27, Frémont left for the east to promote his various projects.[45] In September 1881 both he and Jessie began working, unsuccessfully, to have their two sons transferred to Arizona. Jessie asked that Charley, a naval officer, be assigned to the magnetic survey,[46] and Frémont requested that Frank, a second lieutenant in the third infantry, be transferred from Montana and be put in charge of organizing home guard companies, presumably to reduce both lawlessness around Tombstone and Indian hostilities, a request Jessie supported with personal appeals to both the adjutant general and the commander-in-chief of the army.[47] And to Nelly Browne, Jessie intimated that the Frémont men would be involved in "big big cattle ranch work."[48]

Where Frémont and Lily lived during the governor's brief stay in Tucson is a matter of controversy. Indeed, one scholar concludes that Frémont may never have lived at 245 South Main, which is the address of his residence as given in the Tucson directory published near the end of June 1881 or later.[49] On May 29 and June 2, the *Weekly Arizona Citizen* and the *Arizona Weekly Star,* respectively, informed the public that Governor Frémont had leased the residence of J. J. Hamburg on Main Street and that Mrs. Hamburg, accompanied by Mrs. Ed Hudson, would spend the summer in the east. Hamburg, the manager of the Zeckendorf enterprises, seems to have been leasing the house from Leopoldo Carrillo and his wife, who had obtained it from descendants of José Maria Sosa III. Lily, then, may not have moved into the house currently known as the Sosa-Carrillo-Frémont House until early June 1881. (That its address is now 151

South Granada instead of 245 South Main Street is the result of changes in street designations.) If Lily did not move into the house for more than two months after her arrival in Tucson, where did she live, and where did Frémont live during his brief stay? That we do not know. Possibly they were guests of Judge Silent for the week Frémont was in town, but Lily is not likely to have continued in Silent's home (if indeed he had one; the 1881 Tucson directory does not list a residence for him).

Whatever the house, Lily wrote her mother on April 10 that the rooms were "moderate sized" and that the ladies who had lived in it told her the house was cool. She asked Jessie to send her a six-foot-long cover for the big writing table she had in the parlor. She also added, "The Judge will keep an eye out for other houses, but the chances are so few & his eyes are so busy looking after bigger things that I don't much count on moving."[50] In late August, Jessie, in the east, wrote that Lily had "one of the very best houses" in Tucson.[51]

On October 11, Frémont submitted his resignation as governor, to become effective November 1. He cited the chief executive's lack of authority, funds, and voice in forming policy, especially with respect to Indian affairs, and probably was unhappy with the secretary of war's refusal to transfer young Frank to Arizona. Lily left Tucson for New York sometime in November; the *Arizona Miner* reported November 18, 1881, that she probably went "to assist her Mother in writing a tragedy for the stage, which she is and has been at work on for some time past."

Lily did not write a tragedy. Instead she helped her parents prepare her father's *Memoirs* in 1886 and late in 1887 accompanied her parents to Los Angeles. After Frémont died in 1890, Congress granted Jessie a widow's pension of $2,000 per year, and the women of California built her and Lily a four-bedroom home at 1107 West Twenty-Eighth Street in Los Angeles. Jessie fought valiantly to survive in order to keep for Lily her pension, but her death in 1902 left Lily with almost nothing but the home. Lily ruefully observed to Nelly in March 1903 that she had "laid in bed for the last four days—for Mr. Thomas' interview about those pension papers was too much for me and sent me to bed with appendicitis—consequences which needed the doctor."[52]

Charles F. Lummis had written to President Theodore Roosevelt that in addition to the California home, Lily had but $500 in the world, and in *Out West,* he brought her plight to the attention of the public and reckoned that there was enough manhood in the United States to see that she did not have to enter the Hollenbeck Home for Old Women.[53] This public appeal may have brought some money; family members also offered assistance before their own adversities overwhelmed them.[54] Lily often thanked

Nelly for gifts, such as the money she exchanged for a little black suit or to continue her subscription to *Atlantic Monthly.* She was a frequent visitor in the various Los Angeles homes of Charles Silent, and he as well as other former friends from Prescott—namely, Moses Sherman and his sister, Mrs. Eli P. Clark, who had moved to and prospered in Los Angeles—were sympathetic and diplomatic with assistance to the proud woman.[55] She continued her fruitless struggle to obtain reparations for Black Point in San Francisco, which had been confiscated by the federal government during the Civil War.[56]

As a woman "all alone," Lily first rented rooms within her house to women. Then in 1904 she rented the house itself to a couple and retreated to property she had purchased on Long Beach.[57] In 1912, she sold the house on West Twenty-Eighth Street and also put on the market a bungalow at 2158 West Twenty-Ninth Place, which she had somehow acquired. When it sold, she told Nelly, she would board for a while and then settle into a small flat, perhaps with another woman.[58]

Although she moved often, Lily found time to continue her activities in the Friday Morning Club, of which she had been a first vice-president, and Lummis involved her in early plans for the Southwest Museum. Unanimously elected the first honorary member of the Southwest Museum, she turned a spadeful of earth in 1912 in a groundbreaking ceremony for the building and "as the last of the trio" presented to the museum the flag which her father had unfurled in the Wind River Mountains, and which on his return, he had given to "his young wife and the wee baby [Lily] by her side."[59] In that same year Lily's *Recollections,* written with the assistance of Ismena Martin, a New York journalist, was published. No doubt it was an attempt to make money through writing as her mother had done, but the book could not have been a financial success.

In 1917 a letter came from Frank, the brother she idolized, telling her that he thought he could soon manage monthly installments for the large lot and bungalow Lily had in mind and that he and his second wife would live with her in California. "You have done so much for others, that it is time, and overtime, that you should be coddled and taken care of, and it has been very close to my heart to get to you and 'do' for you. Just now, it looks as if the time had come, and if you will please keep well and contented for a few weeks longer, then dates will be set, and we will all work together for a home, a real home where we can drive nails in the walls, plant pus[s]ley or anything else we want, keep chickens or a burro, and where you can boss us all you like. . . . Now! We do not think you are 'too old' to look after yourself or things. . . . But we think the heat and burden of the days has been yours long enough, and we want to take it off you, and we are going to do so." He concluded by telling her that he had always loved her, "and more and more as time has gone on and I have seen and realized the way through the long years you have fought and sacrificed yourself for the good and comfort of others, have I realized what you are, and how dear you are."[60]

Frank's plan for them to live together never materialized. Lily's obituary two years later listed her as living at 1179 West Thirtieth Street and him in New York.[61] Thirty-six people attended her funeral; Frank was absent.[62] In a poem, "The Daughter of the Pathfinder," Lummis heralded her as the "Unsung and self-effacing third of two that thrilled the world; / The Daughter of their youth, the 'Little Mother' of their age."[63]

Any assessment of Lily Frémont's life brings two major questions to mind. First, why did she not marry? Ninety-two percent of the women born between 1845 and 1849 did so, and Lily's birth year of 1842 roughly associates her with that group. In addressing the marriage question, subsidiary questions arise. Did she see a dark side to her parents' marriage? Did she desire more independence than she thought possible within the confines of marriage? Did she dislike men? Or was it simply a matter of not finding an available man compatible with her interests and intellect?

If she witnessed tensions and disharmony within her parents' marriage, she never expressed it, but she did comment on her father's frequent absence and her mother's depression when he was away. Her diary and letters and the letters of her mother give every evidence of a tight-knit family. Her brother Frank also remembered "an intensive homelife" with "everything centered there."[64]

She is silent on the question of independence. Perhaps she felt she had more independence within her parents' family than she would within a husband's family and at the same time would escape the trials of childbirth and the rearing of children: in the words of her mother, she was not a "baby fancier." As for authority, an issue intertwined with independence, she had from a very early age been managing the household and supervising the servants, and her attitude toward her two brothers—nine and thirteen years younger than she—was maternal. In writing to friends, she frequently referred to them as "our boys," and on the conclusion of Charley's stay at Annapolis, she proudly informed a friend, "our little boy Charley graduates on the 31st." She played a major role in the education of Frank before he entered Peekskill Academy, and when Nelly Haskell began teaching her younger brothers, she offered schoolbooks and counseled "patience."

All during her life, she seems to have had a comfortable relationship with men and rarely viewed them in a negative light, although she did warn Nelly Haskell not to be in a hurry to marry George Browne "unless you feel sure you want to—men are risky, at least some of them of the ordinary sort are—though I know and have known some noble exceptions. I dare say we all do if we live long enough."[65] As a young woman she may have had a brief infatuation, but this speculation is not conclusive. Her diary shows not only her fondness for Judge Silent (in their exchange of personal instructions to and concerns for each other) but a certain desire for a man in the household: "The Judge came up in the early morning & cleaned Mr. Cordis's gun & took it back to him—it felt like the hall at Pocaho to see again a man working at a gun all in pieces."

The second major question is why did Lily not seek a career outside the home, especially after 1875, when all the possessions of the Frémonts were being liquidated? She was a well-educated women, at that time in her early thirties, and could easily have become a librarian, translator, telegraph operator, postmistress, governess, or schoolteacher—all avenues open to young women. Or she might have entered federal government service, although the pay was poor for women. For someone of her talents, there may have been some opportunities in home decorating or architecture. She describes furnishings, sends floor plans to Nelly (including the plan of the first floor to General Willcox's house), and indicates that she likes "to contrive in household arrangements." Probably her parents would have been humiliated had Lily gone outside the home to earn money, just as her Aunt Eliza (Mrs. William Carey Jones) was when her daughter Betty began doing needlework for the "big fancy stores" in San Francisco. Working-class single women found it much easier to find and take employment than did impoverished gentlewomen.

Lily had been held tightly within the family and educated by governesses, masters, or her mother, who was herself ambivalent and confused about woman's role in society. Sometimes girls who are sent away to school become accustomed to a personal independence and also forge friendships that aid in resisting family claims. Lily had been denied this opportunity, and in a sense her mother, only eighteen years older than she, was her sister and dearest friend. Not until she came under the influence of Caroline Severance in Los Angeles did she join a club and the suffrage movement. There is no evidence that she ever rebelled against her long-term role as daughter. In Lummis's words, she "gave up her whole life to be the Angel of the Hearth for her marvelous mother."[66] She did not continue that service in her brothers' families.[67]

The result was loneliness, a predominant theme in the diaries of many nineteenth-century single women. More than once Lily must have felt in her heart the anguish expressed in her diary entry of November 21, 1880:

"A lonesome, homesick day—silly of me but I couldn't help it & a nice letter I had from the Judge only made me want to be near them all the more." She wrote, in an earlier letter to family friend William J. Morton, "I'm sorry you have to be alone for it's a dreary business, being alone is, & hard work don't fill every moment of day & night."[68]

Although lonely at times, Lily had a remarkable ability to make and keep friends, both unmarried and married. Her friendship with Nelly began in 1860 when the Haskell and Frémont families had lived at Black Point outside of San Francisco (and it continued—with a constant exchange of letters and occasional visits—until Lily's death). After her move to Los Angeles, she resumed friendly relations with former Arizonans. Eli P. Clark and Moses Sherman, organizers of the Los Angeles Consolidated Electric Railway Company, presented her and Jessie with lifetime passes for the streetcars. And to the day of his death (just months before Lily's funeral), Judge Silent in California was a bulwark of support, as he had been in Arizona. By 1904, many of the people she had known and corresponded with in the east were dead, but new California friends such as Caroline Severance, Charlotte Wills, Senator Thomas R. Bard, and Charles Lummis were watchful and caring until their own or Lily's death. Lily's sincerity, sterling character, and thoughtfulness won the admiration and respect of all.

Chapter I

West to Prescott

June 8, 1878–January 1, 1879

Lily Frémont, thirty-six years old, begins her diary with an account of Christmas in Prescott and then in a flashback describes her father's appointment as territorial governor of Arizona on June 8, 1878, the reunification of the Frémont family in New York prior to the family's leave-taking of friends and departure for the west on September 2, and their journey to Prescott.

Christmas Day 1878, Prescott, Arizona. When Mary[1] came in to light my fire I was struck with the white light in my room & looking out saw like good King Wenceslas the snow "lying round all smooth, & white & even."[2] The clouds have lifted enough for the hills nearer town & Thumb Butte to show, but Granite Mt. was still hid from sight.[3] Everything was covered with snow which was nearly a foot deep, & it made many new "effects" on the mountain sides, both grand & beautiful; all day through there were heavy snow squalls & glorious clouds ending with a fine sunset & clear starlight night.

The day was kept as a holiday, shops all shut, family & friendly gatherings, the air full of the children's rejoicing in the snow. We had a perfectly quiet family day—Father did a little writing—Mother finished the towel she was working for Mrs. Buffum[4] & we sent her over her Xmas pie; as Mother wasn't feeling at all well (the first real ill turn she has had since we came up here) she only sat up during dinner. Frank spent nearly all his day practising for the organ parts he is to play on Friday Evening at the Masons' celebration. I had a quiet day divided between watching the clouds & the mountains & reading a novel. It was a day of quiet home content for us all & of thorough gratefulness at its difference from last Xmas.[5] There was service only in the Catholic Church, so Mary was the only one who could go to her church.

I must "try back" & tell how we came to be here: when Father was appointed governor of this Territory we were all scattered. Mother, Father, & Frank were in Washington where they had been since early in May—he was appointed June 8th. Charley was in New York with Sally having only a little while before told us of his marriage—& I was staying with Nelly Browne[6] on Staten Island. We all came together July 5th in New York, at a boarding house in West 22nd St. No. 59, where Charley & Sally were already staying & where we expected to be for a few weeks only, but first "business," then Sally's unexpected & dangerous illness kept us till September 2nd by which time our affairs were somewhat settled, Sally was well enough to be left & Charley had settled into working grooves down at the Lighthouse station on Staten Island—a position Mother had been able to get for him which gives him shore duty & ensures him three years with Sally; our two months waiting in 22nd St. was weary work, even apart from the anxiety of Sally's illness & the fear that the great heat (& suspense) would make Mother ill—it was also our very first experience of a boarding house, but it was very quiet & well managed & everyone in it was particularly nice all during Sally's illness; our Dr. Morton[7] took care of her, though her illness was not in his line. He watched Mother too & kept her from making herself ill with overwatching, & helped Frank with all the details of the funeral of the poor little baby, who only lived an hour, about—& was in fact helpful as only a sympathetic friend who is also your physician has the power to be. Charley was very much grieved & broken down by it all & it was well for him he had us with him; Sally's Mother came & went but she doesn't seem to be a very efficient stay in time of trouble. Nell was in town on her way to Kettle Cove with the babies & again when she returned from there at the end of August & went up into the Pennsylvania mts. When Sally could be moved she went down & stayed a while at Nell's in New Brighton [on Staten Island] then returned to 22nd a week before we left.

We saw a good deal of the Darts,[8] even not counting the days Frank & I were at their house sorting over & packing up our things—some to be left with them, some stored & the rest to go with us. Their Aunt Catherine died whilst Sally was ill after a fearfully long & wearing illness which nearly wore out her nurses—the two Fannys & Maggie.

I went up the Hudson with Maggie & Eleanor one day as far as Newburgh, returning with Eleanor. It was a goodbye treat of Mag's who was going on up to Saratoga. Mother & I had one lovely day down at Coney Island with Dr. Morton; splendid surf, high cool wind, not too many people but enough to amuse us & not a jar to a day which we felt it a pleasure to spend together; it was Mother's & my adieu to the Atlantic for how long?

We were very busy when the last days came & the great heat made all the last preparations, which were from necessity crowded into a few days, all the more irksome; Fanny Dart helped us lots. Charley had to go off on duty Sunday evening so that parting with him came then—both he &

Mother broke down under it; the rest were all through Monday, Carry & Mrs. Barlow[9] coming in to say adieu to Mother; Fanny was in & out with us all day. Frank took Sally up to stay overnight with one of her friends as we wouldn't leave her alone in the house where we had all been together & where so much had happened to her. Dr. Morton too took leave of us that afternoon, glad to have us go away from the town where we had gone through such a heavy pull, but somewhat sorry too to quite lose sight of us for an indefinite length of time. (Remember the walk to Macy's & back & the talk over the Bald Porcupine subject—I'm so glad I didn't let him have his way about it).[10]

Mother & Father, with Mary, Thor[11] & all the hand parcels, drove over to the Jersey ferry; Frank & I followed by the Elevated etc. Mr. Kitchen[12] & his brothers joined us at the cars & he made one of our party straight through—they of course returning to their homes. We had a comfortable sleeping & hotel car through to Chicago without change or getting out at all—we crossed the Alleghenies by day, seeing the famous Horseshoe for the first time since July '61 when we went over the same road under all the oppression caused by the defeat at Bull Run, when Father was going out to St. Louis to take command of the Western Dept.

We stopped over in Chicago meaning to stay one day only but staid longer that Father might attend a railroad meeting which included plans of great promise for Arizona & in which [Manuel M.] Zamacona, minister from Mexico, is working in combination with leading Western merchants for the development of the commercial relations between the U.S. & Mexico. We had very fine rooms at the Palmer House, empire furniture of crimson satin & plenty of it, crimson walls, wreaths of olive branches & peacock feathers on ceiling & doors, pictures & statues in one room— about 30 × 40; the other room was all Eastlake olive green with ash furniture & the end of the room was rounded with two great windows having deep set outside jardinières & across the flowers blooming in them one had extended views over the city. We found on leaving that they were Mr. [Potter] Palmer's own rooms & he would not let us pay anything saying "No indeed General you are really my guest."

Mother & Father did the official sights of the city with a lot of city people & Signor Zamacona, special trains & all that sort of thing. Father had to speak at the meeting, too; lots of people came to see us, too, & Col. James (who dates back to '56 & to Bear Valley) was with us off and on all the time.[13] Frank & I had good drives about the town & out through the Park which runs along by the side of the lake—some beautiful residences—& we all had a good sail far out into the lake in a smart little sloop owned by a Swede. Frank sailed her.

Elizabeth Benton Frémont, inscribed "for Mrs. Buffum, from her affectionate friend, Lily Frémont. Los Angeles, December 1896." (Courtesy of the Sharlot Hall Museum/Library Archives, Prescott, Ariz., photo #PO 772.2 pA.)

After leaving Chicago we seemed to be getting really out into the West & the continuous line of splendid big farms was pleasant to look at; at nearly all the stations we passed through during daylight there were crowds waiting to see Mother & Father & wherever we stopped long enough, the people crowded through our car to speak to them & shake

Christmas Day 1878, Prescott, Arizona.

When Mary came in to light my fire I was struck with the white light in my room & looking out saw good King Wenceslaus the snow "lying round all smooth, & white & e-e-e-" — the clouds have lifted enough for the hills nearer town & Thumb Butte to show, but granite Mt. was still hid from sight — everything was covered with snow which was nearly a foot deep, & it made many new "effects" on the mountain sides, both grand & beautiful; all day through there were heavy snow squalls & glorious clouds ending with a fine sunset & clear starlight night. The day was kept as a holiday, shops all shut, family & friendly gathering — the air full of the children rejoicing in the snow. We had a perfectly quiet family day — Father did a little writing — Mother finished the towel & she was working for Mrs. Ruffum & we sent her over to Xmas fire; as Mother wasn't feeling at all well, (the first real ill turn she has had since we came up here) she only sat up during dinner. Frank spent nearly all his day practising for the organ parts he is to play on Friday evening at the Masons celebration; I had a quiet

The beginning page of Lily Frémont's Arizona diary.
(Courtesy of Rare Books and Manuscript Library, Columbia University.)

hands with them—it was so all along the route from the time we struck the West.

At Council Bluffs we were met by Major [James Woodruff] Savage (on Father's staff & some of the household officers in '61–'62) now Judge Savage of Nebraska & living in Omaha. When we had crossed the bridge & we were [at] Omaha he drove us up to his house which was on a ridge some hundreds of feet above the river & commanded a fine view up & down the river & across to Council Bluffs & its fine School House—all along this route & way down into Southern California the school houses were the finest buildings we saw, being the leading buildings in the land-scapes & taking the place belonging in European landscapes to monas-teries & castles. After freshening ourselves, Mother & I spent the after-noon resting & talking with Mrs. Savage; Father & Frank went with Judge Savage & the officials of the Central Pacific [rail]road to look over their machine & work shops, etc. Omaha was all roused by the loss of their big brick hotel which had burned down a few days before & was a great business loss to the community; & the people were grieved about it too as several of the fine young men of the town had been killed in the fire—theirs being the old volunteer fire brigade. In the evening there was a regular reception at Mrs. Savage's—we in our travelling [clothes] only! People we had known before & new ones & many of the officers from the Post, including the General [John Parker Hawkins] commanding—a brother of Mrs. Genl. [E.R.S.] Canby's. Some had been stationed in Ari-zona territory & told us lots about it. We had a quiet morning with the Savages on Sunday, sitting on their porch overlooking the great bends of the Missouri & in Mrs. Savage's old New England room in which every-thing dates back nearly two hundred years & things are all arranged as in the colonial, even to the glass corner cabinet with old vouched-for china & bits of silver. About midday we drove down to the train, where more friends met us & the Savages staid with us to the time of starting—we had a pleasant visit at their house.

On the train were Mr. Paulisson [Paulison][14] & Mr. [Oliver D.] Smith whom Father knew & who were going through to Arizona & were more or less with us after this till reaching Prescott. We had rather a bad feed at Fremont which was our first eating station beyond Omaha. I don't just now remember the incidents of the journey along sharply for I have writ-ten them back to friends so often that they have run together a great deal. We went straight through from Omaha to San Francisco abandoning our original intention of stopping at Salt Lake as the person Father wanted to see was away. Every day's ride had its interest & beauty; what I liked best was the majestic great downs of the Rocky Mts. at the pass through which the railroad crosses them—we had even a sharp snow flurry to make it perfect & Father sitting in a well warmed palace car & looking out through plate glass windows at it, in wonderful contrast to his crossings of them in old times when he made his journeys across them. Then no inhabitants, now comfortable cottages, many with white curtains & geraniums growing in the south windows & women on horseback in real riding habits; mowing machines at work getting in the last crop of hay, & for no length of time, except during the passage of the alkali desert, were we out of sight of the evidence of human habitation & in the Desert itself the fruit trees & alfalfa of Humboldt station show how fruitful it would be with only a moderate degree of irrigation. The two passes into Mormondom, Echo & Weber cañons, were both wonderful & beautiful. I preferred Weber with its sheer mountain sides & swiftly rushing river to the more gigantically fantastic effects of the rocks in Echo cañon; we were delighted with the trim beauty & flourishing looks of the towns & farms in Utah & had delicious fruit there. Ogden is set in view of fine mountains— we met there one of our southern cousins, Mr. [. . .] who stayed with us whilst we were taking our supper which was remarkably good, game & fruit in plenty; also we met people who had been in Arizona.

We passed the Salt Lake itself just as the moon rose giving us a good view of its waters & Father pointed out to Mother where he had gone down Bear river into the Lake & she was delighted to see it first with him. Of course all thro' the journey it was like going back over one of Father's reports to pass over & near to the places so associated with his early travels. We had a most beautiful morning for crossing the Sierras & a perfectly clear view from "Cape Horn"[15]—they are most beautiful mountains & realize all one's ideas of pine clad mts., with rushing rivers at their feet & the road winds wonderfully through them. The snowsheds are a great engineering work & most useful, but they spoil the view to travellers. From the time we began to descend into California I could recognize the old look of the state, its wild oats patches, the manzanita bushes, shapes of the oaks & the peculiar golden look of the sun burned grass, everything took one back to our journey up into Bear Valley now twenty years ago.[16]

Friends came out to meet us soon after we entered the state, first amongst [them] Jerome Davis who was of Father's party in the time when he took California for the U.S. & is now one of the prosperous & leading citizens of Sacramento; by the time we reached Oakland quite a number had joined us including Betty Jones Hughes & Carey Jones (my cousins)[17] & Mr. [Joseph C.] Palmer.[18] The last few hours of the journey the track was right along the bay & the bright cool water was a refreshing sight. We crossed right over to San Francisco, our baggage & small parcels all being taken care of by one of the clerks of the "Palace Hotel," the proprietor of which had telegraph[ed] out into the Desert to use [urge] Father to be literally "his guest" & sent Mr. [. . .] out to Latham [Lathrop] to meet us.[19] They gave us a charming corner suite of rooms, all bay windows, comfortable & pretty & we had everything pleasant about us during the twelve days we staid there. During those days we were a great deal with Aunt Eliza & Betty both over in Oakland & in town, for Mrs. Shillaber made Aunty come over & stay with her most of the time.[20] Mrs. Shillaber gave us a swell reception at which nearly everyone in town was present; drove us out & did all in her power to make things pleasant for us, besides which she has been a thorough true friend to Aunt Eliza during many years.

We went out to a daytime reception at Black Point[21] where the McDowells were very avenant [gracious] to us. I went down & staid overnight with the Palmers at San Jose Mission. We had an incessant run of visitors from the earliest allowable hours up to midnight, old friends & new; a lovely drive out to the Ocean Beach house through the Park—beautiful flowers—in a four-in-hand, Mr. Wm. Boothe [Booth][22] taking us—we had a good look at the Pacific. Father had a fine official reception by the Pioneer Society. The day before we left Betty insisted on sending her chinese cook to us for a year—he has been with her nearly seven—we didn't want her to do such an uncomfortable thing for herself but she persisted & transferred Chung to us. He didn't exactly want to come but, like most of us, money is an object to him & a prospect of increased wages reconciled him to the change. He has already been over a year at Yuma with Major [William Burton] Hughes. Betty also did our shopping for us laying in our groceries & crockery & blankets for us. Another pleasant thing for us was an evening in Mr. Bradford's studio where he showed us his pictures & gave us a running lecture on his stereoscopticon [sic] views which were very beautiful & from which & his little lecture, we gathered several new ideas on the Arctic world.[23]

We left San Francisco on the 24th Sept. Aunt Eliza, Betty & Elsie[24] staying with us to the last only getting off at the second stop in Oakland. Mrs. Shillaber had driven us to the boat. We had a dusty night of it through the San Joaquin valley & were up very early to see the natural beauties & engineering triumphs of the Tehatchpe [Tehachapi] Pass. [Alexis] Godey, who had entered California with Father through that pass, was with us & I stood by on the rear platform of the last car & heard them talking over their memories of that time. We met Genl. [William Tecumseh] Sherman going north just out of Los Angeles. He was returning from an inspection tour which had taken him through Prescott which he praised; he held the two trains for about half an hour whilst he made us a hurried visit in our car. Genl. [Alexander McDowell] McCook was his aide.

In Los Angeles we staid at the St. Charles. Father was serenaded—lots of people called, many of the old Spanish Californians amongst them. Don Pedro Car[r]illo[25] was with us off & on all the time; Dr. Morton's sister, Mrs. Otis & her husband had come down from Santa Barbara to see us, she wanting to see us that she might hear details about her mother & brother; we spent most of the next day with her out at the house of Mrs. Severance[26] of Boston, who has a Nahant like cottage set in an orange grove & flowers in quantity and in perfection. Frank met there some of his Dresden friends. We all liked the [city of Los] Angeles—for itself, for Father's old associations with it of the time when he was military governor there—his headquarters are still standing & from where his battery was we had a beautiful view down over the town nestling in its orange groves, with its fertile fields & vineyards stretching out from it to the mountains behind it & towards the ocean in front & only some thirteen miles away; also it reminded us of our favorite little Nassau.[27] Many of our friends saw us off from the railroad station just outside the town. There was rather an interesting Mexican family on the train returning to their home in Yuma, & an impossible army bride going with her cadet husband to Camp Grant [at the foot of Mount Graham] in Arizona.

We stopped for supper at a really charmingly good hotel at Colton where we had a very good meal. The place was kept by an English woman whose husband had only recently died, & she was sorry [grieving] for him. We made Yuma at about seven in the morning & bade adieu to railroads & palace cars. Major [James Henry] Lord met us with ambulances at the train & after a good breakfast at the hotel took us up to his house at the Army Depot—house built by Maj. Hughes, adobe with thick walls, good big rooms, rinconera [corner] fire places & neat safe beds; queer green Bermuda grass; trees, cottonwood & castor-oil [plants]; lots of water fountains & baths; nice contrivances about the house, which stands on a bluff overlooking the Colorado river & a wooded bottom land opposite. I spent the day in bed from a sort of clover bloat brought on by too many grapes & changing water so often—really bad pain. The rest were all well & more or less busy getting ready for the next day's start.

Sunday morning at nine we started in three ambulances, each drawn by six fine mules in good travelling condition. Father, Mother & I, with Mary, had the inside of the leading ambulance, Mr. Kitchen sitting by Magrath the driver; Frank took the seat on the second putting Thor inside with Mr. Paulisson & Mr. Smith to whom Father offered seats up—also all our hand bags & one trunk went on No. 2—we also had a trunk up behind; the third wagon carried the camp equipage, including a delightful Yankee notion of a table contrived for us by Maj. Lord; blankets, a little Sibley tent, our provisions, one trunk & Chung—who did our camp cooking. Yuma is quite a decent size, all rough adobe houses; the Indian men made a queer effect in their coats, long red sash & bare legs. Maj. Lord had made us thoroughly at home in his house & done everything possible that we should have a comfortable trip, up from the first requisite of good animals & safe drivers down to many a little contrivance which materially [aided] our comfort all along the road.

Soon after leaving the town we forded the Gila, the water reaching much above the hubs; the whole day's drive was through river bottom lands of sand & gravel; mesquite, ironwood, paloverde trees & another of Eastlake tan & green were plenty—some tall cactus. We crossed several ranges of low hills of altered stone, the road running straight up & down with many a sharp jolt. The Colorado was often in sight & we saw two steamboats going down the river to Yuma with their "hoppers" rigged & a man calling out the soundings like on the upper Missouri. We had expected to go up the river to Ehrenberg but the water is so low that Maj. Lord thought it more prudent for us to make the whole trip by land. We reached Castle Dome landing in the afternoon & pitched our tent right on the river bank a little ways from the cluster of adobes which formed the tiny village, a steamboat landing for mining supplies & transportation of ore from the Castle Dome mine, eighteen miles away (& every drop of water has to be hauled to it over mt. roads). Whilst the tent & camp were getting in order we women waited in the private rooms of one of the mine owners, earth floor & wattled roof, big oya [olla] with cool water, opera glasses & worked slippers. Took a sort of dinner at the house. We had a "cup of tea" at the camp by the light of the crescent moon which however soon sank behind the range of low ragged hills on the opposite bank. The stars were splendid & peculiarly reflected right down far into the water which gurled by, muddy but swift. We sat awhile talking comparative botany with Mr. Tyng,[28] nephew of St. George's, who had travelled in Morocco & Spain; we had given him a seat up in the second ambulance as he was going to see the [Castle] Dome mine. We turned in early; Mother & I, with Mary, under the shelter of the tent with our blankets laid on the tent fly which we doubled & used as a carpet; Father just outside the tent on a portion of the fly, the others round about wherever they found soft places in the sand; this was our order every night except that after the first we made a mattress for Mother of the ambulance cushions & the last camp it was so cold we made Father come inside the tent. The first night out we found our beds a little hard & a dust storm which blew over & into us did not add materially to our comfort.

Sept. 30th. Dressed by five; saw Capt. [Edward C.] Woodruff on his way to Yuma, who brought us greetings from Genl. Wil[l]cox;[29] his [Woodruff's] exultant "New York for two years!"[30] Had to wait for breakfast at the station, but got off at 7. The morning's pull was through the dry beds of stony & sandy creeks, with some bits of good travelling over high mezas [mesas] sandwiched in; in the wash beds—which spread out widely— were lots of trees of the paloverde, mesquite etc. & many bushes, but on the mezas we only saw occasional patches of white jimsonweed, in bloom. We halted for a nooning in the shade of some mesquite trees; ate a bit & watered the mules a little from barrels brought along; crossed during the afternoon's pull some very high hills on a very steep grade, with a long range of high jagged dry rock mountains of a red brown tinge stretching away to our right; & from the crest of the range we crossed we had a wide lookout over two large plateaus, on to one of which we descended, & where we offered—at Mother's suggestion—a drink of our canteen water to a tired sturdy looking miner who was trudging steadily along among the cactus under the burning sun. He took [it] cheerfully saying his canteen was empty—& it was still twelve miles to the water station! We gave him a lift in the second ambulance & when he slipped off his heavy pack & sat down he must have felt somewhat as Christian[31] when his load dropped off; it ended in our taking [him] the whole way—Prescott being his bout de promenade [objective]—as he was very helpful to the men & did their camp cooking which enabled the drivers to make earlier starts than they could otherwise have managed.

We passed seven kinds of cactus, from the tall column-like pitaya [pita-haya, now called saguaro] to the small fuzzy ones that resemble the old bottle washers. When we reached the stage station where we had expected to find water they had not enough for a drink apiece to our mules, so we had to turn off the stage road & push on five miles to Horse Tanks— a natural water hole where water never fails & whence it is hauled to the stage station. The road there was very rough from the number of deep, narrow arroyos to be crossed; we wound in & out amongst stony hills until we reached the amphitheatre shaped end of the cañon & there camped amongst cacti & stones with barely enough brush wood for our camp fires, but with plenty of water for the tired mules—for they had had a hard day's pull—& for cooking. A serrated ridge not far away apparently shut us in the cañon & high above us hung the crescent moon on the near edge of our cañon wall—whilst just above us were the Tanks, the basins hollowed out in the rock of graded sizes from that of a bath tub up to a small room; they receive the watershed of the hills round about & may have a spring as they never go dry & to them converge from all the ranges hereabout the well worn Indian trails, showing plainly on the bare rocky sides of the hills. We had a comfortable supper, then turned in after picking away the biggest stones from under our blankets & leaving the small ones to pack themselves level. We managed to have a right good sleep till near dawn when poor Thor plunged into the tent, taking refuge with me—all bewildered & nonplussed by his first encounter with a fuzzy cactus. He quieted down after I had pulled out all the thorns I could reach—those in his mouth bothering him most. We couldn't get to sleep again, so rose early.

October 1st. Venus splendid & the sunrise fine as there were some small cirrus clouds to turn pink & throw the jagged barrier range into blue. We left camp at seven, after coffee & ham. Yesterday's hard pull of 35 miles was rested from & the mules travelled free back to the station ([encountering] two men & some stage horses on [under] a ramada of ocotio [ocotillo]) where we greased the axles then on again, over a plain with better soil than yesterday's mezas—some tufty grasses with yellow & reddish bloom, many little yellow flowers growing low over the ground like seed weed; a sp[ecies] of pus[s]ley[32] & some zinnia looking flowers; no trees till near the end of the day. Sharp high mts. of dry red brown rock enclosed the plateau which was incessantly crossed by the dry beds of shallow creeks & brooklets—for torrents pour down from the mts. in the rainy season, but the water runs off at once leaving the soil, which only needs water to make excellent pasture or grain land, too dry for cultivation.

We stopped soon after twelve to rest the mules—no water for them—& take our nooning; very hot through the afternoon's pull, sandy part of the way too; we stopped at a water hole under the shadow of a big rock towards 2 o'clock, where there was [were] the remains of an adobe house, trees & bushes—some lovely clematis—& an Indian settlement, but they [the Indians] fled like deer when they saw us & watched from behind far away bushes whilst our 18 mules & Thor were being watered. It must have looked like a circus procession to them. We met the Prescott buckboard going to Yuma—that & the Indians [were] the only people we saw. Last night there were no people within 35 miles of us, except the two old men five miles off at the station, & a decidedly wild country all about us but no one even mentioned a guard & we slept as quietly as though we had been behind bolt & bar in our own city. The air is delightful & at night quite cool—today is the first time we have been bothered with the heat.

We made Tyson's Well by 3½ p.m. [The building is a] neat & large adobe; fine well of good water—4, 5 feet deep—the station for two stage lines & all the freighting from Ehrenberg to Prescott; kept by Germans. We sat in the porch whilst the camp was made ready—bought some eggs & canned things from them; picket fence [a]round [the] house enclosure & a grape vine started. We had an ugly camp in the dust on the dry creek bank, [with] low bushes & some trees—wagons too near. Mother bothered by it.

October 2nd. Broke camp at 7½ a.m. Came through a winding pass on a splendid road naturally macadamized; jagged mts. of black altered rock all dotted over with small green & grey bushes; later in the day struck a long sandy plain, heavy pulling for the mules. Passed two freight teams, 3 wagons & 12 mules each; made Desert Station about 1½. Sand plain with small bushes only, but a good adobe house with plenty of water—well 250 ft. [deep]—& a few cottonwoods round the trough, good cows & horses as there is range in the hills near by. Made a comfortable camp on clean sand—day awfully hot, so we women staid in the ambulances till sunset when we took our supper, sat talking about Bar Harbor & the Appletons as publishers[33] for a while, then turned in. Stars glorious & beautiful moonlight. The night was almost cold. Killed a young rattlesnake near camp. The station master here will keep no liquors [because] "the place is too lonesome for drinking."

October 3rd. Ate our breakfast by starlight & were nearly through when at 5 Venus rose; broke camp at six sharp & were on our way before the [sun] rose over the mts. More sand plain with occasional islands of the black rock hills—a rim of mts. encircling the plain. Later in the day we crossed a low range & came into a granite formation with more grass & taller bushes; stopped at Mesquite station—Mexicans—the best water on the whole route—well, 110 ft. [deep]—watered the mules & filled our canteens, also bought some milk; lots of stock & some goodish looking dogs, relations to greyhounds; nice tidy looking Mexican woman; lovely blue-backed, black butterflies; by this time it was hot & we dropped our cloaks which up to this had been comfortable & felt even our dusters to be too much.

Stopped again four miles farther on at Fly's station—well 150 ft. [deep]— where we waited half an hour to rest the mules, & to eat bread & cheese; then on again through more sandy plain, only grass grown now with flowers, some like the California poppy—only smaller. We gathered a bunch of them for [the] memory of Dr. Morton; made camp at Curran's [Culling's] station kept by a Mexican widow whose husband—an Englishman—died six weeks ago & whose third child was only a month old; a courteous, sweet faced young woman sorry for her loss.[34] (Basket cradle hung from the ceiling of ocotio rafters). The house was a big adobe with plank floors to the rooms & an earth floored hall running straight through [to] where the wagons stood & the jerked beef hung from the rafters. There were good large corrals, a rough dove cot & an excellent 360 ft. deep [well], the water brought up by a whim worked as usual by a white mule. Mother & I staid till sunset in the house; had a good wash & talked with the woman of the house. Sun oh! so hot—we made the station at 2. We had passed seven freight teams of 12 mules each; met three smaller ones & the stage. Our tent was pitched back of the corral out on the plain which was very dusty under the light grass. The sunset was glorious, all hues of the Venus saffron & tinting the mts. that completely encircled us, rising to 2,000 ft. with purples fading into blues; the moonlight too was very fine & the stars splendid. The day was furiously hot from about ten to sunset, the night cool to cold.

October 4th. Broke camp at 6 after an early tea & coffee; sunrise fine, crimson colors & many clouds; drove on fertile soil over a good stock grazing plain for some hours with the prickly pear the only cactus, then crossed a divide [making] the ascent through good paloverde & mesquite trees with some pitaya—debouched on to a high plateau with more sand & cactus & perfect groves of the dragon yucca [Joshua tree], many attaining the height & spread of an ordinary apple tree, a queer Doré[35] sort of tree having in its season great bunches of sweet scented white bloom[s] at the end of each branch. The glare was very bothersome & the heat intense— though our driver said it was only *warm* in comparison to southern Arizona. We crossed another divide & came to grass & bush covered hills & soon after made Date Creek station, a real creek with really big cottonwood trees; made a camp at one having come 35 miles. Frank killed a hare this morning & we saw some quail. The creek runs above ground through the cañon, some six miles long, then plunges underground in a wave line pattern so that at times water can be struck at 20 ft. whilst near by it can't be reached at past three hundred; here in the cañon there is always water. We pitched the tent amongst the trees by the creek which made itself many shallow channels through the sandy bottom—the cañon was narrow there with low Otter Creek, Mt. Desert[36] looking rocky hills on which grew tufts of yellow flowers & wind swept bushes which gave them a seaside effect, only disturbed by an occasional pitaya or date yucca. A falcon hawk sat on a rock near by & watched us for over ten minutes.

Gov. [John Philo] Hoyt and Sec. Gosper[37] arrived at about 3, having come out to meet Father. I suggested that as two emperors meet on barges in the middle of rivers so the two governors should stand on a broad plank in Date Creek & discuss the territorial affairs. They took tea with us & brought us an invitation from the Fitch[e]s[38] to come to their house "using it as your own till you can suit yourselves." Gov. Hoyt was très aimable [very pleasant]. Sunset fine, venus saffron changing to pink, clouds right across the cañon, & the moonlight was equally good broken by silver mackerel scales. As the sun set it shown [shone] on the crest of a wind swept, seaside looking hill rising just above the low rocky wall of the cañon, making it into an almost photographic likeness of the Bald Porcupine. We had comfortable beds in the dry sand of the creek bed.

October 5th. Left camp at seven & came six miles through Date Creek cañon, crossing the creek many times, a charming picture all the way, big cottonwoods, willows & rocky palisades, with large quantities of drift wood which showed how the water rose in the rainy season; came out on a grass valley with great beds of a kind of purple petunia. Kept ascending, grassy lands with good cattle range, no longer plains but small valleys now—crossed a high range of granite bowlder mts., road well made—some of the mountains sides perfectly covered with a yellow flower giving the gorse effect; saw a lovely pale blue & a scarlet flower today but the mules were on an up grade & we couldn't stop; asters & the Rocky Mt. sunflower too were plenty. Came down into a large fertile grass valley & made camp at Kelsey's station, on a creek with high banks & rushing chattering brook water such as McLean[39] likes.

The day was nothing like as hot as yesterday—a breeze all the time. A good deal of the land we have passed over today is "taken up." I staid in the ambulance in camp with Thor whilst Mother went up with all the others to the house which was very neat & well kept by an Illinois woman & her husband. She had been on the move all her life, Nevada, Nebraska, Colorado, California & now Arizona & was "most beat out with moving." We got good butter, grape pie & milk from her; her husband is justice of the peace & Father took the oath of office there & issued a proclamation about the approaching elections, Gov. Hoyt turning over things to him there as there was some responsibility about the elections he was to shirk—of course he didn't put it in just those words, but it had to be done today or it couldn't go into effect & that was the reason he came out to meet us. The night was really cold & Father wasn't well.

Sunday October 6th. Broke camp late at 7½ [a.m.] as we had only a short day's journey before us. Passed a really pretty farm, the lines of all the fences hedged with good cottonwoods, fine corn growing; neat buildings—all irrigated by the little creek; lots of cattle ranging; went through a cañon pass, ascending past a wonderful great granite bowlder, isolated & over fifty feet high—& many balanced bowlders—on into another valley, called Skull Valley, where there were many farms with fences & land under cultivation, good houses—all of wood now, cattle & horses ranging— meeting teams often, some ox teams. At one place there was quite a tavern with a very long shed & corral for teams. At Dickson's [Dixons][40] where we watered the animals first there was actually green grass around the house.

I forgot to say about Kelsey's station what a beautiful grass country Kirkland valley was, stretching far around out to the rim of encircling mts., one so odd with a great white blaze on its face & ending in a dome. The grass was so dry we had to be very careful with our camp fires which were built in the creek bed.

After the ascent of the mt. from Skull Valley began we passed really splendid junipers, some trunks over a yard in diameter—saw live oaks & small walnut trees—had beautiful views into folding mts., then as we rose higher struck in amongst the pines, real big trees with great boles & a thorough forest of them. We nooned at Iron Springs where there were many teams around the house, lots of cattle, a very fine spring & a real White Mts. effect of pines & granite boulders. Soon after leaving there the descent began, for on the summit we were about a thousand feet above Prescott—nearly 7000 [6,300 ft.] above sea level. On our right Thumb Butte made just the effect of a lion couchant—at one spot there was a really magnificent & glorious view out over all the mountains—then followed many good views on a smaller scale. The mt. sides near the road are beginning to shew the effect of the axe. About two miles out of town Genl. Wilcox met us in his ambulance with his sons.[41] Mrs. Hoyt,[42] Mrs. Bean[43] & Mrs. Bowen[44] also came to meet us & *the* barouche of the town was also there; so Father with Genl. Wilcox & Gov. Hoyt got in that & led, followed by the ladies' carriage—Mrs. Hoyt however getting in with us—then the Gosper carriage, then our ambulances & Genl. Wilcox's—his with four mules—so we made a procession almost as long as that of a circus company. We stopped at the Fitch house where we went in to a really prettily furnished cottage with water flowing from faucets—blue & silver papering in the room given to Mother, & Eastlake sunflower chintz in mine—the parlor all modern too—& such a really hearty welcome; the family [insisted they would] stay at a friends next door.[45] It took a long time to get the dust off. Ah Chung cooked the dinner as their cook had disappointed them—*6 courses*. We found letters from all our home people—including

Dr. Morton & Dr. Jameson[46]—waiting for us; things were going well with all of them. Dr. Jameson's letter was of Aug. 1st, a nice one in answer to mine telling him we were coming here.

Plenty of flowers along today's road, asters white & blue, goldenrod, sheep's foot—& new scarlet & white ones, also the Spanish bayonet, not in bloom now, & until we got in amongst the pines, the mts. & hills were covered to their tops with the Naples yellow flower, making the most brilliant effects. From Yuma to Prescott by the route we came is about two hundred & thirty-five miles. We brought the mules in in thoroughly good condition; they were good animals & did their work well. Our drivers were all up to their business & Magrath was a pleasant man to have to do with & managed the little caravan well.

Father was right ill for the first few days he was in town which forced the citizens to postpone till the 11th the reception ball they gave him, combining with it a farewell to Gov. Hoyt. Mr. Morgan[47] made the address of welcome & farewell—a good speech—& both Father and Gov. Hoyt replied, then everyone was introduced to us, after which the dancing commenced & soon Father slipped away back to the Fitches as he was tired out. Mother had to dance some quadrilles! Genl. Wilcox & his daughter[48] with most of the officers from the Post were present & were all very cordial in their welcome to us—most of them had already called on us. After the supper which was a very fine one, there were a lot of impromptu speeches, clever & well turned, Mr. Fitch, Genl. Wilcox and Mr. Bean's[49] being amongst the best, but they began to be a little *gay* & we got away about one o'clock, Mother going back to Mrs. Fitch's, but I going up to the Burmister house which Mr. Gosper persuaded Mr. Burmister[50] to let us have for $75.00 a month till his wife returns from Oakland which will be about Xmas.

On the morning of the 12th Genl. Wilcox started on a six weeks tour of inspection through the territory which he had been deferring to welcome Father & be present at the ball given to him. Dr. [Joseph K.] Corson, a real physician looking doctor who seemed nice, started in our ambulance with Magrath driving for Yuma to which station he has been transferred & Mr. Gosper went off by buckboard on a two months leave for the East. Also on the 12th Father & Mother moved up to the Burmister house—neat but not gaudy on the plan of a prosperous mechanic's house in one of Roe's temperance stories,[51] but having all the necessary household & kitchen things, which was handy for us as our baggage, crockery & groceries didn't arrive until the 26th of October sent up in a government wagon for us by Maj. Lord who has literally smoothed our path for us. Father was under the weather for some time, but worked away answering the letters which had banked up for him. Dr. McKee[52] from the Post took charge of him—also he had a report to prepare & send in to the Interior Dept. early in November, the Indian chiefs to see when they came to town to see him & Genl. Wilcox to talk over their grievances. Once they had a big talk out at Fort Whipple at which Father was present with Genl. Wilcox at the latter's request. Also there was the daily business to attend to. Mother soon rested & kept well. There were two local balls we went to; several performances well given at the theatre; visits to receive & return. We had the Hoyts to dine just before they started, then the Fitches; also Col. Booth, Judge Silent,[53] & Judge Archer,[54] Mr. Smith, Mr. Paulisson & Mr. Kitchen; Grace Wilcox[55] & Fanny Weeks[56] breakfasted with us more than once & Mrs. Buffum also took breakfast with us—and maybe some others.

After Genl. Wilcox return[ed], they gave us a very pretty dancing reception at his new headquarters at which all the Post & some of the people from the town were present. I had some nice drives with Mrs. Fitch, one good long one with Capt. Eagan[57] & Mrs. Bashford[58] & Mrs. Goodfellow[59] & another longer still through Willow creek valley with Mr. and Mrs. [Miss] Sherman.[60] Frank had one hunting excursion out to the Black Hills [in Yavapai County] & a mining excursion—horseback—out into the Bradshaw [mining] district [in central Arizona]; he also did lots of outside work for Father & studied parts & rehearsed at the theatre, playing a small part in "Richelieu"[61] & a leading one in [Charles] Dickens' "Dot." We had one snow & rain storm in October. I think the rest of the time the weather was lovely. Father issued the Thanksgiving proclamation in time for it to be generally observed—here in Prescott it was kept as it is in New York. We dined at Mrs. Fitch's, lending her Chung for the day, and met besides her family the Churchills,[62] Mrs. Churchill having only just arrived from "inside," Judge Silent & Mr. Head.[63]

Mrs. Burmister changed her mind & decided to come home earlier—we had only a few days notice of her coming & had to fly round hunting up a house—two were offered us at the Post but we hardly liked to leave the town if we could help it as it would make it difficult for people to get at Father—but we should not have succeeded if Mrs. Buffum & Mrs. Fitch hadn't taken things in hand & made the landlord[64] of the only house in town with bedrooms enough to hold us, tidy up his house & renovate it sufficiently for us to move in which we did whilst the paint was all fresh so that we were all more or less sickened by [the smell of] it.

We moved into our present house on November 29th & have had our hands full ever since getting it into order which is slow work where one has to do most things for themselves, including making the curtains by hand sewing. But I'll tell about the house after I catch up in my notes.

Father & Frank went off in a four mule ambulance, government transportation given them by Genl. Wilcox, on the 7th Dec. to Mineral Park, Mohave Fort, etc.[65] taking Judge Silent & Mr. Churchill with them. Father went to see for himself into the condition of the Indians, both Mohaves & Hualapais.[66] They got back on the 18th looking much the better for their trip & having done the work they set out to do. Whilst they were away we had a good quiet time working at the house, Mrs. Buffum constantly helping us; returning visits; going out to a pleasant little hop the officers gave in their club house at the Fort. We also had Judge & Mrs. Tweed[67] of Mineral Park to breakfast with us—they came to town for a few days only, [after] having met Father's party on the road & given him the keys of their house to use it whilst they were in the Park; also Mr. Anderson, assistant Sect. of State,[68] & Capt. Eagan, a friend of Hannah Lawrence's[69] through the Estells.[70] Mrs. Cory[71] breakfasted with us & Marshall Dake[72] dined with us & Mrs. Buffum often took breakfast with us. Two days before Father got back we were surprised by the Bowen-Ainsworth esclandre which was furious at first & has assumed several colors in turn being now the "whitest of the white" & "only a joke."[73] Of course when the principals view it in that light it is not for us & for the general public to take any notice at all—all the same there must have been a pretty good hot fire for the smoke to rise so furiously & persistently & it came very near splitting "society" in Prescott. Of course we have written home copiously & regularly & we hear frequently from all our friends & from our young people, except from Dr. Morton who has only written once, to Mother, & then said nothing about himself; Charley & Sally are very well & contented.

Christmas Eve we went in the evening to the theatre to see the presents given from the trees to the school children & candy & fruit to all the town children present—it was an interesting sight ending in a dance before which however we came away. Mother was the only grown person who received a present. Her history class—for she has gone over to the school several times on Fridays & given them a history talk—giving her a little work table basket.[74] The theatre was crowded with parents, relations & people generally. The Post band volunteered to play for the children.

Earlier in the month—after Mohave—Frank had ridden down into the Verde valley looking at ranches & taken Thor with him who enjoyed it—60 miles there & back—in spite of swollen paws.

December 26th. In the evening Frank & I went to the theatre where there was a gala performance given consisting of "Barney the Baron," "A Midnight Marriage" & "A Regular Fix," in which Col. [James Porter] Martin acted remarkably well & was well supported; the house was full & all had really good laughs in spite of the plays abounding in allusions which applied to the late smothered scandal & were only too well taken by the audience; all the leading characters in the late affair were present. Mother was not well enough to go & Father was tired.

Friday 27th. Mother had to remain in bed all through the day. Father & I went at seven to the Masons' installation ceremonies in the Court House; Frank played on the organ—a rather out of condition instrument—both a voluntary & for the amateur choir; Mr. Fitch made a very interesting, instructive & bright discourse—short too—after the ceremonies were over. The hall was crowded by a fine looking & respectable audience. The public part of the ceremonies were over early & we [were] home again by 8¾. Several of the Post people were at the installation, Parson Gilmore[75] getting there too late for his share in the ceremonies.

Sunday 29th was a quiet day.

Monday 30th. Mother had asked her class to come & spend the afternoon—photographs, chocolate & cakes—only part could come as some live far away & the weather was so stormy, besides many of them are down with the prevailing cold. Mary was in one of her worse growling fits—helped I'm afraid by a taste at some California wine recently sent to Father—so I had to do everything myself but all went off so smoothly that even Mother suspected nothing. The young people seemed really to enjoy themselves; there are a nice set of frank direct natured young ones & very quick. Grace Wilcox was too sick to come but Fanny Weeks came. Mother was able to be up for the children & staid up to dinner. Mr. Sherman staid some time after the children left, talking with Father & evidently taking clear comfort in so doing. Mr. Paulisson came in during dinner from the mine & mill he & Mr. Kitchen have invested in at Lynx creek, quite enthusiastic over his prospects. The mill is to begin running now & clean up every ten days. Stormy day with constant snow flurries.

Tuesday 31st. Saw to house & New Year's preparations & sewed hard all morning. Mother staid in bed & was in more pain so Frank left word at the Post for Dr. Ainsworth[76] to call which he did towards six, & said it was only a cold of a tedious & pain giving variety but not dangerous. I made nine visits in the town—mud galore & every one in—some nice German people & a Canadian. Mother got up for dinner. Mr. Paulisson dined with us & staid till near 9 when Father & Frank went to a party given by some association in the theatre; of course Mother couldn't go & I got off. Mary's growls burst in a sort of hysteric[al] fit in which she said a good deal she didn't mean—this was late at night & so didn't interfere with the day's routine. Things forgotten:

I took a ride with Miss [Marie] Wilcox & two of the young officers—my horse was a "trooper" buckskin with black points, old fashioned saddle of figured green velvet with an uncommonly short pommel; we rode over an hour, chiefly on a wood road through the pine forest; my saddle was intensely uncomfortable to me but still I managed to have some pleasure from being again on horseback after an interval of five years. A mounted orderly followed us—as I wrote East evidently to pick up the pieces when I came to grief.

New Year's Day 1879. I got up with a stunning sick headache which I carried straight through the day. Dr. Ainsworth called early & pronounced Mother well enough to receive. Of course we were ready by 10 o'clock but the visiting was confined to between the civilized hours of 12–8. Many people making real visits, pleasant ones to us too—all the Post came beginning with Genl. Wilcox, his aide-de-camp Mr. Haskell,[77] & Mr. [Elon F.] Wilcox, who knows Maggie Townsend.[78] We only had chocolate & cakes, as more than enough wines are about in a frontier town on such a day. Sally Upton sent Mother a Shakespeare calendar which got here this morning & is now in place having made a safe & suggesting "topic of the day" for us. I was tired out by my headache & went to bed at 8. Frank went out. Mother & Father had a quiet evening, retiring. The town was quiet.

Chapter 2

Tenth Legislative Assembly

January 2–February 14, 1879

Thursday [January] 2nd [1879]. Morning given to household things but being warned by the calendar that "delays have dangerous ends," I posted off through the mud after breakfast & visited the whole of "Nob Hill" including Mrs. Bowen as people are watching to see whether we call or not & since Mr. Bowen says "it was all a mistake." We are not called upon to see clearer than he does nor are we who have no interest in any of the set to be made to take sides. Personally I must say it was disagreeable to me to have to make the visit & had I been at liberty to do as I chose I should not have made it for I distinctly disapprove of the conduct of each of the principals concerned in that mess; however one has sometimes to be governed by a force majeure [stronger power]. I made eight visits in all, getting home quite tired as I had started out wearied by yesterday's headache & Mary's illtimed unreasonableness. Mother got up to dinner & when Dr. Ainsworth called he found her getting along right well. Father has been busy for some days past on his message [to the assembly]. The weather is mild during the day—which makes the walking bad—but cold at night; & gathering for more storms. This evening the sunset was very fine—bronzed orange colors changing to dull crimson & all against a background of dense grey.

Friday 3rd. "Let us not burden our remembrance with a heaviness thats gone" is the advice of our calendar for today & a principle which I think we as a family have acted up to pretty thoroughly. Mother got up early for her but was in so much pain that we had Dr. Ainsworth stopped as he was passing & he made her go back to bed there to remain till further orders & she was much better by night. Mrs. Buffum made her a visit in the afternoon. Father worked on his message through the day, saw some of the newly arrived members of the Legislature in the evening & retired early. Frank divided his day between outside work for Father & learning a long part given him in one of the new plays. I had indoor things for the morning & visits in the afternoon, clearing the town docket. The mud wasn't quite as bad as on the two other days. Mary came to her senses this morning & I think things will work smoothly again, at least for a few months. I sat up late copying my "notes." Day mild & overcast, with showers from 4 on.

Saturday 4th. Gave the day to odds & ends of necessary indoor work. When Dr. Ainsworth called in the morning he was quite satisfied with Mother's condition, said she might get up & that he wouldn't come again unless sent for—but in the afternoon & evening she did a long piece of copying Father's message—& was a little bothered too so she had a very bad night. Father was busy all day with his message & things in connection with it—saw Mr. Paulisson & the Goldwaters[1] for a while in the evening. Mrs. Fitch, Mrs. Bashford & Mrs. Burmister called during the day. Weather fine.

Sunday 5th. My day was rather quiet, & no writing for my hand is tired out with sewing & writing. Mother had a great deal of pain & we sent for Dr. Ainsworth who changed her medicine & told her to stay in bed—she was better in the evening & slept well. Father was busy with his message & things in connection with it—also he saw Mr. Fitch & Mr. Churchill in the evening.

Monday 6th. Mother had to keep [to] her bed all day but wasn't in pain. Father answered many letters. I sewed at my alpaca skirt, making a botch of it first then getting it right. Frank was in & out. We had nice letters from Charley & Sally—[dated] Dec. 24. The Supreme Court convened & the Legislature met this morning—both adjourned over on account of Mr. Bowers's[2] death, the Legislature without completing its organization.

The Sisters of St. Joseph [of Carondelet][3] who have charge of the county hospital called. Some of the members called whilst we were at dinner which decided us whilst they are here to dine earlier that we may be free for visitors at their early hours. Snow has disappeared from the town but the sunset threatened some kind of storm.

Tuesday 7th. Woke to a howling snowstorm which had already covered everything some inches deep, but cleared off cold & bright about 2 p.m. Mother slept till near noon & had a comfortable day. Father devoted himself to letters except for the brief interval of attending the funeral services at Mr. Bowers's house. Frank went on with the procession to the Masonic burial grounds; it was quite a long & imposing procession being led by the Masons on foot & closed by men on horseback, many varieties of vehicles including the Post ambulances filling in between. There is no hearse so one of the larger express wagons was draped with black & used; the flags were half masted & the bells of the school house & court house tolled alternately. Mr. Bowers had been for four years sheriff of the county doing his duty fearlessly in the days when to have his horse shot under him whilst pursuing desperadoes was not uncommon. Both the Supreme Court & the Legislature attended the services at the house. Mrs. Martin[4] came in just as we were going to breakfast—to borrow some of my riding things for the play this evening—& we asked her to breakfast with us, which she did. Father, Frank & I walked up to the theatre over the crisp frozen snow with the moonlight so clearly bright that we could read writing by it & the whole view as distinct as by daylight, only all altered into a more grand effect. The play was "Led Astray"[5] & well acted throughout, the force of the company being in it—but the [best] was Mr. Fitch's "Cousin Hector." Mrs. Fitch—Armande—had actually lent all her parlor furniture even to the carpet! The coldest day they've had in this town in years, night colder still. Mrs. Bean & Mrs. Bowen called together today.

Wednesday 8th. Mother had a comfortable day, though she found getting up for dinner tired her very much. Father wrote letters, saw people who called & also two committees from the Assembly & Council which came to inform him the Legislature was completely organized & asking him to read his message to them in person tomorrow in the rooms of the Supreme Court, lent to them for the occasion;—in this they follow the practice of the English parliament which California & Oregon have adopted & not that of the Eastern States where the governor's message is read by the Clerk of the Senate.

Mrs. Buffum came across to see Mother & we kept her to breakfast. Mrs. Churchill also called during the day & had her German eyes fill at the sight of our home Xmas cards which we have grouped (with Maggie Townsend's photograph) against the [. . .] of the bay window. Frank carried Father's message, officially as Private Sect. to the Legislature— which they returned at once wishing Father to do the reading. [Frank] did outdoors things for Father, studied his part in the coming play & recited it with me, went to the rehearsal at 6 & at 8 went with some others in the ambulance out to the Post where the regular fortnightly hop was turned into a rehearsal of the coming German, as several of the ladies have never danced it. I sewed, did household things & in the evening wrote to Nell. We had a long Xmas letter from her this morning—also Mother heard from Maggie Townsend & from Nelly Sherwood. Charley

& Sally spent Xmas at Nell's. Day very cold for Prescott, thawing in the sun however; another wonderfully beautiful moonlight night.

Thursday, January 9th. Father & Frank went down to the Court House at 11 where Father read his message—en entre [in addition to] the Legislature there was a large audience including Genl. Wilcox & his staff & Miss Wilcox & several other ladies. I should have gone had I known any ladies were to go. The message was favorably received & after its delivery Father made the acquaintance of most of the members; Genl. Wilcox brought him home; Grace Wilcox & Fanny Weeks took breakfast with us then went up to school. Mr. Sherman had taken the higher class to hear the message read. After breakfast Father & Frank took Thor & went for a long climb on the hills to the east of the town startling hare & many coveys of partridges & in the evening Father went to a terrapin supper at Mr. Fitch's & Frank went up to a rehearsal. Mother had a day without pain getting up to breakfast & staying up late. I sewed in the intervals of other things. Mr. Gosper & Mr. Romberg [Rumburg][6] of Phoenix made a long call in the afternoon. Mr. Kitchen & Mr. [William H.] Hardy, a pioneer after whom Hardyville on the Colorado is named & who has the big flock of angora goats, called in the evening. The evening papers printed Father's message in full with approving editorials. Cool & cloudy morning, clearing off cold.

Friday 10th. Mother was up all day & felt pretty well. Father was busy seeing people & answering letters. Frank in & out. I sewed & did scraps. Miss Wilcox, Miss Parker[7] & the Pines[8] called. In the evening Mr. Gosper & Speaker [Madison W.] Stewart then Judge Silent called. Day cold & bright, but very muddy. Night very cold.

Saturday 11th. Mother was up all day, chiefly writing letters & seeing people. Father worked at the School reports & letters. Judge Silent took breakfast with us. In the afternoon I called on the Sisters at the Hospital, Mrs. Burmister, Mrs. Buffum & Mrs. Churchill—all [were] in.—& on Mrs. Fitch & her mother, [who were] out. Frank went to rehearsal in the evening. Day lovely overhead & very muddy underfoot.

Sunday 12th. Mother only moderately well through the day, more tired & nervous than sick, but almost ill again in the night. Some how the day was an uncomfortable one though nothing special went wrong. Frank went out to the Fort in the afternoon & Mr. Evans[9] stopped in here to tell us he had kept him to dine with "a lot of 2nd lieuts." so he only got home towards ten. Father was busy. Mr. Anderson made a long call; Judge Silent & Mr. Sherman were in & out. I did nothing beyond writing to Maggie Woodruff & reading. The weather was pleasant.

Monday 13th (Nelly Browne's birthday). Father busy as usual through the day & Judge Silent breakfasted with us. Mother had a day without pain & sat up a while in the evening. Mrs. Fitch called in the afternoon. Frank was busy getting his disguise—a monk's gown—ready for the masquerade of the 15th out at the Post. Mr. Bashford[10] & Mr. Anderson wear exactly the same & they expect on intriguing the people; in the evening Frank went to the rehearsal. I mended things & did odds & ends. We had a quiet evening. Grace Wilcox & Fanny Weeks made us a call during recess. Stormy weather threatening.

Tuesday 14th. Mother up again & helped Frank with the masquerade dresses but she isn't yet well enough to go out after night so she had to give up seeing Frank act. Father was busy in the usual way. I sewed all morning. Mrs. Martin & Dr. Ainsworth stopped in for a little visit. In the afternoon I took a drive with Mrs. Fitch—out beyond the Fort. She found it very cold, but it only seemed like a breezy Fall day to me. Father & I went to the theatre together & sat by Mrs. Fitch; the play ("£100,000") was well spiritedly acted & gave the audience—a large one in spite of the storm—great satisfaction. Frank had the lover's role & did it very naturally, one scene between him & Miss Parker exciting quite a murmur of approval from the men present. We came down home through snow ankle deep & the high storm wind beat the snow into our faces so that it was difficult to see our way & made the bright & warm interieure [inside] of the house very pleasant to get back into. The Southern members [of the assembly] were all shaking their heads over Prescott's climate. The weather had been threatening all day but the storm didn't burst till seven in the evening—just in time to prevent many people from coming to the theatre; all through the night it howled round the house—a regular high mountain storm.

Wednesday 15th. Mother well all day & busy with the masquerade dresses. Father busy most of the day seeing people. He & Frank went to the ball at about 9 in a Post ambulance; there was some mistake about the ambulance in picking up the people in town so there were not all present who were expected. [And] at the ball the Legislature didn't understand having a

German after midnight & no more square dances so things were not quite so pleasant as the officers had intended, though there was still a good deal of pleasure & would have been more but for the sourde [voiceless] feeling of antagonism always at work in frontier towns against the army & which is here on the watch for slights. I couldn't go, having nothing just right to wear. Had a combination letter from Sally & Charley; they were in town [New York] and apparently well amused. The day was bright & everything looked smilingly pretty under the fresh fall of light powdery snow, which until packed by tramping, sweeps aside like dust. The night was intensely cold.

Thursday, 16th. Father wrote letters and saw one or two people. Mother was up feeling well all day. I sewed & did scraps. Frank helped us fix things in the house & carried a communication from Father to the Legislature. In the evening Frank & I went across to Major Dake's house where we met a lot of the young people of the town to see about getting up a little sheet & pillowcase party to the Legislature & Post.[11] [That] was the original idea & it was amusing to see how many changes & how much talk it took to finally result in no action. I was entertained & that was about the most result attained & unintentional quite. The citizens and Legislature are very huffy over the ambulance mistake, magnifying it into an intention to slight them. Day bright & clear.

Friday 17th. Father & Mother both busy seeing people through the day, including Mr. Campbell[12] the delegate who goes East on Monday & to whom Mother gave some letters of introduction; also they were busy with letters. I did a lot of copying, papers to be submitted to the Legislature. In the evening Frank went to a rehearsal of "Helping Hands."[13] Mr. Gosper called bringing Mr. Vail[14] of Florence & Mr. Alsap[15] of Phoenix with him. Mr. Vail knew Nassau & Canadian people so we had a subject of common interest to start in on. Fair weather.

Saturday 18th. The day passed in the usual routines of work & seeing people. I did a lot of copying. Miss Sherman & Mr. Wilcox called to see us. Judge French[16] & Judge Silent dined with us—going afterwards as did Father & Frank to hear Mr. Fitch's lecture on "the Indian"—all against them. I retired early. Clear weather.

Sunday 19th. Pretty Xmas cards from Mary Martin[17] in the morning's mail & a good letter from McLean; he was in Paris & had been offered the place of assistant French teacher at Annapolis—a two years' station—which he had accepted & was going to study hard. He only goes on duty June 1st. Morning quiet. Lt. Touey[18] breakfasted with us. Father wanted to see him about laying out some R[ail] R[oad] lines north through the coal fields to San Juan mining district to connect with eastern roads & south to Maricopa Wells to join the Southern Pacific. Mr. Touey though still a very young officer has surveyed most of this Territory & knows clearly what he does know. Mother & Father both wrote during the afternoon & I copied for Father. In the evening Frank went out to the Martins at the Post. Day lowering & threatening.

Monday 20th. Mother moderately well through the day. Father busy over School report. I did some more copying for Father. Frank went to rehearsal after dinner & at nine came back & took me across to Major Dake's where we had a carpet dance—growing out of the Pillow & Sheet talk of the other night—the Pines, Shermans, Miss Parker, Miss Catheroe [Kethroe][19] & Frank & I with a few additional young men, about fourteen in all, made up the party. There was as music a violin & a guitar & Major Dake gave us a supper that would have sufficed for forty; it only took a little while for the people to recover from the newness to Prescott of such a thing as a small dance. After that they all enjoyed themselves very much in spite of the increased work that the Chinese New Year & crowded rehearsals have thrown on the ladies & it was 2 a.m. when we broke up. Day overcast, night mild for the first time in a long while. (All night the Chinese firecrackers were popping off).

Tuesday 21st (Father's birthday). Quiet day with the usual routine. Being the Chinese New Year I gave Chung the day [off] but he insisted on coming back to cook breakfast, which was very unusual as the Chinese generally claim two or three days of complete holiday at this time. Mary cooked the dinner however. Mother went with us to the theatre as the night was very mild & she wanted to see Frank act, which he did as "Dr. Merton" in "Helping Hands." "A Regular Fix" was given also; both were well acted & the audience was evidently very much pleased with the performance. Frank's rendition of the lover being specially well received; the house was crowded. I did a drive with Mrs. Fitch in the afternoon—the sun was warm & it felt like Bear Valley spring weather.

Wednesday 22nd. Father was busy in the morning with the annual meeting of the school board. Grace Wilcox & Fanny Weeks breakfasted with us. At 2 p.m. Father & Mother went up to the School House where the

Jessie Benton Frémont, c. 1863. (Courtesy of the National Portrait Gallery, Washington, D.C., photo #NPG.81.M95.)

scholars gave an exhibition to the Legislature which went off very well & some of the members also made little speeches & Father spoke for a few moments. The whole affair was a success & showed the Assembly what a really good school Prescott has & how much it owes to Mr. Sherman's perseverance. Whilst Mother was out Mrs. Blake, Mrs. Rush, Mrs. Lewis,

John Charles Frémont, engraved from a photograph by Doremus, from *Harper's Weekly*, July 26, 1890.

Mrs. Kelly, Miss Stevens [Stephens][20] & Mrs. Goodfellow called & I saw them all though I was dazed sick with a headache & looking to get my head down on a pillow. After dinner Mr. Hughes & Mr. Kirkpatrick,[21] Judge Silent & Capt. Eagan, who is just back from a short leave with his people in Oakland, called & spent the evening—the Judge staid after the others having a little business talk with Father & then taking a cup of tea & shaking off a little of the homesickness that has been weighing on him lately. Frank was chiefly busy through the day learning the King's part in "Richelieu" & in the evening went to a rehearsal. The lovely mild weather continues. Chung back at work again today. This morning I had a letter from Betty telling us she will go with Maj. Hughes to St. Louis, to which place he is just transferred as QM [quartermaster].

Tuesday 23rd. Usual routine of day—varied in the afternoon by Mother & me in working on a "costume" for me to wear to the Wilcoxes—all old things put together anew. In the evening Mr. Purdy, Mr. Carpenter & Mr. Fay, southern members of the Assembly, called.[22] We had pleasant letters from Sally & from Nelly in the day's mails & also one from Hannah Lawrence. The weather was lovely.

Friday 25th [24th]. I was busy all day working on my dress to wear in the evening. Mother helped me during the morning & in the afternoon she went up to the School for one of her history talks with the upper class, Fanny Weeks & Grace Wilcox coming down for her. Father was busy as usual. The ambulance came for us soon after 9 & we came home at 1 a.m. The getting in & out of the ambulance was a job as the wheels's steps were cover[e]d with mud from the heavy roads; the party was given to the Legislature & as Col. Weeks himself took charge of the transportation it all ran smoothly—it was a very pretty party & thoroughly successful, everyone enjoying themselves; I had a pleasant time personally. The Headquarters house adopts itself to party giving & Genl. Wilcox is so welcoming in his manners that everyone feels at ease in his house. [And] besides his aides, who each worked faithfully at their share of duty, all the Post had resolved itself into a committee of assistance. [And] if the Legislature were not pleased and mol[l]ified the blame must lie with themselves—but everyone did seem pleased & all granted it was the prettiest party ever given in Arizona & the most enjoyable. The weather still mild.

Saturday 25th. Quiet day indoors. Father of course busy with letters & people & Mother doing a little copying for him besides letters for herself. Fanny Weeks came in on horseback & made us a little visit during breakfast, hitching her sorrel to the fence rails. She rides well & likes it. Later in the day Grace Wilcox stopped for a few moments & would have staid longer only her young brothers refused to wait for her; it was very pleasant to be able truthfully to tell the girls how much we had liked the party & how glad we were it had gone off without the slightest contretemps. Frank was chiefly busy with the practisings for the concert to be given early next month. Day lovely—birds singing & air balmy, night very windy, but not cold.

Sunday 26th. A quiet home day. I only wrote to Nelly. Father went across to see Mrs. Fitch & took a walk with Frank after dinner. Frank went to Mr. Foster's[23] in the evening. Very windy but not cold. Mother rested & wrote to McLean.

Monday 27th. Father busy all day answering letters. We had a quiet day. Mr. Touey & Mr. Evans called, the first only stopped to leave some maps with Father but Mr. Evans staid to breakfast & afterwards—"a la '924 Madison Ave'" style[24]—Grace & Fanny were in & out. Thor & I took a short walk in the afternoon. Mrs. Ellis[25] called. Frank went to rehearsal in the evening. Mr. Paulisson—in from his mill for the day—called in the evening. A Bill which commences the struggle about the Capital was brought in today. Weather threatening.

Tuesday 28th. (Charlemagne).[26] Quiet morning. Genl. Wilcox came in to see Father & staid to breakfast. Fanny & Grace came in for a few minutes. Frank & I went out to the Post in the afternoon—in the omnibus ambulance—& made five visits, seeing Mrs. Martin, Mrs. Weeks, Mrs. Biddle[27] & Mrs. Smith;[28] Miss Wilcox was "out." In the evening we went to the theatre. "Richelieu" by request (Frank in the part of the King as Mr. Churchill wouldn't do it again—had stage fright too badly last time). The house was crowded; pleasant people sat near us. The acting was good & understandingly received. The Post, the Legislature & the Judges were all there. Mother was not quite so well today though she managed to go to the theatre. Frank did his king's part right well & looked well in the clothes of that period. Nice letter from Aunt Eliza in the morning's mail; Mother wrote to her and to Betty today. Day very windy with driving clouds & air chilly.

Wednesday 29th. Morning as usual. In the afternoon, I went across the creek & made visits. Mr. Palmer & Mr. [James] Clark arrived about 3 o'clock having come round from Adonde[29] via Phoenix & the Black Cañon. They had lovely weather all the time—houses to sleep in & their animals travelled well, they have good horses & an ambulance made on purpose in Concord; they have rooms in the hotel across the street from us.

Mr. Palmer dined with us & afterwards Father went across & staid some time with them talking over their plans. Mr. Gosper made a short call in the evening, then came Judge Silent & Col. Seamans[30]—the latter from the East & looking over the Territory with a view to investments. Mother had a quiet day embroidering & talking with Judge French who made a long call in the afternoon; he leaves for Tucson soon. Day lovely when you could get sheltered from the wind which blew high—sunset stormy & the snow fell thickly all through the night.

Thursday 30th. Beyond the usual routine of seeing to the running of the house & writing some letters I did nothing all day. Mother had a quiet day too. Judge Silent took breakfast with us & staid for a while afterwards. Grace Wilcox came in as we were going to breakfast, ate it with us & spent her recess here. Mr. Palmer came in towards two o'clock & talked over his plans; & was in again after dinner. Mr. Alsap called in the evening & we had rather a skate-tracky talk with him starting at sugar growing in Phoenix & fetching up at a Drawing room in London. He is an easy man to talk with. It snowed all through the morning but was mostly all melted away by sunset.

Friday 31st. I felt sick & did nothing all morning. Mr. Palmer & Mr. Clark breakfasted with us. Grace & Fanny came in during recess. Fanny was looking really sick so I kept her here to wait for the school ambulance, rolling her up in an afghan & putting her in the bay window, with novels, cakes & cold water, whilst I went out to drive with Mrs. Fitch & Mother went up to the School for her history talk with the children. She had a specially pleasant afternoon with them. I had a nice drive with Mrs. Fitch & got in just as the girls were leaving in the ambulance & Mr. Haskell with Mr. Vail coming to call. After dinner Mr. Palmer, Mr. Clark, Mr. Cordis,[31] Mr. Stewart, Mr. Kirkpatrick, Mr. Thomas,[32] Mr. & Mrs. Beach, Mrs. Kelsey & Miss Wilkins[33] "dropped in" one after another & spent the evening with us, staying till after 10 & seeming to have a pleasant time. Judge Silent, Mr. Touey & lots of others were in & out on business during the day & Father had as usual a busy time. Weather sunshiny & pleasant.

Saturday, 1st February. Usual routine for the morning. Mr. Clark & Mr. Palmer breakfasted & dined with us. I took a short drive with them in their ambulance & four—it does not ride as easy as the one we came up in. Several ladies called during the afternoon. Mrs. Wollenberg's baby[34] with its thick hair being *the* success. Frank was chiefly occupied day & evening with the concert rehearsals. Judge Silent came in after dinner & had a long quiet talk with Father. Mother & I had a pleasant time with our novels.

Sunday 2nd. A constant va-et-vient [coming and going] all day & great excitement over the order from the President making the whole Salt River Valley an Indian reservation thus dispossessing about [1,000?] whites whose farms have been created by their industry in "ditching," & turning over to 1000 Indians nearly a million acres of the best agricultural & sugar lands of the territory & most of the water of the Gila & all that of the Salt River—the reservation extends over & blots out of existence the towns of Phoenix, Meza [Mesa] City & Tempe.[35] Of course it can't stand but before it can be repealed a collision between the whites & Indians is feared, for our settlers in that portion of the Territory are chiefly ex-rebels from Texas & the sugar states, & not as patient as our northern people. Most people acquit the President of anything more than a blunder, but feel sure that others have done it for some job purpose. Father was out at the Fort & Genl. Wilcox was here: other officers also—& Judge Silent too. Our day was very different from the usual quiet Sundays here. Mr. and Mrs. Bean called in the evening. Weather very pleasant but threatening another storm.

Monday 3rd. Day began with a nice letter from Charley—up off Conn. replacing buoys the ice had forced loose. Everyone still immensely occupied over the Pima Reservation question. Mr. Clark & Mr. Palmer breakfasted & dined with us. Genl. Wilcox came in during the morning. Grace & Fanny came in as we were going to breakfast & took their lunch with us. In the afternoon I had a lovely drive with Mrs. Fitch, out over farm tracks to the north west of the town, getting the mts. from new points of view. I saw where Thumb Butte gets its name, the storm clouds of various shades of grey were very fine, a real "winter scene amongst the mts." Topsy was fresh & gay. Mother had a visit from Mrs. Evans & Mrs. [Benjamin] Morgan. Evening quiet as it began to pour about 7 o'clock. Frank was busy about the concert through the afternoon & evening. Mr. Meade[36] called in the afternoon. Before midnight the rain changed to snow & sleet & continued through the night.

Tuesday 4th. Not quiet so many people in & out today on the Reservation business. Mr. Clark & Mr. Palmer took their two breakfasts with us but dined at the Fitch[e]s. Grace & Fanny came in & took breakfast with us. I read a lot of newspapers. Mother wrote a long letter to Charley in the intervals through the day & both of us had a real satisfaction in watching the storm for it rained & snowed all through the day—real "Eastern slope" weather. Judge Silent came in towards five & we kept him to dinner. Frank was busy alternately with rehearsals for the concert & carrying messages to the Legislature. Some people came to see Father on business through the evening & Mr. Alsap & Mr. Anderson made us a visit. Mother had a letter from Dr. Morton this morning.

Wednesday 5th. A busy day with Father's "legislators" in & out all the time. Mr. Haskell in with a message from Genl. Wilcox. Mr. Palmer & Mr. Clark took all their meals with us & were in & out all day; ex-Gov. Safford[37] arrived early from Tucson on S[outhern] P[acific] R[ail] R[oad] business

& came directly to see Father who asked him to return to breakfast, which he did. Mother & I had an "overflow meeting" in the parlor during the last busy day of the Assembly as they are all slightly huffy if they are left waiting by themselves & yet they want each to see Father alone—unless they come as committees. After dinner Frank & I went out to the Fort to a farewell hop given to Lt. Touey who has a year's leave & goes off soon; all the Legislature & many citizens were there & quite a number of ladies [from] Prescott, but the men outnumbered them five to one so all had plenty of [attention]; everything ran smoothly & a spirit of amused pleasure prevailed which made it very pleasant; we came home *early*—2¼ a.m. We packed in with 8 others in the "school ambulance." Night cold with beautiful moonlight. Frank very [busy] with the concert & the Legislature. Fanny & Grace were here during part of the midday recess.

Thursday 6th. Like yesterday as to busy work with the addition of business writing for Mother & lots of copying for me. Besides Mr. Clark & Mr. Palmer, Mr. Alsap of Phoenix took breakfast with us. We dined alone as Mr. Palmer & Mr. Clark dined out but joined us at the concert. After dinner, Capt. Eagan, Mr. Haskell & Capt. [Joseph Henry] Hurst—a new officer on his way to Camp Verde—called. Mother was tired out & lying down to rest up for the concert so I saw them. The concert was a big success & really good music—Mrs. Parker[38] singing "Waiting" really well & the whole thing took. Frank did his duet with the violin uncommonly well—besides which he played all the accompaniments & seems to have lost none of his old touch. Mr. Palmer was overwhelmed with pleased surprise at both audience, performers & performance. "Everybody" was there including nearly all the Post. Day clear but cool. Frank glad to be done with the concert work but pleased to demonstrate the success of music here.

Friday 7th. House full all day with people coming on Legislature business. Mr. Palmer & Mr. Clark got off about 10 o'clock. They expect to reach Tucson in ten days, resting two at Phoenix. Their hearts are set on getting a great cattle ranch in the southern portion of the Territory—mines they have come to grief in & are afraid to try. Mrs. Fitch called. Gov. Safford & Mr. Paulisson breakfasted with us. At 2 Mother went up to her history talk at the School, Gov. Safford joining her & going up with her & whilst there he made a little speech to the School in which he highly congratulated them on the interest Mother took in them & their good fortune in having her to talk to them. Father had an answering telegram from Mr. Schurz[39] to the Assembly memorial he had telegraphed off to Washington—not vacating the "reservation order," but explaining & modifying it. Lots of sharp telegrams about the "Smith divorce" which is included in an omnibus divorce bill[40]—signed before some of the telegrams arrived. Threatening weather.

Saturday 8th. Not quite so busy a day as they have been lately. Genl. Wilcox was amongst those who came on business. We had Dr. Ainsworth come to see Mother—he says it is only reaction from the overstimulating air here, acting like when one stays too long at the seaside. I had a pleasant drive with Mrs. Fitch in the afternoon—part of the time young Wilcox rode beside us on his prancing buckskin. He rides well so it made an effective picture especially as the greyhound was with him. Judge Silent dined with us & staid a while afterwards. Frank went to a performance at the theatre given by the soldiers. Day overcast. I had a nice long letter from Dr. Jameson.

Sunday 9th. Father, Mother, Frank & Thor had a good walk before breakfast, Mother stopping in on her way home & making a visit to Mrs. Buffum who she found had been ill with a bad cold. Judge Silent took breakfast with us. We had an almost quite quiet afternoon. Mr. Clark[41] called in the evening. Father was busy with papers.

Monday 10th. Delegations about Probate Judges & lots of people calling all morning. Judge Silent in & out many times besides breakfasting with [us], which Grace & Fanny also did. Secy. Schurz's telegram in answer to the Assembly's memorial to the President was sent in to the Assembly in the afternoon & made the opening question for tomorrow's session. Everyone appeared huffed at his answering instead of the President, nor did the substance of the despatch please them. Frank was busy all day back & forth to the Assembly & also out to the Fort. Judge Silent came up in the evening after the night session was over.

Tuesday 11th to Saturday 16th [15th]. The days were each & all devoted to the hurried business of the Legislature which left all its real work for the last few days. From early morning to late at night the house was full of people in connection with Legislative business & Father was kept busy all the time. Stormy night sessions were held. At the one on Thursday evening Mr. Purdy made an insulting attack on "Federal officers" & inserted into the appropriation bill a clause granting the expenses for an Envoy to Washington on the Indian Reservation question, but substituting Mr. Alsap's name for Father's. Father having already been appointed the one to go by a joint resolution & having sent in his message accepting, so that it was a settled question. But Mr. Purdy thought by making it a "rider" to the appropriation bill & complicating it cleverly with the political question to carry his point—there were several things about his way of doing it which made it an insulting piece of treachery & it was taken up & resented as such, making of Friday's debate a stormy & prolonged scene which was only ended finally at about 6½ in the evening when Capt. Eagan ran up to tell us the result—he only having heard of it all at four o'clock for the first time & been working vigorously on the Federal side up to the carrying of the measure. Of course Judge Silent worked hard & was in & out a great deal as were also Mr. Fitch & Churchill—& many outsiders who like Lt. Haskell's brother[42] only just stopped in to express their indignation & then went off to add their share to the general work; for such uncalled for action was resented by the whole community. Inside our house for ourselves the day was ominously quiet, for Father, taking the matter as a slap at the Central Federal authority, reserved his action on many of the bills in his hands letting his action be guided by the final result in the Assembly. We were all tired by the time the committee came up a few minutes before twelve on Friday night to notify the Governor they were ready to adjourn sine die [indefinitely]—for more bills had come up during the evening on until after 11½ & many were unsigned by the Speaker & President of the Council, as a tipsy member of the Council (F. D. Welcome) not liking some of them had pocketed a lot & it was late before they could be found & recovered from him. [And] it was a general hurry & scuffle for each man who was needed, as a ball to the Legislature was going on & many of them were at it, only enough remaining in the House to make a quorum. We all went up to the Ball when the Assembly adjourned at midnight, Father & Mother only staying about twenty minutes as they were tired but Frank & I staid till near 2 o'clock—came home & had a long talk with Mother & Father over the defunct Legislature & its acts, which as far as we are concerned all went the way we wanted—& turned in after 3. Too tired & too excited I was to get to sleep for a long time afterwards. This is the gist of the foregoing days. I was too driven & my time too much cut into shreds to be able to write up notes everyday.

Chapter 3

Lily Gives French Lessons, Jessie Teaches History

February 15–August 22, 1879

Saturday, February 15th. Morning spent in finishing up lists etc. belonging with legislative work. Judge Silent breakfasted with us—so did Mr. Weber[1] who staid on & on till breakfast was on the table & we were obliged to ask him to stay, much against the grain. Fanny Weeks rode in & made us a visit—lots of people still coming & going, both on business & to congratulate us on the way things worked at the last in the Assembly.

Sunday 16th. Morning quietly busy. Genl. Wilcox & Judge Silent breakfasted with us. Afterwards a lot of people called; ending up after dinner with Dr. McKee, who is just back from an inspecting tour through the southern portion of the Territory—then Capt. Eagan, who unfolded his plan about Mr. Estell to us. There was very little time in between visits—not enough to settle to anything. We had asked Mr. [P.] Thomas of Pinal to dine with us as he, though a Democrat, had stood by our side in the mission to Washington business, but he had with regret to excuse himself. Weather good.

Monday 17th. Lots to do for the new County of Apache;[2] members calling to make their adieu. Mrs. Buffum came in & made a long visit showing us the paperings for her new house. Judge Silent was in & out. Mr. & Mrs. Fitch spent the evening with Mother & me; Father meanwhile working at papers.

Tuesday 18th. Father & Frank walked out to the Post to see Genl. Wilcox, chiefly about ambulance for Father to go off in; whilst he was away lots of people called both on business & P.P.C. [pour prendre congé; to take leave]; Mr. Vail amongst the latter & we gave him a note to Charley as he goes East this summer. Mrs. Fitch came in & had a long talk with Mother. Judge Silent breakfasted with us. I had a drive with Mrs. Fitch in the afternoon. Fanny Weeks rode in & made us a call bringing Mother some lovely hyacinths. Mother got some Chinese things to send home to the young people & worked monograms on Charley's & Sally's Hkfs [hand-kerchiefs]. Mr. Kirkpatrick was in several times during the afternoon & in the evening Father & Judge Silent walked up & saw Mr. Bean about specimens. Day really warm—no wraps needed in driving.

Wednesday 19th. Day chiefly given to copying & helping Father get his papers ready for his start on Saturday. Judge Silent breakfasted with us & was in & out during the day; so was Mr. Kirkpatrick who also dined with us. Mother had a pleasant drive in Capt. Eagan's new Victoria—pretty but too heavy for these roads. Miss Wilcox & Mr. Haskell also went. Mrs. Lewis & Mrs. Churchill called. Frank was in & around on "Secretary" work through the day & in the evening rode out to the Fort to make his P.P.C.s as he goes with Father as far as San Francisco. Day just lovely & too warm for fires.

Thursday 20th. Morning busy with helping Father over papers, etc. Judge Silent at breakfast showed how two days time would be gained by start-ing tomorrow afternoon instead of Saturday morning. Father at first thought it would be impossible for him to be ready but the Judge won him over, so we were extra busy during the afternoon, especially as sev-eral ladies called, & then we dined en famille out at the Wilcoxes, get-ting home soon after 8 to find Judge Silent & Mrs. Paulisson waiting for us. Mr. Foster & Mr. Kirkpatrick called also. Mr. K. had been in & out through the day & leaves early tomorrow for Tucson. The Judge told us that Mrs. Fitch was going with our set to San Francisco, which was a surprise & under the divorce bill[3] circumstances rather a "circus." We were all non-plussed for a while, but fortunately a bit of business turned up in connection with the lottery Mr. Fitch is interested in which may prevent their going for a few days.[4] Tomorrow early will decide of course only ourselves & the Judge talked it over. The Fitches have not yet spoken to us about Mrs. Fitch's going though he was to go as far as Phoenix on R.R. business.

Friday 21st. The Judge came up early to say the Fitches couldn't go, business stopping them, a disappointment for them but a lucky solution of the question for us, as San Francisco is humming with the Smith divorce case just now, & even to be with them travelling would not be a pleasant complication just now, pleasant as the Fitches are personally. We were as busy as bees all morning—people in & out on all sorts of territorial business, last letters for Father to answer & all the final odds & ends before a journey. The Judge was equally busy at his end of the town even holding court till 11½ when he ran up & breakfasted with us, was off again & back at 1½ when the ambulance & baggage wagon, each with six good mules, came in from the Fort for Genl. Wilcox has given Father transportation as far as Phoenix—& were packed & at sharp two they were off— our people sorry to leave us but glad to be off & Father looking forward to a very useful journey, both in regard to the territory & to ourselves. Judge Silent will follow Father East in a short time, on business & will see our young people there. Some ladies called in the afternoon, but we had a quiet evening & were glad of it as we were tired out. Cloudy weather.

Saturday 22nd. A quiet resting day. Grace made a short visit in the morning, then Fanny came in & staid some hours, quietly pottering over embroidery & I put her on her horse when she left. I'm going to teach her how to spring up; yesterday Mrs. Weeks was here & told us about young Wilcox's behavior. Capt. Eagan called in the evening. Mr. Anderson came in to see if he could be of use. Mother had a note from Father at Agua Frio [Fria]—so far all well. He asked Mother to see if anything could be done to extend the transportation facilities beyond Phoenix. Capt. Eagan undertook to see to it. Weather lovely.

Sunday 23rd. An absolutely quiet day, mostly spent in reading. No one came in & we didn't go out, but just enjoyed a whole day of quiet. Weather lovely. Col. Weeks wrote Mother that he had telegraphed Father to keep one wagon on to the R.R., which settles favorably the transportation.

Monday 24th. Quiet morning with lots of pleasant letters: from Charley, Sally, McLean, Mrs. Barlow, Mrs. Mattie Brown, Aunt Eliza & Mrs. Palmer[5]—also New York papers. At noon we had a despatch from Father, at Phoenix this morning & to leave in the afternoon "all well." Fanny Weeks rode in & spent an hour with us. She had a little plan which may result in my riding with her occasionally. Mother & I were just starting out to make some visits when Genl. Wilcox, in his ambulance with the four grey mules, & Grace with him, came to ask us to drive with him, so we dropped the visits & went for a lovely drive in & out amongst the low rocky hills & under big pine trees towards Thumb Butte, having many varying views of the butte which culminated in a giant lion's head where we turned just at its base & on a lovely little ranch with two tiny log cabins & a tribe of towheaded children. On the way back we passed Miss Wilcox & some others who had been on a riding party up the Butte. They looked tired &

bored. Mother spent the evening at the Fitches. I staid in & wrote to Nelly. Charming weather. . . .

Wednesday 26th (Ash Wednesday). Mrs. Buffum dropped in & took breakfast with us & stayed part of the afternoon. Then we walked down through dust & warmth & returned Mrs. Wood's visit as she leaves tomorrow for Tucson.[6] In the evening went over & told Mrs. Fitch goodbye. She leaves per buckboard tomorrow for a trip East via San Francisco.

Thursday 27th. Quiet Day. Nice letter from Father in the evening's mail—written Tuesday morning just as they were leaving Phoenix, which in its spring dress of apricot blossoms & green fields of wheat & alfalfa with the running water of the large sequias [acequias, irrigation ditches] pleased him very much. Also a despatch from Burk[e]s[7] station which they had reached all well & greatly obliged to Col. Weeks for the transportation. . . .

Saturday March 1st. Mother & I walked across to the Post & made a visit at Mrs. Biddle's before breakfast. Thor went with us. I did a little shopping in the Plaza shops in the afternoon, part of which Fanny Weeks spent with us. Mr. Clark made a short call about his leave East in the evening. Had a telegram from Father in the morning dated Yuma, 28th, all well so far on their way. Weather still lovely.

Sunday 2nd. Read & staid indoors, high wind & beautiful clouds. Mr. Sherman made us a visit in the afternoon & brought up our mail in the evening. Mr. Anderson also looked in to see if he could be of use.

Monday 3rd. Too windy to go out of doors, but not cold. Bonnet trimming and dressmaking were the chief objects of the day. Mr. Gosper came in to ask a business question in the morning. Dr. McKee, Mr. Estell & Mr. Foster called in the evening.

Tuesday 4th. Mother embroidered, finishing the sachet for Mrs. Fitch. I worked at dressmaking. Fanny Weeks came in to breakfast & sat in pleased quiet watching Mother embroider all the afternoon. Thor & I walked out with her to the Post just before 5. Dr. McKee called during the evening. Weather lovely in spite [of] some gusts. Had letters from Father at Los Angeles—all well.

Wednesday 5th. I sorted Mother's papers & she read during the morning. Mr. Foster brought us a mince pie of his own making & we reciprocated by some freshly baked home made bread. Mr. Gosper called in the evening. Rather windy day. . . .

Friday 7th. Did a little dressmaking & read. Mrs. Cory made us a visit before noon. Fanny & Grace called in the afternoon. Mr. & Mrs. Churchill dined with us. Capt. Eagan (with his feathers all ruffled), Mr. Foster & Mr. Kitchen called during the day & evening. Furious wind & dust all afternoon.

Saturday 8th. An eventless day with furious wind blowing. Very pleasant San Francisco letter from Father finished Monday 3rd. Major Dake & Mr. Kitchen made a fashionable call at near 10 in the evening. Cloud effects over Granite Mt. fine all through the day. Mother made Mrs. Cory a call after dinner.

Sunday 9th. Less wind. A peaceful day, chiefly spent in reading. Mr. Foster made us a visit in the evening; he looks in for a minute almost every morning to see if there is anything he can do in Frank's absence.

Monday 10th. Began the day with nice letters from Father (dropped at Sacramento en route 4th) & from Charley who is at Nell's whilst Sally is avoiding the March winds by a visit to her people in Kentucky. Charley just learned by Press telegrams that Father had started East. Pleasant drive round about in the hills with Capt. Eagan in the afternoon. Mrs. Bowen (!) sat with Mother. In the evening mail another nice letter from Father (beyond Colfax) & one from Frank (in S.F.) in which he tells of Dr. Morton's engagement to "Mrs. [Elizabeth Campbell] Lee." Mrs. Otis had told him—we thought Dr. Morton was acting in an almost "engaged manner" before we left the East, but were too thoroughly friends to ask questions. A lull in the winds gave us a lovely day. Mr. Gosper called in the evening. . . .

Wednesday 12. Pleasant letter from Sally in Elizabethtown, Ken. Mrs. Buffum came across from her rooms where she is cleaning house [preparatory to moving] & took breakfast with us, so did Fanny Weeks & Mr. Evans who came in just as we were going to table. Later Genl. Wilcox called, Grace with him. Mr. Sherman called in the evening. The event of the day was the arrival—by Express—of two boxes of oranges & one of sweet lemons which Father had sent to Mother from Los Angeles. I spent most of the morning rubbing & shelving them. They came very free from bruises; here in town each lemon sells at "two bits" as they are luxuries. Pleasant weather.

Thursday 13th. Nice letter from Father, posted at Ogden. He goes into N. Y. via the Erie R.R. Mother sewed & some ladies called in the afternoon. Mrs. Buffum took breakfast & dinner with us. I took a walk in the hills with Thor in the afternoon.

Friday 14th. I spent the day fighting a big headache & went to bed right after dinner. Mother went up to her history talk in the afternoon & made some visits. The Shermans dined with us & spent the evening. Nice letters from Father—Omaha—& from Father (S.F.) & telegram of 13th from Father at Washington—all right.

Saturday 15th. Just a quiet day. Fanny Weeks came in to say goodbye as she goes tomorrow to stay two weeks at Camp Verde; she is really a nice little girl. Mrs. Fred Smith came to ask us to take lunch with her on Tuesday. Mr. Foster called to report his return from Verde river & see if we needed anything. Mother found some of Balzac's novels she hadn't read at the Churchills yesterday & they amused her. I read the "New Republic"—clever & amusing. There is a lull in the wind storms just now & the weather so mild that we sit with open transoms & without a fire in the evenings.

Sunday 16th. Mother & I spent the day chiefly in talking over future plans. Mrs. Buffum brought over some new samples of papering for her house to show us & staid to dinner. Mr. Anderson called in the evening. Weather pleasant.

Monday 17th. Grace Wilcox & Lt. Evans drove in on a low buggy & Grace staid with us whilst Mother took a drive across into the pine woods with Mr. Evans. They staid to breakfast. Mr. Evans knows French history much more than is common & is fun over it, including of course Napoleon. Letters from Father near Omaha—& from Maggie Woodruff with account of Belle Chevalie's wedding & also Belle's cards. Mrs. Weeks came in & sat with us whilst waiting for the arrival of a friend from Tucson by the evening buckboard. Mother wrote a lot of letters.

Tuesday 18th. I went over to see Mrs. Cory & take her some oranges. Then Grace stopped to ask me to drive with her which I did & we went quite a way out on the stage road. Lt. Smith called with an ambulance to take us out to the Fort but we had already arranged for the barouche & to take Mrs. Lewis with us, which we did and had a very pleasant lunch & afternoon at Mrs. Smith's—a pretty & friendly menage. Mrs. Weeks was there also. Mrs. Smith has been in both China & Japan & met many people we knew. Mr. Smith brought us back in an ambulance. Mother went across to see Mrs. Churchill & borrowed a lot of books. In the evening Dr. McKee & Mr. Foster called. Weather mild but threatening a storm; rain is needed. Telegram from Frank saying he would leave San Francisco today.

Wednesday 19th. Mrs. Cory made us a visit in the morning. Mother sewed most of the day at my dress. I felt sick & read Wraxall's memoirs.[8] Mr. Foster called in the evening. Mother had a faint turn in the evening, room too hot, too much sewing through the day & some little I'm afraid due to the high dry air—but she slept well. Gusty day.

Thursday 20th. Mother felt rather languid through the day but brightened up in the evening. I read & sewed. Mr. Gosper called in the evening, so he did yesterday also. Mr. Foster spent most of the evening with us & brought us up the mail—2 letters from Father posted at Chicago & Cleveland. Weather still threatening a rain. . . .

Saturday 22nd. Quiet evening. In the early afternoon Grace & Mr. Evans called & Mother went for a drive with Mr. Evans whilst Grace staid with me; while Mother was out the General's ambulance & four grays came for us to take a drive, which of course we had to miss. Miss Sherman called. I squeezed a lot of sewing into the day & some reading. Had a telegram from Frank at Phoenix saying he would get here via Date Creek tomorrow evening. In the evening we went with Mr. Foster to see a performance of the Mattie Taylor troupe at the theatre, which was crowded; lots of the Post people sat near us & Capt. Eagan walked home with us; the star of the troupe is a little girl who does her parts really well.[9]

Sunday 23rd. Letter from Father in New York 11th hadn't seen any of our people as they were all dispersed; another from Aunt Eliza, they had reached St. Louis all right. Mrs. Cory breakfasted with us. Mother wrote & read; I only read. Frank arrived about 7, having come via Wickenburg & joined the Yuma stage at Date Creek. We talked steady till after midnight; he had thoroughly enjoyed his trip "inside" & had lots to tell us & it was very nice to have him back again. Mr. Foster came in to see Frank & welcome him back, but only staid a little while.

Monday 24th. Talked most all day with Frank & did scraps of sewing. Mrs. Martin & Mrs. Bean, Mr. Foster & little Mattie Taylor called. Frank went to the theatre in the evening. Weather pleasant.

Tuesday 25th. I spent the day chiefly in talking with Frank & sewing in the afternoon. Frank went out to the Post to deliver parcels he had brought down for Mrs. Smith & Genl. Wilcox. Grace called & with her Lt. [George L.] Scott of Camp Verde. In the evening's mail Mother had a nice letter from Father at Washington 14th saying that the big Reservation would be rescinded & the smaller one at the mouth of the Verde used temporarily whilst the whole question was gone into. He was very pleasantly received by the President, Schurz & Genl. Sherman. Also Mother had an agreeable little letter from Fanny Weeks at Camp Verde. Warm day.

Wednesday 26th. Mrs. Bean called early to ask Mother & me to lunch tomorrow. Then Mattie Taylor's sister called bringing us Mattie's thanks for the cake we sent her yesterday & tickets for the evening's performance. In the afternoon I drove Mother—in a shakelty low buggy with a lazy but unreliable buckskin bronco—across the creek & out to the Post & we made *nine* visits. We got home well tired at five o'clock. After dinner Dr. McKee & Mr. Haskell called, leaving when Mother & Frank went to the theatre. I staid at home & read a novel. Weather clear & very warm.

Thursday 27th. Genl. Wilcox & Grace called, the General wanting to talk over the Episcopalian church venture here with Mother. Mrs. Buffum brought us some preserves of her own making & staid to breakfast. Mother & I walked up to Mrs. Bean's lunch; eight ladies, some from the town & some from the Post. Got home by four. Capt. Eagan & Capt. [David Johnston] Craigie called in the evening. Howling sandstorm all day & on into the night.

Friday 28th. Mother went up for her "history talk"—now on the U.S. to the School in the afternoon. Frank was mostly down town & in the evening he went to a meeting of its Dramatic Club in the theatre. Mr. Foster & Mr. Gosper called during the evening, *separately;* and Mr. Anderson had called in the morning & told us of the bad accident to his hand.[10] Good letter from Father, N. Y. Wind still roaring high, though not as bad as yesterday.

Saturday 29th. Just a quiet day reading & sewing & for Frank a little going about down town & pleasant letters from Nelly, telling us of Father's arrival & of McLean's successful passing his examination for Master, U.S.N., & from Fanny Dart. Day really hot but night pleasantly cool. Stars wonderfully brilliant.

Sunday 30th. Mother spent her day chiefly in writing letters; Frank & I in reading. He went out to sunset parade & dinner with the Smiths at the Post. Mrs. Buffum & Asa[11] spent the evening with us. Soft gray day threatening rain which fell slightly in the night beginning with a very heavy squall of wind.

Monday 31st. Frank was home most of the day, reading. Mother & I did a lot of sewing. Fanny Weeks was in for a few moments to tell us she was back from Verde—& looking much improved in health. Lt. Evans dropped in during the afternoon & made us a pleasant chatty visit. Stage arrived too late for distribution of the mails. Delightful gray day damp air with several slight showers & splendid masses of driving clouds all shades of grey & catching on Granite Mt.

Tuesday April 1st. Good letter from Father—New York, 20 ult.—very busy with strong prospects of success on mining affairs. Mother spent the day chiefly in cutting shirts out of the new stuff Frank brought back from San Francisco. I did scraps & made Mrs. Cory a visit. Grace Wilcox came in for a short visit. Frank was busy making a right handed violin into a left handed as he means to take lessons. Mr. & Mrs. Lewis & Mr. Cordis called in the evening. Gray day & moist feeling air, heavy showers in the night. Short letter from Charley, everyone all right.

Wednesday 2nd. Mother wrote letters & I sewed; Frank worked on his violin. Fanny Weeks rode in & made us a short visit—the poor child has her headaches back again; air too rarified. Mrs. Buffum came in just as we were going to dinner & staid to dine with us & spent part of the evening. Frank went out to a rehearsal; Mr. Foster also called. Lovely masses of clouds & the pleasant moist air, but no rain.

Thursday 3rd. Good letter from Father Washington 21st. He had good long talks with Schurz & with Col. Rogers.[12] They both thought well of the plan of letting in the Gulf waters into the Desert & Father was to see the President that evening; as it is a new idea to them all of course it will take time to germinate.[13] . . . I spent part of the afternoon with Mrs. Cory who isn't well. Windy day.

Friday 4th. Went out driving with Miss Wilcox at 11. Too windy for pleasure so we turned in at the Fort. Mrs. Weeks was also there; we sewed, talked & Mrs. Weeks sang some. Lt. Wilcox & Major [Reginald] Fowler came in to lunch, going right back to a court martial. I got back home about 3. Mother had gone up to the School for her "talk." Fanny Weeks & Grace Wilcox—without concert (or harmony) had breakfasted at our house—staid a while after. Dr. McKee made us a visit during the evening. Frank went up to a rehearsal. Furious howling wind & dust storm all day & nearly all night. When I went to bed the dust completely hid Granite Mt. & almost hid Thumb Butte. Genl. Wilcox with three of his officers & a whole company of cavalry left this morning for Camp McDowell where he meets Indian Inspector Genl. [J. H.] Hammond. Two companies of infantry are marching to the same point & the situation there is a very delicate & critical one, as Capt. Eagan says, for the San Carlos Indians have for nearly two months past been on *five* days rations for *seven* days & they are fretting under [it] & just at this time it has been decided to disarm a large band of Apaches belonging to that Reservation—so that an outbreak is probable though it may be avoided; the whites would rather like it but all that can be done to avert it Genl. Wilcox will do. The village is full of rumors, all the more numerous as the telegraph has been down for some days, so we could get no authentic news.

Saturday 5th. Mother had had a bad night's rest which left her with a heavy spasmodic headache which only cleared off during dinner. She was up most of the day however. Grace Wilcox came in for a while & later sent us quite a pretty bunch of wild flowers. I went over & staid a while with Mrs. Cory who is better & expecting the Fitches back in a week. Miss Wilcox & her brother took dinner with us—we asked only Mr. Foster to meet them as six is the largest number our dot of a dining room can hold with comfort; we gave them a pretty little dinner, for here, & they seemed to have a pleasant time, everything running smoothly & not a jarring topic turning up. They left at 9, Frank going down town at the same time. Then Mother & I read & talked till bedtime & she went to bed quite relieved of her headache. Pleasant weather. . . .

Monday 7th. Nice letter from Sally in Kentucky & from McLean, on the wing to the Boston Navy Yard. He is to go on the Woodruff round the world expedition, if it sails—a really fun thing for him.[14] Usual routine of the day inside, outside a howling wind & dust storm. . . .

Wednesday 9th. Letter from Father full of pleasant & promising business news and two nice ones from McLean. We read, talked & I went over to see how Mrs. Cory was getting along. Mr. Gosper called. Fanny Weeks walked in to see us & was tired out so we kept her to dinner, telegraphing to Mrs. Weeks. Lt. F. A. Smith & Mrs. Smith dined with us & we had a pleasant little evening; they taking Fanny back to the Post with them. Ice last night, morning shivery cold, afternoon dazzlingly warm, & sharply cool again at night.

Thursday 10th. Letter of 28th March from Father to tell us that the preliminaries of a very advantageous & large business arrangement had been *concluded.* Mother & I spent the day as usual & some ladies called, Mrs. Churchill making a pleasant visit. Lt. Evans took 5 o'clock tea with us. Frank was in & out. High wind all day.

Good Friday. (Mrs. Thibodo,[15] Scotch, sent us over some Hot Cross Buns, joining us in the keeping of her home customs). The weather was overcast, with frequent snow & hail squalls & really cold. Mother trimmed Fanny Weeks' hat. I read. Frank did as usual. Capt. Eagan called in the evening. No Protestant church service.

Saturday 12th. Morning chiefly given to talking over home letters from the East—business & Father all right, but Mother worried by hearing through Nell that Sally's father's family is consumptive. Lt. & Mrs. Evans took breakfast with us & spent the afternoon. They are Mississippi from the Yazoo river & Mr. Evans' older brothers were killed on the Rebel side I've been told, but they never talk "lost cause" & are really nice Southerners. Fanny Weeks rode in to take a look at her hat & was storm bound by a snow squall, staying however only while it lasted, which just covered the breakfast hour. Mr. Gosper called in the evening. Frank was in almost all day. The evening we gave to looking over a pile of Mrs. Churchill's "Art Journals" with lots of nice pictures. Day cold & stormy, with frequent snows.

Easter Sunday. Nice letter from Charley whose fête day it is; good business letter from Father & good telegrams in the "Bulletin," San Francisco, about the success of Father's plans East including Indian, letting the water into the Colorado Desert & mining operations—nothing but the Indians squarely concluded as yet but all looked on favorably. I wrote letters & read. In the afternoon Mother went up to the empty theatre where Frank

& Mr. Macmillan[16] played for over an hour, & Mother made Mrs. Cory a little visit. No church services to go to. Weather raw & stormy.

Monday 14th. Mrs. Parker & her sister-in-law[17] called early in reference to forming a church choir for the expected Episcopalian church. Mother & Frank wrote letters in the intervals of visits from Fanny Weeks; Lt. Evans who did his first French lesson; Grace & Orlando Wilcox; and whilst we were at dinner, Mrs. Buffum. I went across to see Mrs. Cory during the afternoon; Frank went to rehearsal in the evening. Fanny & Mr. Evans each rode in; his horse is pretty & grey. Yesterday he & Mr. Wilcox came up to the door in the most fringant [dashing] manner to the great delight of the Sunday School children who were just leaving church.

Tuesday 15th. Mother, Frank, & I went out to Mrs. Evans's to lunch & spent the afternoon going & coming in an ambulance. Dr. McKee & Mrs. Biddle were also there at the lunch; the San Francisco Mts. were splendid with a fresh coat of snow. Mr. Evans came in with us—told us about his patent for packing ammunition, in which we were all interested. Mr. Churchill called in the evening.

Wednesday 16th. Through Mr. Churchill we heard of Mr. Fitch's starting for the East yesterday & why.[18] Just the usual routine; Fanny Weeks in for a while. Mr. & Mrs. Masterson[19] called.

Thursday 17th. Lots of letters from home people in the East. Mother staid & embroidered. I went over to see Mrs. Cory & then went on up to Mrs. Buffum's new house where I spent some time with her, both indoors & inspecting the attempts at a future garden. In the evening we went to the theatre—"Still Waters Run Deep"—the Martins played very well. Frank had only a thirty word part. Mother wasn't very well.

Friday 18th. Mother not feeling very well but still went up in the afternoon for her "talk" to the school. Lt. Evans, Grace Wilcox & Fanny Weeks—each separately—happened towards noon & staid to breakfast with us; and Mr. Evans did a French lesson with me. Quiet evening. . . .

Sunday 20th. A furious wind & dust storm—the worse I've seen lasting all day & way into the night. Everyone staid housed. Our day the usual letter writing & reading. . . .

Tuesday 22nd. Mr. Evans, Mr. Churchill, Mrs. Evans & Grace Wilcox called at intervals. In between time Mother embroidered & I sewed. The town is getting to have a deserted look as all the unsettled populations are drifting off towards Tucson & Leadville.

Wednesday 23rd. Mr. Evans came in & breakfasted with us, doing a French lesson with Mother afterwards. Miss Wilcox & Grace, then Mrs. Buffum called. The Churchills dined with us & after dinner Mother & Mrs. Churchill went over to see to Mrs. Cory who is not well. I spent the day fighting a headache. Weather very pleasant. . . .

Sunday 27th. Quiet day & Mr. Gideon Tucker[20] of New York, just arrived, dined with us. Day hot. . . .

Tuesday 29th. The Smiths, from the Garrison, called in the morning. He goes off tomorrow on a three weeks tour of duty inspecting telegraph lines to the south. Mrs. Buffum came in whilst we were at dinner & staid with us. Genl. Wilcox & Grace walked in & made a short visit & the other Wilcoxes stopped a moment as they rode by. In the evening Frank & Mr. Macmillan played at the Churchills & Mother went up to listen. We have both been over often to see how Mrs. Cory was getting on. Day very hot, about 94°.

Wednesday 30th. Grace came early & took me [on] a drive, Fanny was here when we got back & both the girls staid on till the ambulance came for them at 12. Quiet afternoon. In the evening Mr. Tucker, Mr. Haskell & Dr. McKee called. The officers told us of the President's vetoing the army appropriation bill with its Democratic "rider." Day hot but evening & night chillily cool. We have steadily good letters from Father—final decisions not arrived at however & he distrusts the mails too much to write details.

Thursday, May 1st. Quiet day. In the evening Mother & Frank went to the Churchills where Frank & Mr. McMillan played. I went to bed well enough but waked before one o'clock with about the worse headache I've had in years. They have been growing steadily worse all the time up here. I even went to Frank's room for the morphine ointment which didn't help apparently and after a nuit blanche [sleepless night] had to wake Mary & try a mustard football before 5 o'clock, but it didn't help either; so I dressed & sat round & it gradually wore off during the day, but had hurt so much that I saw Dr. Ainsworth about it in the afternoon & he has provided me with medicine to fight the next one when it begins. Mother went up to the School in the afternoon & also called on Mrs. Cory in the evening. She is better. Fanny W. came in to ask us to drive but we couldn't & anyway a fierce wind storm rose before midday & lasted till on in the evening. . . .

Wednesday 7th. Good telegram from Father saying "business moves on very satisfactorily." Mrs. Buffum & Grace called in the afternoon. Mother spent the evening at Mrs. Cory's; otherwise day as usual.

Thursday 8th. Judge Tucker, Fanny & Grace, each separately, came in during the morning & they all staid to breakfast, Grace staying part of the afternoon, too. In the evening we went up to the Churchills where Frank & Mr. McMillan played. Young Mr. Fitch,[21] Dr. McKee & Mr. Haskell being there besides ourselves; very good music. Mr. Churchill has a very good business telegram from Mr. Fitch this afternoon. Weather again windy.

Friday 9th. The Fort people stopped by for Frank at eleven to go with them on a picnic & climb to the top of Thumb Butte. He went in the Weeks's ambulance; we were asked too, but refused. In the afternoon Mother went up to the School for her "talk"—and came straight home as it was blowing a gale. Frank got back just before 6 p.m. He, Mrs. Weeks & Fanny had climbed quite to the top where they left Mrs. W.'s hkf. as a flag; view fine. I sewed & read through the day. The wind flurries me even inside the house & everything is so charged with electricity that when I touch anything it goes off with a "spang" that stings my fingers. It blew from sunrise to sunset. . . .

Sunday 11th. Frank took Thor & went out early for a long walk & "look for" quail with young Fitch—getting in just in time for breakfast. Quiet reading day for Mother & me. Lt. Haskell called in the afternoon & went with us up to the empty theatre where Frank & Mr. McMillan practised, Mrs. Parker coming in for a while & trying over some songs. In the evening Frank beat Mr. Foster at chess in the club. Mother & I read. Not windy—a fine mountain day. . . .

Wednesday 14th. Cool morning & I had a pleasant read of a history of Scotland borrowed from the Churchills. Mrs. Smith & Grace came in towards 12, staid to breakfast and on till 3 when Miss Wilcox came for them. Pleasant evening at the Churchills, Frank & Mr. McMillan playing well. The event of the day to the village was Miss Pine's wedding—the first church wedding Prescott has ever had.[22]

Tom Fitch in his Prescott law office. (Courtesy of the Sharlot Hall Museum/Library Archives, Prescott, Ariz., photo #PO 2227p.)

Thursday May 15th. Quiet morning filled with content by a good business telegram from Father. About eleven Mrs. Buffum came in to bring us a lot of wedding cake sent us by the bride, Miss Pine, who also sent her regrets at not having a big enough house to have asked us & other friends to a reception, but was obliged to keep to strictly family friends. We kept Mrs. Buffum to breakfast. Nice letter from [Nell], with dear pretty photographs of her baby girl, now 3 years old, and telling us she is packing up to leave Cairo for Europe. Pleasant cool day in the house. The stage gets in at all hours now. Dr. McKee called during the evening.

Friday 16th. Morning as usual. Afternoon Mother went up for her school "talk" with the children, quite annoyed that Mr. Sherman had asked Mr. Tucker & Mr. Churchill to be present. She slipped most of the talking over on to them & afterwards took Mr. Tucker over & introduced him to Mrs. Buffum at her new house & he being struck with the neighborhood talked of buying the Head cottage next [to] hers. Frank & I did a solid two hours work in answering Father's mail. In the evening Capt. Eagan called—all "Peck imbroglio" & things have [come] to a serious pass about the mine.[23] Then Mother went for a while to listen to Frank & Mr. McMillan at the Churchills. The day was delightfully cool indoors without being windy. The stage someway failed to bring the letter mail in today.

Saturday 17th. Frank's 24th birthday. Good business letters from Father. We read & wrote letters. Frank was in & out. Miss Wilcox called in the forenoon, bringing with her Lt. Kingsbury[24] who is just in from a scout among the Hualapais, to the northwest. He says they are quiet but underfed entirely & liable to break out from want of food. Grace called in the afternoon. Had a nice little birthday dinner for Frank, then he took a walk with Mr. Churchill & afterwards played chess at the Club till midnight. The day was quite cool, with an overcast morning! . . .

Monday 19th. Morning chiefly reading. Pleasant letters from Sally in the mail. Fanny Weeks rode in and staid in the afternoon. Frank & I worked at Father's accumulated mail. In the evening Mother went up to hear Frank & Mr. McMillan practice at the Churchills. Another windy day, but in the evening clouds to the SE.

Tuesday 20th. I went early up on the hillside wild flower hunting & was a little successful though between the drought & the donkeys the flowers don't have much chance. Housekeeping & reading till breakfast. In the afternoon Frank & I worked at Father's mail. Mother read & sewed.

Wednesday 21st. We each felt flurried & nervous on account of these steady wind storms & our day went in scrap[p]ly reading & the evening was spent with music at the Churchills—trying over the "Pinafore"[25] & Dr. McKee brought us Stanley's "Dark Continent."[26] . . .

Saturday 24th. The ambulance came at 7 a.m. for Frank who goes with Lt. Haskell to spend a few days at Camp Verde. Mrs. Cory is quite in a flurry over the "marching orders" which reached her yesterday as the Fitches

Francis Preston Frémont,
photograph by Bradley and Rulofson, San Francisco.
(Courtesy of the Southwest Museum, Los Angeles, photo #36487.)

have taken a house in New York for a year—at Madison Ave. & 75th St.![27] We had a quiet reading day. Mrs. Churchill & Mrs. Buffum dined with us. Very pleasant weather, cool without wind. . . .

Monday 26th. Good letter from Father; Judge Silent is almost at San Francisco & may be here next week. I felt a little racked from my headache fight yesterday & spent the day in doing nothing. Mother read & sewed. Grace came to ask us to drive & Fanny rode in & made a short call. Mrs. Bit[t]ing & Mrs. Thorne, wives respectively of the leading faro & gambling saloon keepers here called;[28] quiet nice women who were, Mrs. B. especially, rather nervous as to how we would take their calling &

Prescott Free Academy, late 1870s. (Courtesy of the Sharlot Hall Museum/Library Archives, Prescott, Ariz., photo #BU-S 5025pb.)

left all smoothed down. (drôle de pays! [what a strange country]). I went across to see Mrs. Cory in the evening. Mother has sprained her knee & can't walk easily.

Tuesday 27th. I went out early to a dressmakers to have my pongee let out & have a polonaise made of the rest of Charley's pongee. Then took over to Mrs. Cory some things Mother sent her to make her long journey easier on her—the old lady was delighted. Mother sewed & read. Frank got back at 4, charmed with Camp Verde & its military team & very much interested in its relics of the cliff-builders, he having spent a whole [day] in exploring their ancient dwellings near Camp Verde; his trip was a real pleasure to him. Very good letters from Father, also a draft for four hundred from him. Weather windy again. Bettie J[ones] H[ughes] to go to N. Y. for 1 month. . . .

Thursday 29th. Dr. Ainsworth was called in to see Mother & says her knee is only sprained & will right itself, which eased her mind. Mr. Evans came in to breakfast & staid most [of] the afternoon amusing us with a description of his tournée [tour] in the southern part of the Territory & Tucson especially. Judge Tucker & Maj. Dake's cousin, Mr. [Ed.] Dake of S.F. also called. Frank & I contrived to do a little at Father's mail. In the evening Frank walked out to the Fort & made some visits. There was an alarm of fire at 11 p.m. which scared us but only damaged a shanty; as a breeze was blowing it would have been a bad thing but for the prompt action of all the men in town, who turned out at the first cry of "fire" as there is no engine & the town is of wood.[29]

Decoration Day. Mother tried to get a holiday for the school children but the school board wouldn't grant it, but Mother did not go up to the School & gave her reasons "that the day should be kept in grateful memory of" etc. & as there are no soldiers' graves here sent a bunch of flowers with the red white & blue tied on, by one of the schoolboys to be left on Mr. Gosper's desk, as he has lost a leg from wounds received leading a charge. There is a good deal of rebel feeling in this Territory. Frank & I did our stint at the mail in the afternoon; Fanny Weeks was in for a while. In the evening Mother & Fanny Weeks went up to the Churchills for the music practise. I felt cross from the wind & staid home, reading a "Harpers" which Mr. Churchill brought over to me.

Saturday 31st. Mother's birthday. Quiet morning with pleasant letters from our people in the East. Mr. Gosper called & made his thanks, with evident honest sincerity, for Mother's remembering through him Decoration Day & its meaning. Judge & Mrs. Tweed of Mineral Park dined with us, but left early. They were only in town two days en passant [on their way] to Phoenix where they are going to live. Otherwise we shouldn't have broken in on a home day. Weather pleasant.

Sunday June 1st. We had hopes of Judge Silent's arriving this morning but instead came a telegram to adjourn court to the 16th as he remains in San

Francisco a while. Just a quiet day. Frank got an inning into the Democratic movements in the Territory & their present Head centre.

Monday 2nd. Maj. Dake called early to offer us his pony phaeton & horse—warranted mild—for a drive this evening, which we accepted. Then Mrs. Weeks called with Fanny & Merle. In the afternoon I helped Frank with the mail & Mother wrote letters. I made Mrs. Cory a little visit after dinner. Frank went out to the Fort to see Genl. Wilcox & make some visits & I drove Mother to call on Mrs. Noyes & on Mrs. Brooks,[30] who both live beyond walking limits. Mrs. Brooks had a really good flower garden with lots of roses—she has been there *fifteen* years! And Mrs. Noyes told Mother, apropos to books, that she was the niece of Silas Wright of New York.[31] I staid in the carriage to mind the horses. Fanny Weeks was riding by & joined me for part of the time. When we came back to the village, I left Mother at the milliners for a few moments & turned the horse over to Maj. Dake. It was a mild beast, but didn't like holding back on a down grade—and came in. Soon afterwards Dr. McKee & Mr. Haskell called & spent the evening. The Doctor came to take leave as he goes on Wednesday for a month's rest to San Francisco. Mr. Haskell was to have gone with him but has to stay & do some extra duty. Pleasant men, both, & the doctor is very nice in lending us his books. Warm day, night cool.

Tuesday 3rd. Quiet household morning. Mr. Evans came in & breakfasted with us & afterwards did a French lesson with Mother. Genl. Wilcox & his son called & asked us to join a picnic to Maple Grove tomorrow—we can't as we are afraid of the sun. No letters came for Father so Frank & I were off duty. Grace, on foot, & Fanny, on horseback, came in for a while after dinner. We spent the evening at the Churchills listening to music & looking at a glorious harvest moon; several other people were there including Mr. Haskell & Mr. Smith from the Fort & the Lewises from in town. Day hot, night chilly.

Wednesday 4th. *Very* good letter from Father. I walked down to ask after the Mother Superior at the Hospital as she is very ill—say[s] Sister Mary.[32] Had beef tea made & sent to the M[other] S[uperior] & to Mrs. Cory, who is also having another ill turn. Read & did scraps. Day extremely hot. Capt. Eagan called to say goodbye. He also goes on leave today, going inside at the same time with Dr. McKee. Mother spent the day reading & writing. The morning's mail brought no letters for Frank to answer. After dinner Mother & I returned Mrs. Bitting's visit as she leaves for Cal[iforni]a. tomorrow. Mother went on to the Hospital & saw the Mother Superior who was slightly better—then in returning called on Mrs. Ellis.[33] A quiet reading evening till bedtime. The night was cool enough.

Thursday 5th. Carry Crawford's wedding day. I went out early & did some shopping before it got hot. Grace breakfasted with us & spent the afternoon, going home in the School Ambulance. We did a scrapy reading & sewing whilst she was here, Frank going in & out. There were no letters to answer. After dinner we drove out to the Fort in the barouche, Frank going with us, & made a tour of visits to all the ladies there. The Smiths were out, Mrs. Martin & Mrs. Biddle sick, but we had variedly pleasant visits at the General's, where we saw the whole family, at the Kingsburys where we sat on the porch, saw the roll call, the Flag run down & sunset gun fired & met Lt. Haskell; at the Evans in front of whose house was an open ditch for new water pipes which Mrs. Evans got across & received our visit sitting in the carriage with us whilst Mr. Evans sat in a chair on the ridge of earth thrown up from the ditch; in the "middle distance" black Johnny with Charley Wilcox's help (?) was tying cords for the hop vine to run up against porch & a glorious rose & yellow sunset was throwing its tints on the far San Francisco Mts. Then two decorous indoor visits at the Weeks & the Fowlers,[34] the new Paymaster's family. The south breeze was sweeping cool up over their country-like porches & the view over the valley from Staff Hill was really fine. We got home before 9 & had a good read before bedtime; I at the second volume of "Stanley's Dark Continent," which Miss Wilcox had turned over to us. Mrs. Cory is better; the Mother Superior is worse. Hot day but pleasantly cool night. . . .

Sunday 8th. Mother & I spent the day mostly in planning our future home in Washington, as we have decided we like life there better than in any other American town. Frank was in & out. Mary staid the night at the Hospital so that the two Sisters might take turns sleeping as they are beginning to wear out under the heavy pull of nursing. Day pleasant, night cold.

Monday 9th. A fine good letter from Father in Washington & pleasing ones from Sally & from Nelly. Betty Hughes is with them. Mrs. Churchill came to breakfast with us & spent the afternoon, Mother helping her to make a sleeve part of her special pattern. Mr. Evans also took breakfast with us, after which he & Frank did a French lesson with me; then went to the club for billiards, coming back in time for Frank to answer the morning's mail before the stage went out. In the evening we went up to Mrs. Churchill's for the music—both Frank & Mr. M[cMillan] were in view. The Lewises, Mr. Gosper & Mr. Haskell were there. The day wasn't quite hot, the night cold.

Tuesday 10th. I gave the early morning to finishing Stanley's "Dark Continent" which has interested me greatly, in spite of the trail of "Herald correspondent style" which permeates his writing. But he unquestionably knows how to lead an expedition. Mrs. Churchill breakfasted with us, then Mother devoted another afternoon to the jacket which is turning out very well & gives Mrs. C. clear comfort. Frank spent the afternoon going down the Congo with Stanley. Day coolish.

Wednesday 11th. Morning as usual. Judge Silent arrived in this morning's stage at 10 o'clock. He came up about 1, staid quite a while giving us a full account of business, as concerns us, in New York. It is an almost accomplished condition which if completed will be *very* satisfactory for us, & even if this special enterprise fails it will have paved the way for future successes. They have had intensely hard *waiting* work. The Judge came back & dined with us staying till after 9 & we did a lot of talking & planning & see our way very well to calm future. The first thunderstorm & rain of the season came this afternoon, from 3½ to five, accompanied by a double rainbow with intensely bright colors, & leaving a mass of clouds which turned to golden brown & melon pink at sunset. The air became cold, mountain cold. Mr. Sherman came in to call, but finding Judge Silent knew we must have lots to talk [about] & didn't stay.

Thursday 12th. Judge Silent breakfasted with us & had a very long business talk with Mother & Frank whilst I gave Mr. Evans his French lesson. In the early morning Mother & I had a walk on the hill, the air was delightful after yesterday's rain & piles of glorious cumulus clouds gave the play of light & shade which is usually routine to this landscape. Mother stopped a while at Mrs. Buffum's. When Frank went to post Mother's letters toward five, he found a registered letter from Father in our box which had been overlooked in the morning. It was written on Mother's birthday & had the most satisfactory business intelligence, & told us of Judge Thacker's[35] coming out to look at &, in almost certainty, conclude all arrangements about the mining business. This of course was to be shared with the Judge so Frank went down to the Court House & brought him back to dinner; after which we had another business talk, telegraphed status here—good—to Father & Frank went out to see Genl. Wilcox. Pleasantly cool day. . . .

Saturday 14th. (The Mother Superior died at 5 a.m. Mother Basil[36] had arrived from Tucson on Thursday so the dying Sister had the comfort of seeing & talking with her; her death was perfectly calm, without pain & quite conscious to the last & glad to go.) Morning as usual. Fanny Weeks & Judge Silent breakfasted with us & after breakfast we had a long planning talk with the Judge, our plans including a future house & pied à terre [lodging place] at Santa Cruz. Fanny left soon but the Judge staid on till Mrs. Churchill came in at about 3 to tell us she was going over to Mrs. Brooks to get white flowers & make a cross for the Sister, which she did & showed it to us late at night as beautifully done as if a florist had done it. Grace came whilst we were still at dinner to ask Frank to come out for their Saturday choir practice which he did, & spent the whole evening playing whist with the General! Mr. Churchill called to explain his proposed law partnership with Judge Tucker! Mother & I each went down to the Hospital in the afternoon. . . .

Monday 16th. Rising early I found Mary crippled with a slight attack of rheumatism brought on by needlessly sitting in a draft at the Hospital on Saturday night. She couldn't get up so I had her share of the housework to do & she missed the funeral. As the Sisters had asked me to be one of the ladies to tie the crape on the pallbearers I went to the Hospital soon after 9 & with Mrs. Brannan [Brannen][37] of the Post got everything in our department ready. Genl. Wilcox & four other officers from the Fort, Frank, two of the Supervisors & four of the leading men of the town made up the number of pallbearers; they had rigged up quite a regulation looking hearse out of a wagon & draped it in black with white streamers—working late & early at it out at the Fort wagon yard—& Genl. Wilcox had lent them all the ambulances. The little church was packed & in a soft scared voice Carry Wilkins blundered through the singing part of the Mass whilst Father Becker, who knew better, gabbled through the fine Latin Mass. All [the] Mexicans followed on foot as is their custom & so did many others whilst the rest of us followed in the ambulances & in most every sort of vehicle, for all respected the Mother John & turned out to shew it. Mother was at the church & Fanny Weeks represented the ladies from the Post— they with Mrs. Churchill, Bean & Lewis rode to the graveyard in Genl. W.'s own ambulance; & Mother thought to ask Mr. Sherman to have the School bell tolled which he willingly did. We were home by 12. Mr. Evans came in for his French lessons which he did thoroughly with Mother & with me. Judge Silent dined with us & staid a while after; Mr. Church made us a short call, then came Mr. Cordis, who brought us friendly messages from Mr. Kirkpatrick whom he has been seeing in Tucson lately. The morning was rather cool with a strong breeze which changed to a sandstorm & gale in the afternoon lasting on into the night & causing Lux to break his bridle & run off home. We hear continually from Father— all his letters are cheerful & point to a speedy conclusion of business in New York.

Tuesday 17th. Day as usual. Frank lunched at the Wilcoxes and took Thor with him. The Judge dined with us. After dinner Mother Basil & Sister Mary called to thank us for what we had been able to do for Mother John. They made quite a visit & we found they belonged to the same sisterhood as the nuns Mother had sworn in for war nurses in St. Louis in '61 & whom we knew again in Wheeling, Va. later on in the war. After the Sisters left we went up to the Churchills where Frank & Mr. McMillan played extremely well & Mrs. Lewis & Mr. Estelle sang. Besides ourselves, the Churchills & Lewises, Miss Wilcox & Grace, Dr. Ainsworth, Mr. [Frank] Fitch & the Shermans were there. Day warm & night cool. Mary better.

Wednesday 18th. Lovely cool morning which I gave to the reading of my Scotch history; Mother & Frank were not around very early. The Judge & Grace took breakfast with us, after which Grace got me to give her a French lesson whilst Mother had a long talk with the Judge who is blue at being away from his family & sleepless & tired from his journey—so we made him come back to dinner with us. Mrs. Gosper called bringing Capt. Hancock[38] of Phoenix with him & we arranged with them that they should get up a slip pamphlet showing the advantages of the Salt river valley for agriculturists for us to send in answer to letters asking about farms in Arizona. Quiet evening.

Thursday 19th. Frank, taking Thor with him, went out to the Fort & spent the day with Mr. Evans. The Judge both breakfasted & dined with us. Mrs. Behan,[39] Mrs. Luke[40] & Mrs. Rodenburg[41] called. The last is a typically pretty German woman from Bremen & each of the women was pleasant in her way. In the evening Mother went down to see the Sisters & show them the permission she had got through Judge French from the Catholic Bishop[42] at Tucson for them to wear wash stuffs & cooler veils during the hot weather. They were charmed. I went across to see Mrs. Cory. After we came in Mr. Churchill called. Good telegram from Father.

Friday 20th. Mr. Gosper brought Mr. Griswold of Chicago & Mr. Caldwell of Cleveland—both interested through Mr. G[osper] in Big Bug mines[43]—to see us about 9 a.m. They were just leaving town; they were intelligent men & we had a pleasant visit from them. The Judge came up to breakfast & so did Mr. Evans. Mother went up for her really last talk at the School, where most unexpectedly to her she found the desk all dressed with flowers & a pretty present—silver sugar tongs & spoon—given to her by the class & Mr. Sherman; the presentation speech made by Harry Thibodo. All the boys & girls were as tidy as could be, nearly all with blue cravats & blue ribbons as they thought that was Mother's color & the boys each with a flower in their buttonholes & all wearing coats. The children have really enjoyed Mother's talks; one girl today told Mother she was reading "Lucile"[44] which would have been incomprehensible to her in many parts, she said, but for Mother's accounts of European ways to them & Mr. Sherman tells Mother that in many ways the class has improved visibly. Mr. Evans did a solid French lesson with me, [ending] with billiards at the Club with Frank. The Judge dined with us & got a chance to tell me that he heard from New York that his & Father's present mining plan would fall through—that he had already taken steps & written to start another which he had reason to think would be more successful & that he would write to Father about it & tell him to come back, as I am afraid it will wear too much on Father to be there alone under these reiterated delays & disappointments. We don't tell Mother as Father may be back & the other plan well started before she need know the failure of this one, which has not yet publicly failed—the Judge's information being from the inside. Mrs. Lewis spent the evening with us. Day & evening very warm.

Saturday 21st. Quiet morning. With the Judge's news in mind, I didn't feel like settling to anything. The Judge breakfasted with us & went back to court right afterwards, not coming up again to dinner. Mother & Frank wrote letters till 3, when they went across to the Churchills where Frank and Mr. McMillan practised till 5. The Sisters came in to thank Mrs. Churchill for the flowers she had sent to Mother John & were persuaded to stay to listen & enjoyed the music, especially Mother Basil who teaches it in the Tucson school. Just as we were through [with] dinner, Fanny Weeks rode up on an ugly roan, her pretty little horse not having yet recovered from the hurt at the picnic; and soon afterwards Mr. Evans rode in to talk over with us the news of the Prince Imperial's death in Zululand.[45] Haskell had telegraphed it in to us early in the afternoon, for the Fort is very kind in sharing news with us. It seems a hard fate for the "Petit Prince" & must strike awfully on the Empress, bringing back to her the fate of Maximilian.[46] Grace too came in for a while. Then Mother went over to see Mrs. Cory & when she returned, before 10, I turned in. Hot day.

Sunday 22nd. Quiet indoor day, the Judge breakfasting & dining with us. Mr. Haskell sent an ambulance in for us at 6 to come out & see [the] dress parade & listen to the band. We took the Judge with us & drove to Mrs. Evans & sat on her porch where Genl. Wilcox & his boys, Mr. Haskell & others joined us & we had a pleasant time. Genl. Wilcox offered Frank a letter to the Sect. of War asking for him to be appointed to his own regiment, the 12th; & later on Mr. Haskell talked over the ways to urge it on, for all the officers here are very nice in wanting Frank in their regiment. We came in early but Frank staid on, walking home towards 11. Day hot with high gale.

Monday 23rd. Father's letter this morning (12th) is impatient of delays in business & says we may expect him sooner. The Judge both breakfasted & dined with us. Mr. Haskell came in in the afternoon to talk over Genl. Wilcox's letter about Frank's appointment with him & took him back to the Fort whence Frank sent a despatch to Mr. Rogers, the President's Priv. Sect., & then letters to Mr. Rogers & to the War Secretary enclosing Genl. Wilcox's letter; then Elon Wilcox called. Mother went across to see the Fitches, who arrived this morning.[47] Hot day with high winds.

Tuesday 24th. Usual quiet morning with nice letters from Father & Sally. The Judge & Mr. Evans breakfasted with us. At 2 Mother went up to the School Examination & afterwards called on Mrs. Bashford & Mrs. Burmister. I gave Mr. Evans his French lesson in the intervals of billiards & Lux running away. The Judge dined with us. In the evening Mother called on Mrs. Lewis & I on Mrs. Fitch. Mrs. Churchill made us a little visit. Frank dined out at the Wilcoxes, riding with Miss Wilcox & Elon after dinner & then playing whist with the General till after midnight, when he walked home. He had gone out in an ambulance with Fanny, Grace, & Nelly Biddle[48]—a nice little girl of ten. More lift in the air today & the night cooler & all with less wind.

Wednesday 25th. Quiet morning. The Judge, Fanny & Grace took breakfast with us, after which Fanny went across to the Churchills to listen to Frank & Mr. McMillan's practise. Judge Silent went back to court. Mother, Grace & I went up to the School & "assisted" at the last day of examination. It was Miss Sherman's class & the little things did remarkably well, even to repeating their pieces which were well selected with clearness & right information; in their geography, spelling & arithmetic they were little marvels & there was no mauvaise honte [reticence] about them, though the room was crowded with their relations & the examining board. It was the first time I had seen a public school exhibition & I was very much interested in it. I came straight home out of the glare & the heat, but Mother stopped in to see Mrs. Fitch & Mrs. Cory. Judge Silent dined with us; after dinner Mr. & Mrs. Evans drove in to ask us out there for breakfast tomorrow—only staying a minute; then later Fanny rode up with Mr. Evans & Mr. [William Wallace] Wotherspoon, who has just been transferred here from Verde. Mother & I spent the evening at the Churchills listening to the last practise as Mr. McMillan leaves this week for the East. They played remarkably well & we had a quiet time as only the Lewises & Mrs. Fitch were there. Mrs. Churchill & I took clear comfort in listening whilst we sat outside in the moonlight which softened the mountain line around us. Day hot, night not very cool.

Thursday 26th. An ambulance came for us at 12 & we drove out to the Evanses, where we took lunch & spent the afternoon till 4½ when we drove back, Mr. Evans coming in with us, but going right back. Besides the Evanses & ourselves only Genl. Wilcox was there & we had quite a pleasant time, discussing agencies for Pimas & Papagoes amongst other things. Judge Silent came up for a few minutes in the evening to show us a very good telegram he had just received from Father, endorsed "Certificate with Controller. Agent will be appointed with Power"; which settles the point about the Judge's having overstaid his leave & makes the business success almost a certainty. So we were all glad together, & glad too that Father is so near through with the long strain of waiting. Frank went to the School party where he met nearly all the Fort people & they all turned in to dancing with the children & amusing them; things went off pleasantly except for the Beach set who were cut by the Fort for their recent unnecessary & untrue attacks on the army. Mrs. Fitch walked across & spent the evening with us until called home to lead the hunt for her toy terrier, which had gone astray. Some thunder & lightening today, with a tiny shower & splendid piles of cumulus clouds ending in a glorious bronze & yellow sunset, succeeded by a clear sky & beautiful moonlight. Not so hot as yesterday.

Friday 27th. Quiet morning. The Judge breakfasted & dined with us. Mother was busy all the afternoon writing letters in continuation of yesterday's talk with Genl. Wilcox about the Pimas & Papagoes: writing to Mrs. Martin[49] & Mrs. Meagher.[50] Frank also answered letters. Ida Burnett called. She has done well with her Walnut Grove School & returns there in August. She is only just over 16, but perfectly capable.[51] Mr. Haskell came in for Frank to go out to a small dancing party at the Wilcoxes, where Frank had a very pleasant time & Mr. Haskell walked back with him at 2 a.m.! We were asked in a side fashion by Grace & so managed not to go. Mr. Churchill called to see what we thought of getting Judge Silent to marry Mr. [Eugene W.] Risley & Miss [Eleanor] Merrill this evening after Court had adjourned; we thought it would be just right as there is no real clergyman here & the Justices of the Peace are not people one would care to be married by whereas if Judge Silent does it it will feel real & legal and Miss Merrill [wants] it as she has come through alone from Boston so as to avoid the expense & loss of time it would have been to Mr. Risley to go after her. He is reporter to the Court & also clerk to Fitch & Churchill— the engagement a five year one. The Judge did marry them at 10 p.m., the Fitches & Churchills being present & the bride went straight to her house which was in readiness for her, she having arrived by this morning's stage & stayed the day at the Shermans. The day was so hot that I wore out in the afternoon & could do nothing, but Mother was all right. The night was cool enough.

Saturday 28th. Less hot than yesterday, so I was busy redding [readying] up odds & ends & sewing till dinner time. Mother also did some sewing. Grace spent most of the afternoon with us. The Judge breakfasted & dined with us. Mr. Evans also took dinner with us doing his French afterwards, and we arranged for night school now [that] the hot weather has set in. After dinner Mother went down to the Hospital to see Mother Basil who returns to Tucson on Monday. Evening & night really cool.

Sunday 29th. Quiet day chiefly given to writing letters to our home circle in the East. Judge Silent breakfasted with us but dined at the Lewises. He is about well again now. I went down to the Hospital after dinner to tell Mother Basil adieu as she leaves by the Black Cañon Stage at 8 a.m. tomorrow. She is content with her visit to Prescott & pleased with us for the little we were able to do for Mother John. Mrs. Churchill made us a little call in the evening. Frank took Thor & walked over to the Fort after dinner, making some visits there. The day though hot was not oppressive; night cool.

Monday 30th. Not a hot day. Mother & Frank did quite a lot of writing; I only read. Miss Sherman & Mrs. Otis[52] called & Mr. McMillan called to say adieu as he left in the afternoon stage. In the evening I called on Mrs. St. James, Mrs. Thorne & Mrs. Thibodo. Judge Silent dined with us.

Father's letter this morning had several good business points in it, among others that Ros Raymond[53] will probably be the expert sent out to examine into & report on the mines they have in hand. Night pleasantly cool.

Tuesday 1st July. Quiet day. Mother sewed; Frank wrote letters & I read. Judge Silent dined with us. Grace made a short call. In the evening Mother, Frank & I walked over & called on Mrs. Risley, the bride, who seems a pleasant mixture of the Illinois & Mass. woman. As we came home we met Mr. Evans, Fanny & her brother[54] who is on leave from Annapolis, out riding. They had been at our house, but missed us. Mother turned in at Mrs. Fitch's & made a call there, I came straight home. Frank went on to the Club where he won two games out of the tournament & Mrs. Otis called this afternoon. Rather cool day, a light frost in the hills. The fire in the woods is sending great clouds of smoke sweeping over Granite Mt.

Wednesday 2nd. Lovely cool morning. I had a good read in my Scotch history sitting by my window, the outside light hadn't its usual glare. Judge Silent & Fanny Weeks breakfasted with us, Fanny spending the afternoon. Mr. Evans came in & having tied up Lux with a regular cable, did a good French lesson with Mother & with me. Frank went out to the Fort after dinner. Miss Wilcox & Dr. Ainsworth called *together,* later in the evening Mrs. Lewis & Mrs. Churchill turned in, & Mrs. C. told us of their intended move across the creek to the Weber house, a pretty place, but a disagreeable walk to reach it. The idea of moving makes the little woman low in her mind, but "business" required it. Evening & night icily chill. The forest fire has crept along till now it is just back of Thumb Butte & rolling dense clouds of smoke across over the village.

Thursday 3rd. (Dr. Morton's birthday). Usual morning routine & Judge Silent breakfasted with us. Mother & I both sewed on her blue wrapper in the afternoon. After dinner Fanny Weeks came & took Mother & Frank for a drive in their ambulance which is easy to get into. Judge Silent came in for a moment to get Charley's address that he might telegraph through him to Father that the "Black Warrior"[55] would be lost unless immediate action can be taken. Mrs. Fitch came & took me [on] a drive with Topsy. We were all in again by 8 after which Mrs. Churchill & Mrs. Lewis stopped in for a while on their return from a tour of visits. Weather still pleasant.

Friday 4th July. Quiet home day for us, with little visits in the evening from Fanny & from Judge Silent, who had been to the Picnic held at Iron Springs—& been bored—where they had the band & quite a turnout, likeness a ball; there was a meagerly attended ball at the theatre also. None of us went. Pleasant weather continuing. . . .

Sunday 6th. Hot day, but so continuously overcast with thick grey clouds that everyone hoped for rain, but they cleared off in a very beautiful gold bronze sunset, leaving the air, however, less dry & less disagreeably charged with electricity than it has been lately. The Judge breakfasted with us & as Mr. Churchill was out of town we sent across for Mrs. C. to dine with us, which she did & enjoyed it—going home right afterwards as Mr. C. returned early from Lynx Creek. Grace came for Mother & Frank to go out to sunset parade which they did, sitting on the Evans' porch & got back before 9. I didn't care to go.

Monday 7th. Mother wasn't well all through the day, having one sharp turn of neuralgia, but everyone is out of condition from the weather. Fanny Weeks & her Mother called, Fanny staying to breakfast & part of the afternoon. Judge Silent dined with us. After dinner, I went to see Sister Mary at the Hospital, Mrs. Churchill & Mrs. Fitch. Mrs. Weeks & her son from Annapolis walked in & made us a short visit in the evening & Frank walked back to the Fort with them. Threatened rain all day & sprinkled a few drops—day hot, but night reasonably cool.

Tuesday 8th. Mother was better today but felt tired. Mrs. Churchill called early & I walked with her over to the Weber house, which we inspected together, staying over there till near 12 o'clock. It is a right decently comfortable place for here, though following their usual fashion up here the bedrooms are shrimped for the sake of having several parlors! Mrs. C. has decided to move over. We had a quiet afternoon. The Judge dined with us & after dinner Mr. Evans rode in & did a solid long French lesson. The day was partly overcast, but still hot, sunset beautiful, mixed gold colors & pink on deep blue. Night warm—guitar serenade to the Fitches & Lewises at 2 a.m., which sounded well.

Wednesday 9th. The day was mostly broken into bits by visits—Mrs. Evans & Mrs. Lewis—& by watching the storm clouds; there was a small shower in the town & heavy rain to the South & S.W. In the evening I went to see Mrs. Fitch & when I came in I found Prof. [Alonzo J.] Sawyer of Chicago, now in mines at the Big Bug. Mother asked him & his friend to breakfast tomorrow. After he left Judge Silent came in & had a goodbye talk over matters here & in New York, as he leaves at 6 a.m. tomorrow for Mineral Park. Sunset fine.

Thursday 10th. I spent a lazy day fighting a middle sized headache. Mother worked on a pincushion for Grace. Frank went out to the Fort in the 9 o'clock ambulance to spend the morning & lunch with the Evans. Dr. Caldwell of Cleveland & Prof. Sawyer of Chicago breakfasted with us & we had an interesting talk with them over the prospects of the Territory. They go East on Saturday to return in some months. Mother & Frank wrote important letters to Father & to G[eorge] B[rowne]—Judge Silent's testamentary directions before leaving for Mohave [County]. Fanny rode in in the evening. Day partly overcast & not hot inside the house. Sister Mary & Mrs. Wollenberg called in the afternoon.

Friday 11th. A quiet morning. Mr. Evans, Lt. [Henry Peoble] Kingsbury of the 6th Cavalry, & Mids[hip]m[an]. Weeks breakfasted with us & had a gayly disputatious time of it; they adjourned to billiards soon after leaving us to a quiet afternoon of reading & sewing. At 8 the ambulance came for us & we drove out to Mrs. Evans' where there was a little dance given to Grace & to Fanny, as Grace starts next week for school & Fanny is to follow soon. Nearly all the garrison were there. Genl. Wilcox is off to where his boys are camped. We were the only ones from the town. We had a very pleasant evening—I chiefly sat on the broad porch overlooking the parade ground & listened to the band which played well and talked with the different people who went & came, making the acquaintance of some new officers & having to dance a little: we got home by 12½, having each enjoyed ourselves. Pleasant weather. Jupiter, Mars, Saturn & a quarter slice of the old moon—with numerless [sic] lesser lights—were brilliant in the sky as we drove home.

Saturday 12th. Cool morning & commenced quietly enough but we were all upset by the news that the stage had again been robbed & the mail riffled—just south of Phoenix—which mail contained Mother's and Frank's letters of the 10th important as to business & containing personal matters which we had decidedly not intended for the public. Fanny came to breakfast & after her came Grace who brought with her Lt. [Palmer G.] Wood, from Verde, (she must have made him think we had asked him, as he doesn't seem to belong to the order of those who come uninvited). They left between two & three—then Frank rewrote his letter to GB. In the evening Mother went over to the Fitches. Mr. Haskell called here. . . .

Monday 14th. Still day mostly spent in reading. Mother & Frank wrote some letters to replace those lost. Mr. Haskell sent us in some scraps of the lost letters which were forwarded amongst others to the Military

Headquarters. Mr. H. also sent me in a spare mirror to replace my "bias" one he had heard me speaking of at the Evans', which I will use till he has a good opportunity of forwarding it to the officer for whom he originally meant it. Frank went out to the Fort for a while, ambulance both ways. In the evening I went to see Mrs. Lewis. Afternoon hot, but rain signs thickening. . . .

Wednesday 16th. Grace Wilcox came in early & staid till 4½ p.m.! Mother wrote letters—we have had no letters from the East for several days. The afternoon was pleasantly spent in watching the first rainstorm of the season which lasted some hours & was accompanied by heavy thunder & very brilliant lightning & cleared off in a glorious sunset—mists of gold dust curtaining off Granite Mt., whilst many shades of smoke color & of pink in the dense clouds came out strongly against the clear light green of the sky—the air after the rain was delicious. Frank went out to a little dance at the Fort.

Thursday 17th. No letters in the mail—four days now since we have heard from Father. Frank & I spent the morning in watching the splendid grey & white cloud racks which came before the storm that burst about 11 & lasted some hours with heavy rain, thunder & lightning. Mrs. Fitch, who had stepped across for a moment, was storm bound, spending the morning & breakfasting with us. The rain has only just come in time for even the dry grass was failing & stock beginning to suffer, the milk & butter supply running very short—twenty cows giving three gallons at a milking. Mother & Frank wrote letters in the afternoon & I gave Mr. Evans, who rode in on "Lux," a big French lesson. In the evening Mrs. Churchill, then Mrs. Lewis called. Guy Huse has graduated at West Point 21 in a class of 66; & is assigned to the 4th cavalry which is scattered over Texas & the Indian Territory.

Friday 18th. Pleasant & reassuring letter from Father in the midday mail. Mrs. Evans called with Lt. Kingsbury who came to take leave as he has won the [competition] here in shooting & goes on to San Francisco there to further contest for being one of the teams sent to Creedmoor.[56] Mrs. Churchill took dinner & spent the evening with us. After dinner I had a drive with Mrs. Fitch, during which she called on Miss Wilcox & on Mrs. Smith. Day rather hot.

Saturday 19th. After the usual Saturday morning housekeeping, I took some papers across to Mrs. Churchill's & then went on up to Mrs. Buffum's where I made quite a long visit. She told [me] Mr. Buffum had gone out to his mine, the "Genl. Crook", with an Eastern capitalist who had come on to see it on Father's endorsement of Mr. Buffum's reliability. Mrs. Churchill, Mrs. Lewis & Mrs. Cory breakfasted with us & spent part of the afternoon, evidently enjoying themselves. Mother wrote full long letters to Father which Lt. Kingsbury will post in San Francisco which will ensure their getting through—also some notes of introduction for Mr. Kingsbury. Mrs. St. James called right after dinner, then came Fanny Weeks with their carriage & its five mules & took Mother & Frank for a drive, I staying in to "entertain" Mrs. St. James, Grace, Orlando & Charley Wilcox, who all left before dark. Mother felt much freshened by her drive. Weather not hot indoors.

Sunday 20th. Mother had a nice letter from Charley & I had a good long one from Dr. Jameson. Mr. Evans breakfasted with us bringing us a splendid big watermelon from Verde; he has the promise of being sent East in charge of an insane officer which gives him expenses to Washington & causes his leave to date from there. Frank went out to the Fort in the evening. Judge Silent got back from Mohave this evening & came to see us. He is in quite a cheerful frame of mind about business.

Monday 21st. Judge Silent came up early to show us a very good telegram just arrived from Father who asked some questions about mines & said "finish next week" dated 19th. The Judge & Fanny Weeks breakfasted with us, Fanny staying the afternoon. Mr. Evans rode "Lux" in for his French lesson & staid to dinner. Grace dined with us by invitation as she leaves on Wednesday for school in Oakland, the General taking her "inside." After dinner I drove with Mrs. Fitch out to near the race course to call on Mrs. Powell [Powers] of Miss[issippi] who has come on from Otero, N.M. with her husband & two other gentlemen over the Mogollons in their own ambulance.[57] When we got to their camping ground we found they had moved camp to Miller Flat so we drove quickly back & were joined on the road by Mr. Evans, who called with us—& made a good genre picture as he stood in the dull blue uniform by grey "Lux" under a tall pine with low sweeping boughs, with a low tent, black ambulance & camp trappings, all picked out against a near background of jagged cream tinted rocks. The camping party are nice people & Mr. Evans soon found they had Miss. acquaintances in common so he asked Mrs. Powers to stay with them whilst the men of the party go up into Mineral Park where one of them owns a mine. They have been seven weeks on the road from Otero.

Genl. Wilcox & Miss Wilcox had called whilst I was out, the General to say goodbye & they had taken Frank home with them for whist. Judge Silent came up a moment to show us a beautiful &, I believe rare, moth—the Peach moth which was caught in the Court House. A pleasant telegram to Frank from Mr. Haskell about vacancies in the army & hopes for Frank's "quick appointment." Mr. Churchill—on his return from Mohave—& Mrs. Risley called during the afternoon. Day lowering & hot. Sunset wonderfully beautiful soft canary yellows on dull grey brightening into burnished gold & fading away into softest Venus saffron—& Venus herself at one moment appearing with "trailing robes" of shimmered saffron—then a baby crescent moon. Night warm.

Tuesday 22nd. Mother spent most of the day at Mrs. Fitch's, helping her arrange a jardinière of artificial flowers for the next play. Judge Silent breakfasted with us. He had good letters from Father. Day lowering & hot, but no rain fell in the town.

Wednesday 23rd. Another good letter from Father. Day chiefly spent in reading the weekly papers from London & New York. Mrs. Lewis called with Mrs. Eugene Aram.[58] . . .

Thursday 24th. Usual routine of day—Frank adding a good bit of studying. Judge Silent breakfasted with us. Mr. Evans came in late in the afternoon, did his French with me, dined with us & then went to the theatre with us. "A Scrap of Paper" was right well given, from an American point of view that is for it was not at all the "Pattes de Mouche" I remember. The Churchills & Lewises sat right by us & nearly all the Fort were present— several of the officers "visiting" in the necessarily long entractes [intermissions]. (Gov. & Mrs. Powers returned my visit this afternoon). Two very heavy showers during the afternoon.

Friday 25th. Quiet morning. Young Mr. Weeks breakfasted with us. Mr. Churchill brought & introduced to us Mr. Robbins, correspondent of the Chicago *Inter-Ocean,* who staid quite a while talking about the Territory. Mr. Sherman called to take leave as he starts tomorrow for an official tour amongst the schools of the southern part of the Territory—& possibly an outing to Guaymas. Judge Silent dined with us & brought us a basket of very good Wickenburg peaches. Mrs. Churchill & Mrs. Lewis spent the evening with Mother. I walked with Frank to the Fort, calling on Mrs. Evans—out—Miss Wilcox—in—& the Mrs. Weeks who was in also, & a

Lot of people on her porch where there was a pleasant breeze, good view of the quiet moonlit valley & of Venus; we got home soon after 10. Day really hot, night pleasant.

Saturday 26th. Despatch from Father to say "Business concluded, I leave Monday. Experts accompany or follow same week. All right here," which naturally filled us with thankfulness & content. Our morning was chiefly given to talking over Father's telegram & its good consequences. Fanny Weeks spent part of the afternoon with us. Mr. Evans took his French lesson & staid to dinner. Judge Silent & Mr. Robbins dined with us—the Judge had also breakfasted with us. After dinner Frank walked out to the Fort with Mr. Evans & staid the evening. I called on Mrs. Buffum & on Mrs. Churchill, coming home before 8. Mother spent the evening at the Fitches. Day hot, but pleasant south breeze after dark. . . .

28th. Judge Silent breakfasted with us. A Dr. [George B.] Abbott of Chicago called with letters from Genl. [Napoleon Bonaparte] Buford of Illinois—he had just arrived by private team from Santa Fe, 26 days, & with his mother[59] is stopping at the hotel. After dinner I crossed over to the hotel & called on Mrs. Smith[60] of Chicago—in, on Mrs. Abbott—out, Mrs. [Francis A.] Shaw & Mrs. Alsap of Phoenix, both out. Came back home to find Mrs. Fowler & Fanny Weeks—both had ridden in—Miss Wilcox & Lt. Wotherspoon calling—& later on Dr. McKee, just back from San Francisco, & Mrs. Lewis called. Mother trimmed a hat for me during the day. Frank answered letters & studied. I read scraps. Day hot & showers by turns, night pleasant with one very heavy shower.

Tuesday 29th. Quiet morning. Mr. Evans came in to breakfast & just after, Frank read in the telegraphic column of the "Bulletin" the appointment by the President of "Francis Frémont of Arizona" as Second Lieut U.S.A.—at which we were naturally greatly delighted, as we agreed with Frank in wishing it for him. He & Mr. Evans went off together for a game of billiards; & I went with Mrs. Fitch for a longish drive down the Verde road, which gives quite new points of view of the mountains round Prescott. The sky was overcast with heavy storms to the north & we just got back to the village before the rain fell there too. Mr. Evans was still at our house & I had time to hear his French before the ambulance came & he & Frank went out to the Post where Frank dined with the Evans[es] & then called on several of the officers who are all charmed with his appointment & want him in their regiment, 12th Foot, as Frank will have a pleasant time if assigned to it. Fanny Weeks came for us to drive—with the mules—after

Rebecca Evans Buffum and her son Asa, c. 1870. (Courtesy of the Sharlot
Hall Museum/Library Archives, Prescott, Ariz., photo #PO 130p.)

dinner. Mother & I went & had a pleasant drive. Fine sunset; day not hot &
night cool.

Wednesday 30th. Quiet day. Judge Silent dined with us. After dinner
Frank went out to the regular Wednesday evening dance at the Post.
I called on Mrs. Bowers,[61] Mrs. Bashford & Mrs. Buffum. Fine sunset

& sultry during the afternoon. Mrs. Churchill, Mrs. Thorne & Mrs. Bean called. . . .

August 1st. Two good business letters from Father. Quiet reading & talking day. Frank studied & I heard him repeat. Mr. Robbins—Chicago—called; Fanny also in the afternoon; and in the evening Mrs. Churchill, Mrs. Fitch & Judge Silent called in succession—the Judge very much pleased with Father's letters. Frank spent the evening at the Post with the Biddles. Day overcast with rain in the near neighborhood, but none in town; fine sunset, sharply cool breeze from the south from sunset on.

Saturday 2nd. Another good letter from Father. Usual routine of day. After dinner Judge Silent called & we learned how ill Mrs. Smith of Chicago had been. I went over to see her, then on down to the hospital & saw Sister Mary; coming back to the house, I found Mrs. Bowers, Mrs. Bashford & Mrs. Burmister making a short call. Later on Mother went across & staid two hours with Mrs. Smith who is much better & has old Katy to sit up with her. Everyone went to the minstrels. We thought it might be rather loud & we could hear storms of applause; the crowd coming back over were in a bright good humor—& the usual Saturday night "25 dollar Keno" of the Whisky row was omitted, which shows the favor the Minstrels were held in. Overcast day with no rain in the village, though plenty on Granite Mt.

Sunday 3rd. Splendidly stormy day—heavy rains with thunder & lightning & a superb Garibaldi yellow & storm blue sunset with a few hazy pink clouds: the creek rose so that we could hear its rushing roar up to our house. We sent food across to Mrs. Smith who is doing well. Frank went out at 9 a.m. to the Fort & spent the day there chiefly with the Evans[es] & Biddles. Judge Silent called in the evening. Mother & I had a quiet day.

Monday 4th. Letter from Father received this morning said he would certainly leave on the 28th ult. Mr. Evans came in to breakfast & after his French lesson we discussed with him plans & ideas for his European tour, as he, yesterday, received a twelve months leave with permission "to go beyond the seas." Judge Silent both breakfasted & dined with us. Frank studied pretty much all day. I called on Mrs. Allen[62] after dinner. Fine driving clouds all day & a big shower. . . .

Friday 8th. Mother nearly well; usual routine & Frank studied. We had a good letter from Father & I had a nice long one from Fanny Dart—chiefly about the Northampton College to which she goes in September as matron of one of the girls's dwelling houses, which will be a pleasant work for her. In the evening I made visits & Mrs. Lewis & [Mrs.] Churchill called here. Frank went out to the Biddles. Delicious sweeping cool breeze from 8 p.m. on through the night.

Saturday 9th. Mother well again. Mr. Evans came in for breakfast & staid till 5 having a solid French lesson & working over plans for his stay in Paris. After dinner I called on Mrs. Rodenburg & brought home some German books. Judge Silent called in the evening. Frank spent the day chiefly indoors studying. Only a small shower today, but not hot.

Sunday 10th. No mail as the heavy rains south have made a break in the railroad. Frank went out to breakfast at the Biddles & dined at the Evans[es], getting home towards 9 & we talked over his army prospects. Mother & I had a quiet day. One lovely shower right over the house with the sun bright & hot over the whole landscape.

Monday 11th. Telegram from Father dated Council Bluffs today, saying he would "reach Maricopa the 18th," which made us all rejoice. Judge Silent dined with us to talk over the telegram & transportation combinations. Fanny & Merle Weeks spent the afternoon with us. Frank went out to a rubber with Miss Wilcox. Dr. McKee & Mr. Haskell called in the evening. Afternoon hot, rest of the day pleasant. Letter from Nell with babies on Gould Island, R.I. Sister Mary called in the afternoon.

Tuesday August 12th. Frank received his orders to report for examination to Fort Whipple, which greatly pleased us as it spared the expense & time needed for the trip to West Point. Mrs. Evans & Mrs. Weeks happened in & staid to breakfast—at which was also Mr. Evans—& Mrs. Evans staid on till the 4 o'clock ambulance. Mr. Evans (who did his French, too) remained till on in the evening, talking Europe, etc. when Frank, who had staid in all day, walked back to the Fort with him. Mr. Haskell on "Fox" & Fanny on "Baldy" stopped by on their way home & made us their congratulations on Frank's having received his first orders. Mother spent the rest of the evening at the Fitches. Day pretty hot. . . .

Thursday 14th. Pleasant letter from Baker[63]—in Bruxelles on leave. Judge Silent came in early with a lovely bunch of wild flowers he had gathered on the hills across the creek; he had a bit of very interesting news about "Acting Gov." Gosper whose stage robber proclamation—a relic of the

Middle Ages—we also discussed.[64] The Judge came back to breakfast when we had Col. Rogers's pleasant letter to Father—"our associates"—to discuss. Frank studied & Mother wrote letters all the afternoon. Fanny Weeks rode in & made us a short visit after dinner. Frank went to the "Minstrels." The day was very hot but in the night it turned sharply cool.

Friday 15th. Mother wrote letters most of the day. Frank boned & I heard him review; also I wrote to Dr. Jameson, & read a little but it was too hot to enjoy doing anything & the clouds cleared up in a gorgeous red & gold sunset without giving us the shower we were hoping for. Fanny W. drove in after dinner with messages from Col. Weeks about the ambulance to meet Father at Maricopa—arranged for by telegram from Genl. Wilcox. Fanny took me [on] a nice drive with her strong grey out to the stage road. Mrs. Churchill spent the evening with us & Frank spent his with the Biddles.

Saturday 16th. The Fowlers asked us some days ago to go with them to a big picnic given Fanny & Ed. Weeks as an adieu. Mother didn't care to be out all day & so backed out when the General's new ambulance with its six brown mules came for us at 9½. So Frank and I went alone to the Weeks where we waited till starting time; nearly all the Post people went. Mr. Evans was sick & his Mother staid with him. There were three six mule ambulances, one four mule provision wagon, two little two mule ambulances, the Weeks & the Wilcox carriages & the Smiths' pony phaeton in the procession which drove quickly out to Cooks' ranch[65]—Fanny & Mr. Haskell & Mr. Wilson made the load of our ambulance in going out—where five open tents were pitched under good sized walnuts & a large sized unfinished house was utilized as our dining hall. The children—there were eight of assorted sizes—dispersed about enjoying the day amazingly. After a little rest & talk under the trees, I joined Mrs. Weeks & the working party in the dining room & helped there till lunch was prepared, when our set adjourned to our particular tent. The set was Dr. McKee, Mr. Haskell, Wilson, Frank, Mr. & Mrs. Smith, Fanny, Merle & I. When the rain threatened Mr. Haskell wanted us to go under shelter, but we all preferred to risk it & consequently got more or less wet for it was a big rain which boxed the compass & was beautiful to watch for we were on a small plateau up out of which Granite Mt. rose like a magnified Porcupine Island. We got shelter in the ambulances etc. whilst the shower lasted & towards four started home. Fanny & I, Frank, Mr. Haskell & Merle in our same ambulance. We left Fanny & Merle at their house & Mr. Haskell came on with us to our door whence he hurried back to avoid the coming storm. We had had a really pleasant day. Mother had a quiet day & interesting, too, as Judge Silent had breakfasted with her & talked over a new & splendid mine on his list—in the Tonto Basin. In the evening I made Mrs. Fitch a short visit. The day was hot, the rain & the clouds fine.

Sunday 17th. Despatch from Father at San Francisco to say he leaves the 18th. Frank studied hard all day as his examination is ordered for Tuesday morning. In the evening Frank & I walked across to the Fort & called to see Fanny & found her with a slight cold from yesterday's wetting. Judge Silent was at our house when we came in. Rather hot day, with a shower & lovely gold brown sunset.

Monday 18th. Despatch from McLean to tell us he is ordered to China & leaves in Sept. Fanny Weeks breakfasted & spent part of the afternoon with us. Later in the day young Weeks made his P.P.C. call. In the evening Mother, Frank & I drove out to the Fort & took leave of Mrs. Evans & of Fanny. They go Wednesday, Mrs. Weeks going with them to the railroad. Mr. Evans stays a fortnight longer. Both Fanny & Mrs. Evans were sorry to tell us adieu. The rain, which lasted partly through the night, caught us at the Fort. Frank sat up late studying. Day not hot.

Tuesday 19th. Frank went out to Fort Whipple for Examination & passed the medical part, then stayed on to the Evans' auction, coming home to dinner & report progress of examination, then returning for the serenade etc. of the bouquet d'adieu to Fanny, Ed, & Mrs. Evans. Mrs. Lewis & Mrs. Churchill breakfasted with us—to make the acquaintance of corn pudding. Mrs. Evans—P.P.C.—& Miss Wilcox called; also Ida Burnett who goes tomorrow to her school in Walnut Creek. After dinner I called on Ida Burnett, Miss Kethroe & Mrs. Luke, Mrs. Powers & Mrs. Smith—all in. Day not hot.

Wednesday 20th. Frank went out to the Fort earlyish & went on with his examination—working till 3 when he came home, tired too. Fanny & her brother with Mrs. Evans left at 2, Col. & Mrs. Weeks going to Maricopa with them. Mrs. Smith of Chicago & Mrs. Powers took breakfast with us—by invitation—& spent part of the afternoon. Judge Silent dined with us & brought a big bunch of lovely wild flowers. After dinner Mother went to see Mrs. Buffum & Mrs. Fitch, coming back in time to see Mr. & Mrs. Otis, Mr. & Mrs. Churchill who were still at the house, but missing Dr. McKee, who had called earlier in the evening. Day not very hot.

Thursday 21st. Frank went out to his examination & passed as he knew though he could not be officially informed as the papers have to go on to Washington before the finding can be made public—"passed splendidly." He was very tired when he got home at 4 & went to bed at 9 which is a wonder for him. We had a telegram from Genl. Wilcox, dated last night, saying he & Father had connected at Maricopa & would start homewards. Mrs. Noyes called. Judge Silent came up to talk over Father's approaching arrival & plans belonging with it & he returned to dinner. I drove with Mrs. Fitch in the evening. We were all tired & went to bed early. The day had a tinge of Fall in the air.

Friday 22nd. Frank went out to the Fort for an hour in the morning to finish quite up. Mr. Evans breakfasted & dined with us, spending the intervening time part[ly] with us & partly at the Club. He is still limp from his recent illness. Frank went out to the Biddles for the evening. Mother went down & spent the evening at Mrs. Lewis's. Only hot in the afternoon, the nights now are frostily cool. Telegram from Father this morning said he would be home Saturday.

Chapter 4

The Arrival of the Mining Experts

August 23–October 20, 1879

Saturday, August 23rd. Elon Wilcox rode in earlyish to let us know that Father might arrive by noon, which kept us on the look out all day. Frank answered a pile of letters. Mother wrote & sewed. Just as we had finished dinner Father arrived well & not much fatigued, though as they had relays of mules on the road they had travelled fast, making today sixty mountain miles. They had met the Weeks' party in Phoenix where they all put up at the same hotel. There were two murders in Phoenix that night & next day some hours after they had left a "Law & Order" committee hung the two murderers![1] Of course there was a big talk amongst us all & Father sent for Judge Silent to give him the business points. The day wasn't hot & there is a touch of frost now in the nights.

Sunday 24th. Judge Silent breakfasted with us & had a big & very interesting talk with Father over business—past, present & to come & "concerning copper, mica, antimony, silver & gold," the Judge having an "assorted lot" of mines on hand & Father knowing parties who want them. In the evening Dr. McKee, Lt. Evans & Mr. Churchill each made short visits on Father. The rest of the day was talkee, talkee, & overhauling Father's trunk, which came by a second ambulance & of course had something for each of us.

Monday 25th. Judge Silent breakfasted with us & Mr. Evans dined with us. Several gentlemen called to see Father who was busy nearly all day writing back east in concert with Judge S. who was in & out. Frank also wrote letters & went out to the Fort in the evening. Mother read & did a little sewing. I called on Mrs. Fitch in the evening. The nights & mornings are quite cool, but the afternoons are still too hot, autumn heat however.

Tuesday 26th. Day chiefly given to letter writing by the rest of the family. I copied some for Father & read. I went a short drive with Mrs. Fitch.

Judge Charles Silent. (Courtesy of the Research Division, Arizona Department of Library, Archives and Public Records, Phoenix.)

Mother went across to her house & made her a little visit & Mr. Fitch called on Father. The day was tiringly hot with clouds & a gorgeous gold & red sunset, night cool.

Wednesday 27th. Letter writing was the order of the day. The Judge breakfasted with us. Frank went out to the Fort in the evening & was storm bound there till 1 a.m.! for after a glorious red gold sunset we had the heaviest rain storm of the season lasting till nearly 2 a.m., coming from S.W. & accompanied by heavy thunder & vivid lightning.

Thursday 28th. Letter writing & copying was the bone of the day. Judge

The courthouse in Prescott, looking northwest, c. 1880. (Courtesy of the Sharlot Hall Museum/Library Archives, Prescott, Ariz., photo #BU-G 507pf.)

Silent breakfasted with us. Mr. Evans came to tell us that he would start on Monday on his twelve months leave for Europe, leave to date from the time he turns over to the Washington National Asylum a crazy soldier he takes on from Camp Grant, A.T. He staid to dinner. In the evening Mother & Father went to see the Buffums about the terms we hold this house on as we are not quite pleased with our landlord's failure to do some necessary things about the house. Several people called on Father through the day, which was not a warm one.

Friday 29th. I went to see Mrs. Buffum early & she suggested our trying for the Thibodo's house as she knew they want to go east & it is the only one large enough for us, which resulted in Mother's seeing them & getting the refusal of the house for several days. Father drove out to the Fort in the morning with Delegate Campbell to consult with General Wilcox about the Hualapais Indians, who are in pressing need of food & together they telegraphed the War Dept. about [it]. Frank spent the day & night at the Fort. Genl. & Miss Wilcox called in the afternoon. Mrs. Buffum & Mrs. Fitch called in the evening. The morning was stinging cool after a sharp frost & Mother some way caught cold. The air was delightful.

Saturday 30th. Several people on Territorial business came to see Father through the day. The Judge also was in on business. Mother had a "miserable" day with a cold, but managed to go out in the evening with Father & Frank to a band musical at the General's—Foster & the four greys came for them. Genl. W. himself was in bed with a cold which is epidemic just now. Everybody of the Post was there except the Weeks[es] & Mr. Evans. Only the afternoons are hot now. Moonlight fine. . . .

Monday September 1st. Father busy on Territorial & mining matters. Mother wrote lots of letters. Judge Silent breakfasted with us & came up again in the evening & each time had good, long business talks. Frank was in & out to the Post etc. on business for Father. I went up on the hill with Frank to see the full moon rise just back of a peak & with a few clouds near it—very fine. Stopped in & made Mrs. Cory a visit; got home to find Miss Wilcox & Mr. Walsh[2]—passing thro'—had called & Mr. Sherman & his committee for a short call. Afternoon hot.

Tuesday 2nd. Just one year since we left New York. Usual routine of mixed territorial & mining business; the Judge breakfasted with us & came again in the evening. Frank went out early with Mr. Murphy[3] to look at a mine sixteen miles south of the town which Mr. M. wishes to sell to Father's syndicate. Frank got back before dinner well pleased with the mine. Mother's cold nearly gone. I went across to see Mrs. Churchill in the evening. Clouds through the day & very fine moonlight—not however quenching the brighter stars.

Wednesday 3rd. Capt. Eagan, who was sent for by Father on Territorial business, told us he was busy getting off supplies to the Hualapais. Usual routine of the day. Judge Silent dined with us. I took a little drive with Mrs. Fitch after dinner; Mother went across & spent the evening at Mrs. Fitch's. Mr. Haskell called to take leave as he starts tomorrow on an extended tour among the camps in the southern part of the Territory. Lt.

[George Spencer] Wilson was with him. Frank spent the evening at the Fort. Day hot, in spite of some clouds.

Thursday 4th. Usual routine of the morning was broken in upon by a big fire in the N.W. end of the village, luckily the wind was slight from the south so the sparks etc. were blown into the fields or we should have had a real conflagration—as it was two nice families were burned out, a barn & a warehouse—full—destroyed; the furniture was saved & so would have been the contents of the warehouse but that the cry of "powder" was raised—it was afterwards known it was only giant powder.[4] Everyone in town & part of the military fire co. were on hand & saved three residences which but for hard work [would] have gone too. There is no provision against fire in the town, it has to be s[. . .] work & almost no water. I went in the afternoon to see the burned out & nearly burned out families—Wollenberg, Rodenburg, & Burke. Also called on the Sisters; two new ones have arrived.[5] Frank was at the fire. Mr. Haskell called in the afternoon; he got off later in the day—he goes on an Indian mission to induce some hundreds who escaped from the San Carlos reservation during the last agent's time, to return to the reservation. If he fails then force will have to be used. No one knows of this state of affairs & it is to be kept quiet. We don't know of it through Mr. Haskell, who supposes us as ignorant as the rest. Prof. Maynard,[6] one of the experts connected with Father's mining business, arrived by the morning stage, & both breakfasted and dined with us. Genl. Wilcox came in to tell Father that the War Dept. had granted sixty days rations to the foodless Hualapais & that the commissary was busy buying & sending off the supplies to Mohave; this is prompt action on the joint application made from here on the 29th ult. The Genl. staid to breakfast with us; and Judge Silent breakfasted & dined with us. Mr. Maynard staid in the evening talking over his stay in England & business travels into Russia & Asia—almost to Khiva.[7] Dr. McKee called. Not hot.

Friday 5th. We have asked Mr. Maynard to breakfast & dine with us while he is in town; Judge Silent dined & breakfasted with us, & they had a long consultation over mining work. In the evening, we drove Mr. Maynard out to the Fort, stopped for a moment to see Mr. Evans who is still ill—then went up to Genl. Wilcox, where we made quite a long visit, driving home by moonlight; Frank staid to whist at Col Martin's & remained all night at the Fort.

Saturday 6th. Dr. Einhorn,[8] the second expert, arrived at noon by the stage & tired out; next week they will start off on their inspecting tour of the mines. Usual routine of mixed territorial & mining work. Mother not quite well. Dr. Einhorn dined with us—as also did the Judge & Mr. Maynard. In the evening those three went with Frank to hear the local "Minstrels" at the theatre. Weather pleasant.

Sunday 7th. The Judge & the two experts breakfasted with us & the experts dined with us & spent the evening. Frank went out to the Fort in the evening. I went to evening church with Judge Silent—an act de presence [a token appearance] as a new Methodist preacher has just come to town.[9] I didn't like him or his style which was a mixture of cant, personalities & diffused repetition, delivered in alternating high & low tones, the loud ones nearly deafening one in this thin atmosphere; but I think his congregation liked it. The Judge staid a little while setting the programme for next week's work. In between times we wrote letters—I to McLean, who is in San Francisco & sails thence for China on the 13th, & to Nelly. The stars were splendid before the moon rose, & even after.

Monday 8th. Frank walked out to the Fort early with Mr. Maynard who had been ill in the night—with the cramps and fainting—which so many have in the first days of their stay here—and wanted to see Dr. Ainsworth. Dr. Einhorn & Judge Silent breakfasted with us; Dr. Einhorn & Mr. Maynard dined with us. The Judge was in & out through the day, talking things over & getting ready for a start on Wednesday. Mr. Maynard is every way nice & a life long friend of Jack Howard & Ros Raymond. Dr. Einhorn is different— having the obstinately bumptious conceit of a young German, & rather expecting everything to be ready on tap here as it would in a large eastern city: so he has to be ménagé [jollied] somewhat—not that he means it disagreeably. Father has lots of letters & territorial business to keep him occupied. Mother is almost quite well again. Frank took Dr. Einhorn out to the Post in the evening & they were asked to stay the night, which they did.

Tuesday 9th. Besides preparations for tomorrow's start & mining work, Father did lots of territorial business with the Marshall, Auditor Clerk & Mr. Sherman & letter writing. Judge Silent was in & out often. He & both the experts breakfasted with us. Mr. Evans called during the afternoon; so did Mrs. Lewis; and in the evening Dr. McKee. Frank, Mr. Maynard & Dr. Einhorn dined with the "young officers" mess at the Fort, so we had a quiet dinner alone.

Wednesday 10th. We were all up early, Father & Frank having their coffee at 6½. An hour later the ambulance & four mules came over from the

Fort—for it has been arranged that Father is to travel with government transportation—& as everyone was ready they started at once; Father, Frank, Judge Silent, Mr. Maynard & Dr. Einhorn. This time they go to the Bradshaw Basin, inspecting the Tiger & many other mines & return on Sunday. Mr. Evans breakfasted & spent the afternoon with us—a visite d'adieu as tomorrow morning he starts for the East via Tucson & Santa Fe, picking up his crazy man at Camp Grant & travelling by ambulance, stage, & rr. We shall quite miss him & have given him piles of letters to our friends in the East & in Europe. Mrs. Churchill spent part of the evening with us; Mother going to see her home spent the other part with her.

Thursday 11th. Just a quiet day with [a] nice long letter from McLean, still in San Francisco; & a pleasant little visit from Genl. Wilcox in the afternoon. In the evening Mother called on Mrs. [Lucinde] Adams, the wife of the new preacher; and Mrs. Buffum called here to say goodbye as she goes "inside" on Sunday for a six weeks absence. Day hot with an enervating Fall heat. Mr. Evans got off at 8 a.m. this morning via the Black Canyon. . . .

Saturday 13th. Reading & sewing morning. Mother had a nice letter from Fanny Dart enclosing a photograph which is a charming likeness of her. Dr. & Mrs. Adams, the new Methodist preacher, breakfasted with us. Mrs. Thibodo called in the afternoon. Mother & I dined at the Fitches, Mother staying on in the evening later than I did. Afternoon hot. . . .

Monday 15th. Mr. Gosper, then Mrs. Weeks called during the morning. Mother sewed most of the day & after dinner made a short visit to the Sisters Hospital where she saw the Catholic Bishop, who is up from Tucson, & asked him to breakfast tomorrow. Dr. McKee spent the evening with us & showed us lots of his European photographs. We had a message that Father was detained by the necessity of pumping one of the mines to be visited free of water, & may not be back for days yet. Afternoons still hot.

Tuesday 16th. Mrs. Smith of Chicago called & gave us a very amusing account of her camping out experiences with the Powers. Bishop Salpointe breakfasted with us; the talk was chiefly on the Papagoes. He left early as he is busy organizing a school for the Sisters here & starts back for Tucson tomorrow. I went across to see Mrs. Churchill in the afternoon. In the evening Mrs. Fitch called & Mother returned with her & sat awhile on her porch which facing south catches the cool breeze. We half expected Father.

Wednesday 17th. I had a nice letter from Dr. Morton! Just a quiet day till 4½ when Father & the others got back & devoted themselves till dinner time to removing dust. They had driven, ridden & climbed, besides walking lots & were all somewhat tired. Mr. Einhorn [was] so tired out that he didn't put in an appearance. I was not expecting them, so Chung had to "fly around" to get a dinner for seven instead of two as was planned for. Dr. Adams called on Father after dinner. In the evening, Mother, Frank, & I drove over to the Parker-Bashford wedding, taking the Churchills with us. Father was too tired to go. It was a pretty affair, both in the little church nigh the house & in the big roofless marquee under the pines—for the house was too small to hold the guests—& lit by rows of Japanese lanterns. The bride was in the regulation white silk, veil & orange blossoms & looked well; so did her bridesmaid, *Mrs.* St. James. The supper was very correct; the Fort band played decently well. Only Genl. Wilcox & family were asked from the Fort. The invitation question was quite a matter of heart burning in the village. In coming back we made room for Mrs. Smith who had failed to secure return in the hack.

Thursday 18th September. The experts were busy sorting ores in the dining room all evening. They and Judge Silent were in & out all day. They dined at breakfast with us. In the evening Father, Mother, Frank & the experts went out & spent the evening at the Wilcoxes, the General sending his four greys & "Cinderella" in for them. I didn't feel well & staid at home. The experts leave tomorrow evening at six with Judge Silent for the Big Bug district to look at a lot of mines there & be gone three days. . . .

Saturday 20th. Father was busy writing a report to the Dept. of the Interior on the Territory & incidentally at the mining work. Frank received his first envelope addressed officially from the War Dept. to "2nd. Lieut. F. P. F." It was his appointment & oath of office, a very scorchingly severe one which of course was easy for him that must come hard on unreconstructed southerners. Judge Silent & the experts got back just as we were going to dinner; he dined with us & reported on the trip. Mr. Maynard called during the evening.

Sunday 21st. Judge Silent & the experts were coming in & out thro' the day. Mr. Maynard breakfasted with us, but they all dined elsewhere. Father was busy with letters, etc. I looked over Dr. McKee's European photos. Frank got back from the Fort—where he had spent the night at Lt. Wilson's quarters—in time for breakfast. Just as we were going to dinner Indian Inspector General H. Hammond called & we asked him to dine with us; he is on his way up to the Navajoes & on into New Mexico, travelling buckboard, arrived this noon, leaves tomorrow morning. He spent most of the evening with us. Father went down to Judge Silent's room where they held a meeting with the experts about the telegrams to be sent to the N. Y. Syndicate tomorrow morning. Our evening took the form of thin grey clouds that veiled the sun all day & gave us a touch of sunset—the first in a long time.

Monday 22nd. People in & out all day from 9½ on. Genl. Hammond, Judge Silent & the experts breakfasted with us—after which Father & Frank drove out in Genl. W[illcox]'s ambulance to the Fort to call on Genl. Wilcox & had a long talk on Indians & railways with him. Mr. Maynard staid a while talking to Mother. Col. Benjamin[10] of Little Rock, Ark., who is travelling through the territories with a view of settling in one of them, and Mr. Maynard dined with us & afterwards Mother & Mr. Maynard called on Mrs. Bashford & Mrs. Bowers, & on Mrs. Fitch. Night cool.

Tuesday 23rd. Genl. Wilcox called with Genl. Hammond, who came to take leave as did Col. Benjamin. Mr. Maynard breakfasted with us & the Judge dined with us. Others came in & out. The day was chiefly devoted to mining work. Frank went out to the Fort in the evening.

Wednesday 24th. The experts went out of town for the day to examine a mine for a Mr. Ross.[11] Father was busy on his territorial report & with Judge S. [who] was in & out & ate with us. Dr. McKee called in the evening. Night sharply cool. The mining work is waiting on telegrams from N. Y. The electrical weather is back again & both Mother & I had headaches.

Thursday 25th. A partly satisfactory telegram was received from N. Y. & answered after several consultations had been held. This & its side issues was the principal work of the day. The Judge & Mr. Maynard both breakfasted & dined with us & Mr. Einhorn joined us at dinner. A gale, like in the Spring, blew all day. Mrs. Bowers made us a P.P.C. visit.

Friday 26th. Mining business was the ruling thread through the day. Judge Silent & Mr. Maynard took breakfast & dinner with us. A grey day like in the East & a heavy & most unexpected rain in the evening & night.

Saturday 27th. It rained all day, a real soaking eastern rain which only cleared off at sunset when there was an absolutely perfect double rainbow—the "double" looking like an ordinary rainbow, the other more intensely vivid in coloring than any we had ever seen, out of a shower; the light clouds blew swiftly by over them only softening not obscuring them, & under the arch a great pile of saffron white cumulus clouds rose like glacier mts; whilst in the west was a sunset of soft yellow shading to "manganese smoke" on a dull grey ground, with the mts., white & softened, as a base line. The rain postponed a trip Father was to have made with the experts to examine a copper mine some twenty miles from town. Judge Silent took an overdose of a tonic having strychnine in it & was partially numbed by it for some hours & we were all frightened about him; but he seemed all right by evening. A careless village doctor ordered it for him. The Judge and both experts dined & breakfasted with us. It was so damp a day that we had fires. The whole countryside is rejoicing over the rain, which the telegraph tells us has been a general one.

Sunday 28th. A lovely day, cool & with scudding white clouds against a blue sky. I walked with Frank & Thor almost to the Fort before breakfast; and in the afternoon took Mr. M. up on Reservoir Hill to see the view. Judge Silent almost well again; he and Mr. M. breakfasted with us & Mr. Maynard dined with us, going across with me afterwards to call on Mrs. Churchill whilst Mother went in to see Mrs. Fitch. Father & Mother had written some letters; otherwise having a quiet day. Frank spent the evening at the Fort. The judge was in & out all day.

Monday 29th. Father, Mr. Maynard & Frank—after early tea—got off at 6:40 with Mr. Richards[12] to examine the Black Hills copper mine, taking saddles with them in their buggies as part of the trip is to be made on horseback. The judge took breakfast & dinner with us—he seems quite well again. Mrs. Churchill spent the afternoon with us, looking over Dr. McKee's photographs & some of ours, which I showed her whilst Mother wrote letters & sewed. Mrs. Fitch called. We had [a] quiet evening, reading & going to bed early. A cool breeze & packs of drifting clouds beautified the out[side] view all day.

Tuesday 30th. Mrs. Fitch took me on a pretty drive south to Curtis's mill. We were gone from 10–12, lovely Fall day. Saw some pretty wild flowers. In the afternoon Mother went with Mrs. Lewis & Mrs. Churchill in the barouche & called on Mrs. (bride) Bashford & others across the creek & then out at the Fort—ten visits in all. Father & the others got back at 3, having had a pleasant time in beautiful scenery, with deciduous trees & plentiful grass, & seen a fine copper mine. Judge Silent was with us at both meals & Mr. Maynard dined with us, going afterwards with Frank to the theatre where the plays were so badly acted that they were amusing. The Fitches have quite retired from managing at the theatre. Mr. Einhorn called in the evening.

Wednesday 1st October. Father devoted most of his day to work on his report. Miss Wilcox called early & took Frank home to lunch with her—& he stayed to dine & the night with Lt. Wilson. Judge Silent & Mr. Maynard took dinner & breakfast with us. I called on Mrs. Churchill in the morning & Mrs. Fitch in the evening. Mother did some sewing & wrote letters. The pleasant cool weather lasts.

Thursday 2nd. Father worked all morning on his report, Mother helping. Judge Silent & Mrs. Maynard were with us at meals. I made visits on "Nob Hill" in the afternoon.[13] Frank went out to whist at the General's in the evening. The Mining Works wait just now on telegrams from N. Y. where they are slow in acting not realizing how valuable time is at this end.

Friday 3rd. Father & Mother busy together all morning on the report. Judge Silent & Mr. Maynard breakfasted with us & Mr. Maynard dined with us. They are all getting fretted over the loss of time—& possible loss of rich mines, the bonds for which are expiring—occasioned by the N. Y. slowness in replying to telegrams. Miss Wilcox & Mrs. Smith (of the Fort) & Elon Wilcox called in the afternoon. Frank went out to Col. Biddle's in the evening. I wasn't well—took a walk on the hill in the morning & staid most of the day in my room.

Saturday 4th. The report was still the morning's work for Father & Mother. Judge Silent & Mr. Maynard breakfasted with us & as they all thought it best Father sent on a telegram to Mr. Howard[14] asking into the delay—it was sent at 2 & at 8½ the answer came, quick work between this place & Brooklyn, N. Y. It said delay was caused by the absence from town of some of the parties in interest but a deciding meeting would be held on Monday. In the afternoon I went out & made *seven* visits. The Judge & Mr. Maynard dined with us, Mr. M. staying a while afterwards & telling me about Ros. Raymond & Jack Howard, who are both intimate friends of his. Frank spent the evening at Col. Biddle's & the night at Lieut. Wilson's. Showers in the night!

Sunday 5th. The Judge & Mr. Maynard breakfasted with us & Mr. M. dined with us, the Judge coming in afterwards to consult over a despatch urging prompt decision in N. Y., which Frank—who had come home at noon—took out between showers at 7 p.m. We had a day of magnificent clouds & splendid light & shade effects on the mts. & many really heavy showers thro' the day & on into the night. The day was a rather resting one to all of us.

Monday 6th. Just a year since we reached here. The report and letters for Father & Mother. Scraps for me during the morning. The Judge & Mr. M. both breakfasted & dined with us. Mr. Gosper came "on business" to see Father. I called on Mrs. Fitch, to say "thank you" for their kind reception of us a year ago today. Then went in to see Mrs. Churchill & called on Mrs. Risley—out. In the evening Mother & Father went across to the Fitches & staid some time. The Judge staid & talked about his home on the Alameda San Jose—one of Charley's old lots—with me.[15] Frank was in & about all day. The weather was boisterous & cool with some scudding clouds.

Tuesday 7th. The report & letters made the morning's work for Father & Mother. The Judge & Mr. Maynard took both breakfast & dinner with us; the Judge had a long business consultation with Mother & Father in the afternoon. I walked out to the Fort with Mr. M. in the late afternoon & we called on the Wilcoxes; they were all in. After dinner another business talk took place which ended by sending an urgent telegram to Mr. Howard urging an answer from the Syndicate. Frank took it out to the Fort—the telegraph office in town having been closed. Mr. Einhorn called for a few moments during the evening. A windy day, fine yellow-brown sunset, cold night with rain toward morning.

Wednesday 8th. Everyone aux aguets [on the watch] for the delayed telegram—the slowness of the N. Y. action jeopardizing the property. The Judge and Mr. M. took their meals with us & were in & out frequently—others called also. Frank went out to the Fort in the evening. Dr. McKee called here. Day very windy & quite cold—splendid clouds & fine sunset—heavy frost in the night. Letters & telegrams from Mr. Palmer about a big "gravel mine" he has bonded in Cal. & wants Father to help in, & also have a share.

Thursday 9th. Finding it too risky to wait any longer a telegram was sent to other parties in [the] East for necessary preliminary funds—two days will be allowed for an answer. If it fails then to come, Judge Silent will go on to Cala. & Mother to New York—in that case she will probably stay some months coming & going between Washington & N. Y. The business part

John Charles Frémont, Jr.
(Courtesy of the Southwest Museum, Los Angeles, photo #36488.)

will be tiresome for her, but she will be a good deal with Charley & Sally & amongst friends & on the whole I don't think it would hurt her. The day was chiefly spent in business consultations. Mr. M. & the Judge in & out as usual & also ate with us. Frank went out twice to the Fort with telegrams. I sewed all morning & went for a drive with Mrs. Fitch in the afternoon, making calls on Mrs. Noyes & Mrs. Brooks. Pleasant in the sun.

Friday 10th. An inadequate & pointless telegram received from Mr. Howard in N. Y., which only angered, by its want of comprehension of the situation here, Father & the others. Lots of business talk & some work at the report. Col. & Mrs. La Motte[16] called. Frank went out to the Fort in the evening. The Judge & Mr. M. took their meals with us & were in & out frequently. Frank helped Mr. M. pack the ores. Weather still very cool & pleasant—fires needed morning & evening.

Saturday 11th. Answer from Pittsburg[h] party refused to advance a loan so preparations went ahead for Mother's start Eastwards. Both Judge Silent and Mr. M. were in the house. Lots of copying and sewing were the order of the day. The Judge and Mr. M. took breakfast & dinner with [us]. Frank walked out to the Fort in the evening with telegrams.

Sunday 12th. A big washout in the Colorado Desert made a break in railway travel in S. Cal., so today we got the accumulated mails of four days. The day was an anxious one as there was the possibility of a slip in obtaining the thirty day extension on the S[ilver] P[rince][17] for action on which Mother goes East. Mr. Maynard & the Judge breakfasted with us & Mr. M. dined also; the Judge coming back in the evening. Frank took some telegrams to the Fort. Frequent showers thro' day & night. In p.m., F. drove to the Fort to ask for ambulance for her, but Genl. W. "couldn't."

Monday 13th. Day chiefly given to preparations for Mother's start. In the evening we went across to tell Mrs. Fitch & Mrs. Churchill & take leave. They were out so we only saw Mrs. Cory. Showers thro' day & night. Gorgeous sunset, flame colored & grey west & south; blue edged with pink East & N.E.

Tuesday 14th. Just after breakfast—at which the Judge & Mr. Maynard joined us—came a telegram from Mr. [J. C.] Babcock saying conditionally that he would take the Silver Prince; Mr. M. replied accepting conditions & stating tomorrow was the last day. This made an exciting day for us all. The Judge & Mr. M. also dined with us & in the evening Mrs. Lewis & Mrs. Smith & Mr. Fitch called. Frank went out to Col. Biddle's. More showers, with—towards sunset—snow flurries.

Wednesday 15th. No telegram from Mr. Babcock, but late in the evening two from Mr. Palmer on the "gravel" business & one from Maggie saying they can sell the Adirondack property—& asking if we have done anything about it. Orders came assigning Frank temporary duty at Fort Whipple, so he reported at once, but no action was taken. He went over again in the evening with telegrams. Mother went up & took leave of the school children—had a nice time. Sewing, copying & discussing were the chief [things] of the day. The Judge and Mr. M. were in & out as usual. Dr. Einhorn left without calling. Dr. McKee & Mr. Churchill called.

Thursday 16th. Day chiefly given to copying last reports of Mr. Maynard['s] & doing things in connection with him; he & the Judge breakfasted with us & were in & out—all expecting an answer from Mr. Babcock which failed to come. Mr. M. left on the stage at 5 p.m. for mines near Yuma belonging to outside parties. He will either return here directly or after a hasty view to N. Y. Some preparations for Mother were also worked out. Frank was out at Whipple in the morning to report—he was given leave till Saturday at Guard mounting when he goes on duty. In the evening, [he played] whist at the General's. Mrs. Weeks called. Mr. Buffum called to see when Mother would reach Los Angeles that Mrs. B. might meet her there.

Friday 17th. I was busy all day getting Frank's kit ready for his move over to Whipple tomorrow. Mr. Wotherspoon has asked him to share his quarters till he receives more definite assignment, which is every way very nice & spares Frank the expense of furniture, etc. Also we were uncertain till 5 p.m. whether Mother & the Judge would get off tomorrow or not till Monday, which latter day was decided on. *The* telegram didn't come but one from N. Y. W[estern] U[nion] Telegraph's manager *did* saying the telegrams had been delivered to Mr. Babcock, so all responsibility rests with him. One from Maggie misunderstanding Father's telegram & saying she wouldn't sell Adirondack property "as he had arranged for it" which necessitated a counter telegram which Frank and Thor took out in the evening & brought back one from Mr. M. at Phoenix asking for news. I turned in early as I had had a bad headache all day. Father was busy preparing papers for Mother to take with her. Mother made some farewell visits. Mrs. Churchill, Mrs. Otis & Miss Sherman called. The Judge was in & out & took his meals with us. Mother had a pleasant letter from Mrs. Shillaber with warm messages from both Genl. & Mrs. [Ulysses S.] Grant.

Saturday 18th. Frank went out to the Fort to report at 9 a.m.—all of us feeling the goodbye to the home part of his life that it was; though it couldn't be done more pleasantly & though it is by our own wish that it is done. Genl. & Miss Wilcox called to tell Mother goodbye; so did Mrs. Hargrave,[18] Mrs. Lewis & Mr. Campbell. The Judge was in & out, nearly worn out, & desponding, but he brisked up by dinner time. The day was chiefly given to packing Mother's trunk & getting papers ready. Both

Mother & Father feel sanguine as to the business results of Mother's trip. No telegram from Mr. Babcock of Adams Exp. Co.

Sunday 19th October. 38th anniversary of Mother & Father's wedding day. Judge Silent in better spirits, breakfasted with us & was in & out through day & evening. Mr. Hotaling [Houghtelin],[19] Mr. Sherman, Mr. & Mrs. Fitch & Mrs. Churchill called to say goodbye. There was a lot of letter writing & last review of papers for Mother & Father & a mass of copying for me. Frank came in for dinner & staid till after 10. I turned in early as I have had a three day headache, & then it left Mother freer for Frank.

Monday 20th (Z. E. K.)[20] Up by 4½. Had early tea at 6, & were all ready when Judge Silent & the stage came up for Mother, who started in *quite* good spirits & had a lovely Indian summer day for the beginning of the journey. Mrs. Bashford goes as far as the Bowers's ranch, her woman Maggie on thro' to Phoenix—& she will be a convenience to Mother. Col. Head all the way to San Francisco—& of course Judge Silent who only turns down to San Jose when they reach Martinez, Cal. After they left Father went at his report; & I with Mary's help turned her into Frank's room & her room into a storeroom. Father took a good tramp with Thor in the afternoon.

Chapter 5

Selling the Silver Prince

October 21–December 31, 1879

Tuesday, October 21st. The morning Father gave to his report; I to a headache. Mrs. Fitch took me [on] a long drive out past Cook's ranch in the afternoon. Father had a good walk with Mr. Churchill & Thor. Telegram from Mother—in Phoenix all right. . . .

Thursday 23rd. Father worked at his report & some letters & walked in the afternoon. I was lazy all morning & made ten visits in the afternoon—everybody in! & crossed the creek too. Met Frank in the street. We've had two postal cards & a telegram from Maricopa—Mother all right.

Friday 24th. Father worked at the report & had his afternoon's walk with Mr. Churchill & Thor. I finished redding up things in the morning & in the afternoon went with Mrs. Churchill & returned 7 visits. Weather warm Indian summer.

Saturday 25th. Home things in the morning & Mrs. Cory called; 5 visits in the afternoon. Father worked some on his report & saw Mr. Churchill in relation to Judge Silent's letter from Yuma on the "Curtain"[1] question; he also took a walk with Thor.

Sunday 26th. Quiet home day. I had a letter from Baker—Nice—announcing his coming marriage to Miss [Reese?] which I answered in the evening & also wrote to Mrs. Evans & to Mr. Babcock. In the day I read "Homo Sum"[2] which Baker had sent Mother from Nice. Father wrote letters & read & in the evening made a short visit at the Churchills. We had a P.C. from Mother at Yuma—all right. High north wind all day, but not cold. . . .

Tuesday 28th. The morning mail brought letters from Globe City asking Father, as Gov., to help the citizens there to procure arms as they are uneasy as to the conduct of their near neighbours, the San Carlos Apaches, under the prolonged excitement of the Indian wars in Colorado & New Mexico & referring to their petition to the Gov.—which only came to hand late in the day, signed by all the leading citizens of Globe. Father walked right out to the Fort & saw Genl. Wilcox who arranged to co-operate with him & obtain permission from the War Dept. to issue arms on a company requisition from Globe. Genl. W. drove Father back; & then Father sent telegrams to Globe via Florence stating what had been done. We had despatches from Mother & from Judge Silent in cipher to say that they had succeeded in San Francisco & that the Judge would return here "immediately with money in hand." Mother leaving eastwards this morning awfully happy "over this quick result of her mission which saves the leading mine here & lays the cornerstone of our future thorough success." Prof. Sawyer of Chicago & Big Bug spent the evening with us.

Wednesday 29th. Father worked on the report. Prof. Sawyer breakfasted with us. I called on Mrs. Churchill & on Mrs. Fitch. Father had his afternoon walk. Mrs. Luke called to take leave. Good letters from Mother.

Thursday 30th. Frank came in earlyish, staid to breakfast & was made happy by our news from Mother. Father went out to the Fort in the morning & had another talk with Genl. Wilcox about Indian affairs. Mr. Churchill called to take leave—goes "inside" this afternoon for three weeks. Had telegram from Mr. Maynard, just leaving Yuma for San Francisco—evening 29th.

Friday 31st. Father worked on his report. Mr. Buffum & Mr. Curtin called to talk over with him the big strike in the "Silver Prince"—1000$[3] ore four feet wide—& in the afternoon he took a walk. I went to see Mrs. Churchill in the morning; called on Mrs. Luke & on Mrs. Lewis in the afternoon.

Saturday 1st November. Letters from Mother & from Judge Silent of the 27th ult. fully confirming our reading of the cipher telegram & giving details—both happy at the result. Father telegraphed the Judge to hurry his coming here. The excitement of all these things makes the report uphill work to Father; he had his walk & I a drive with Mrs. Fitch in the afternoon. Lt. & Mrs. F. A. Smith & Mrs. G. R. Smith[4] with Frank called in & made us a visit which I missed. We are all very happy at the business result in San Francisco. A Mr. Hays called to see Father in the evening.

Sunday 2nd. Father went out to the Fort in the forenoon, saw Genl. Wilcox on the Globe business—the Sec. of War has granted use of arms—& saw other officers, including Frank. I had a quiet reading day. Weather still lovely, but big storm ring round the moon this night.

Monday 3rd. Nice letters from Mother at Ogden. She is to have two hours in St. Louis & has telegraph[ed] to Aunt Eliza and to Dr. Eliot.[5] Frank came in to breakfast & gave the surprising news that he has been assigned to the 3rd Infantry, Co. H. & ordered to join his company at Fort Missoula, *Montana*. I'm afraid of the cold there for him, otherwise it's all right as the 3rd is a crack regt; he gets off on Saturday. Father was busy day & evening on his report, except when seeing people & taking a short walk. Day overcast. We had hoped Frank would be left at Whipple over the winter. . . .

Wednesday 5th. Usual routine. Frank took breakfast with us. Mrs. Hargrave called to ask me to join a party of ladies for a drive & climb tomorrow, Genl. Wilcox having lent them an ambulance. Telegram from Mother to say she had arrived "all well & found everyone well," dated Staten Island. Father took his afternoon walk. Dr. McKee called in the evening.

Thursday 6th. After arranging the house to run the day without me, I went across to Mrs. Churchill's where the ambulance with Mrs. Hargrave picked us up at 8¾, then went for the other ladies—Mrs. Lewis, Mrs. Smith of Chicago & Mrs. Masterson—& we drove off. Mrs. H. was captain & as she was not sure how to get to her mountain we boged around a while & finally brought up at Clark's sawmill, five miles out of town & some three miles north of her mountain. We didn't attempt to reach it but substituted Thumb Butte which was nearby & leaving the ambulance at its base by some cabins belonging to charcoal burners, we all set off each climbing as much or as little as they wished to. I only climbed up the eastern face as high as the base of the stone butte itself & being warned by loss of breath & a twinge in the side stopped there, having the same view as I should have had from the summit—that is out over Prescott, Whipple, Point of Rocks & across Lonesome valley great stretch of pale yellow to the blue peaks of San Francisco, Mogollon & Bill Williams Mt. to the north; the Black hills meza line to the east, Granite Mt. slightly N. W. & a lot of wooded mountains southwards. Mrs. Churchill & Mrs. Lewis gathered dwarf ferns & some few autumn flowers farther down. Mrs. Masterson & Mrs. Hargrave climbed on to the Butte itself, but not to its highest point which is very difficult of access. Then we all met up for our lunch on some shaded rocks near the ambulance & were watched as we ate by a flock of brilliant blue birds with great black topknots—of course as each had contributed towards the lunch there was much more than we could eat, even after the driver, an obliging & civil man, had had his share, so we sent all that was left up to the children in the two cabins. We drove straight back to town, getting in at 2½. Later Mrs. Blake & Miss McClintock[6] called. Father had a busy day with official work; he took his walk in the late afternoon.

Friday 7th. Father wrote letters & worked at report & took a little walk with Frank in the afternoon. I went across & saw Mrs. Churchill, who is going to mend the blue afghan for Frank—was busy with odds & ends for Frank during the day. Frank came in to breakfast & staid with us going about after last things & in the evening making P.P.C. calls on Mrs. Lewis, Mrs. Fitch & Mrs. Churchill. Day threatening & high wind.

Saturday 8th. Day began with a despatch from Mother asking Frank "what assignment do you desire" evidently looking toward moving things in Washington for a change; which Frank doesn't wish & besides he wants things to run the regular Dept. course with him. Everyone at Fort Whipple is sorry to have him leave—all the officers there really liking him & the last days were full of all varieties of goodbye fêtes to him. Dr. McKee says we need not fear the cold up there for him as it is of the dry variety & besides Frank is well & strong again. All the day belonged to Frank, helping him pack etc. & chiefly hanging around with him. He had his dinette at 4 & at 5 the four horse stage came for him & he was off—the only passenger, with plenty of wraps & as comfortable as we could make him. But it is a long way off from us, is Fort Missoula & I wish he could have been left nearer by—for our sakes that is. The night wasn't a cold one so we think he must have gone over the mountains in moderate comfort. In the evening Mr. Cordis called bringing with him Judge S[. . .] who is passing through Prescott. Day lowering.

Sunday 9th. Nice letters from Mother, posted Fremont, Neb. She was travelling comfortably along. Father worked some at his report & read. I wrote a lot of letters. Quiet day. The morning began with snow flurries which changed to rain by p.m. & continued on all through the night accompanied by a gale of wind—the heaviest rainstorm I have seen here & very welcome now that Frank is safely down in the plains.

Monday 10th. Father walked out to see Genl. Wilcox on Indian matters in connection with McMillanville[7] & Genl. Wilcox was at our house on the same business in the afternoon—the McM. people have got scared by the

Fort Wingate burning canard. Father was busy the rest of the day on the report. The storm held up during part of the morning, the clouds lifting & showing us all the mts. snowclad, but closed in again for the afternoon; no rain in the night however.

Tuesday 11th. Father worked at his report in the morning—in the afternoon walked out to see Genl. Wilcox about the Pima Indians at Phoenix this time. Mrs. Lewis & Mrs. Churchill called in the afternoon. I went up to see Mrs. Buffum—just back from "inside" & Mrs. Ogier,[8] in the afternoon. Mr. & Mrs. Smith of Chicago called in the evening. Had letters from Mother at Jefferson City, Mo., all well. Day clear again.

Wednesday 12th. Father worked some on his report; several people called to see him. The telegraph line was in working order again & we got a batch of telegrams—all delayed: one from Mother said "Don't commit yourself, unimpeachable channels offered me here" & asked actual status of the Belt[9] & Prince; one from the Judge at Lathrop on the 10th said: "very sick child prevented earlier leaving," which brings him here on Friday the 14th. One from Frank was also the 10th at Maricopa—got there all right though it rained heavily from Wickenburg on. There was another telegram from Mother to Judge Silent—we were authorized to open it— about needing "books," which is part of our cipher & we could not understand her need & Father was flurried by it. We sent Mother an answering telegram. Father went for a short walk in the afternoon.

Thursday 13th. I did some copying in the morning & in the afternoon made seven visits, including Mrs. Gov. Bashford[10] & her daughter, who have just arrived & the Sisters. Father was busy seeing people & the report till four when he went out with Thor. Shortly after he left Col. Martin, Mr. Wilcox & Mr. Staples,[11] now from Apache but having served under Father in the Mt. Dept., called to see Father & failing him made me a visit. We had a quiet evening. No letters today, but good telegram from Maynard about Hydraulic property.

Friday 14th. Father & I were up & at work—he writing & I copying, on the report, so as to get through some work before the stage got in as we expected the Judge on it. It got in at 9 & about 10 he came up to the house having since his arrival got through some necessary preliminary business & arranged for a conveyance to take them out to the mine. He looked pulled & tired, but said his telegrams had kept him posted about the child who was better. He only staid a short time, but came back at 12 & took a hurried scrap of breakfast; then the "vehicle" came & they started, Father, the Judge & Mr. Hotaling to the Silver Prince which they will formally take possession of & return here Sunday. Quite an excitement in the village about the Prince.

Saturday Nov. 15th. My 37th birthday. I had a quiet day finishing bits of copying, writing letters & reading. The "Arizon[i]an" is crowing pleased over the taking of the "Silver Prince" through Genl. Fremont & Judge Silent—the "Miner" grudgingly allows that it "supposes" they have bought the mine. Mrs. Churchill dined with me & spent the evening. Mrs. Lewis came in during the evening, too. Mr. Lewis called for them & took them to their respective homes. It was Emmy Lewis's birthday[12] & I had sent her down a cake & a Japanese object—remembering how I used to like birthday presents at her age.

Sunday 16th. Quiet reading day. Father & the Judge got back at 4, having successfully terminated the taking possession of the Silver Prince & met with cordial congratulations everywhere. The Judge dined with us & after dinner Father & he sent off a long telegram to Mother telling her how things stood & of the last rich strikes in the Prince & Warrior. Weather cold now. Mrs. Churchill came in for a moment to bring me some fruit.

Monday 17th. Two notes from Mother written at Nell's & at Dr. Morton's—all well. Father was busy seeing people & working on report, but took his walk in the afternoon. The Judge was in & out & dined with us. I copied & sewed in the morning; in the afternoon took some telegrams out to the Fort & called on Mrs. Fred Smith, Mrs. La Mott & Miss Wilcox. Dr. McKee called in the evening & the Judge brought Mr. Lewis in to see the fine specimens from the "Prince" & "Warrior." Weather sharply cool.

Tuesday 18th. Lots of people in & out to see Father who worked in between on business things. The Judge was in & out, busy packing rich specimens from the Prince, Warrior, Belt & Eureka[13] mines which left by express in the afternoon stage; he took breakfast & dinner with us. Genl. Wilcox called in his light ambulance, Foster driving, to take us out. Father was really too busy to go, so the General obligingly took me; a lovely & very rough drive over a scarcely broken road—& at times no road—which wound amongst the low boulder strewn & pine overgrown hills to the west of the town till we came to the Treaty Stone, an Indian "painted rock"—an oval boulder which crowns a group of the usual piled up boulders & which has carved into its slightly flattened western face a line "/\/\/\/\/\", something like that & which is on all their pottery & on the Navajo blankets, then a herd of deer—6 I think in single file, the leader, pausing startled—as well he may be for facing him stands a double deer, two heads & antlers & two sets of forelegs but one body—then a man with on either side of him a group of three hissing snakes, standing upright like the serpent in Paradise—then a long low thing which the General said was a Colorado river canoe, & some hieroglyphics.[14] Two other stones had a few marks cut into them but not clearly like the stone. At the western base of the group were quantities of broken glazed crockery, broken into fragments. It is supposed to have been a tribal meeting place. I was very much interested as it is the first thing of the kind I have seen. I had a pleasant drive too & the weather was lovely—the ambulance well swung like a carriage. We came in by the stage road. Judge Silent staid on after dinner discussing with Father the Wyoming project for next summer.[15] I was over at Mrs. Churchill's a moment in the afternoon. . . .

Thursday 20th. Father worked on his report & I sewed all morning. The Judge took breakfast with us. Mrs. Martin called; I walked out to the Fort & called on Mrs. Weeks, Mrs. Biddle & Mrs. Fowler; also a moment at Mrs. Churchill's on my way back. Father took an hour's real tramp up the mountains with Thor. In the evening Mr. & Mrs. Fitch called. Father had business telegrams—& answered them—from Mother, Mr. Palmer & Judge Porter.[16] Mr. Palmer's will require Father's meeting him & others at Yuma early next week on the gravel business. The weather is lovely, though all the northern slopes of the mts. are still covered with snow. . . .

Saturday 22nd. Father was busy with papers all day & only took a short walk in the afternoon & went down with telegrams in the evening staying a while in Dr. Lincoln's[17] store which is a species of club now—that is, the nice people turn in there for talk in the evening. I copied & sewed. Mrs. Churchill came in for a few moments. Judge Silent took breakfast & dinner with us & staid a little while in the evening. We had a business telegram from Mother. Lovely weather.

Sunday 23rd. Father was busy finishing up his report & I copying. Judge Silent took breakfast with us. Mr. Shipman,[18] a mining expert, was with Father for a while. We worked till eleven. Judge Silent came in for a moment in the evening to see if Father could possibly start tomorrow morning & take advantage of a private team going then. That not being possible, he arranged for Father to connect with the team in Phoenix & go on to Maricopa with it which ensured him a night's sleep before taking the cars for Yuma.

Monday 24th. I copied steadily all morning. Father answered letters & did a lot of official business all day & evening & sent off the report. Judge Silent dined & breakfasted with us. Father went up for a few moments to see Mr. Buffum & give him Mother's address as he leaves for New York on Saturday & having just come in from the Peck district he can give her the latest news from the Prince & Warrior.

Tuesday 25th. I finished up odds & ends Father left me to attend to, wrote some letters, read & sewed. Miss Willcox called & asked me to dine with them on Thursday, but I've already asked the Churchills here. Mrs. Churchill called. Judge Silent breakfasted & dined with me. Court is sitting now. Father left in the Black Cañon stage at 7 a.m. & had a mild day for his journey out of the mountains. He will reach Yuma on Thursday evening & expects to get back Dec. 3. We were up at 5 a.m. which gave me the chance to see Venus—more wonderfully & beautifully brilliant than I could have imagined even here. At half past six, while the rising sun lit all the air & tinged the clouds into brilliant pink, she was still shining brightly—looking just about as Sirius does in the eastern skies.

Wednesday 26th. I had a quiet reading & sewing day & a nice letter from Frank at Salt Lake City. Mrs. Lewis came in during the morning to ask me to dinner tomorrow. I declined on account of the Churchills coming, but later in the day I learned that Mr. C. goes to Mohave with the Judge on Friday morning, so I proposed to Mrs. C. to adjourn our dinner to Friday, knowing she must want to have Mr. C. all to herself after his month's absence; they agree, so I'll be alone tomorrow, which doesn't bother me. I had a telegram from Father—received 4 p.m. in Prescott—to say he had made Maricopa comfortably. Strong wind & clouds all day which broke in a sleet & snow storm about 7 & though not lasting long made quite a little fall. . . .

Thursday 27th. Thanksgiving. Just a quiet reading & sewing day. The Judge breakfasted with me & was in & out several times during the day. He dined at the Lewises.

Friday 28th. Quiet day nursing a cold, reading & sewing. Mrs. Churchill dined & spent the evening with me. The Judge & Mr. Churchill got off at

4 a.m., driving themselves in a buggy. The Curé[19] called to ask me to see how the Post liked the idea of a school kept by the Sisters. P.C. from Frank, at Blackfoot, Idaho. . . .

Monday December 1st. I did a little shopping at Brays & went up to Mrs. Churchills for a moment in the morning; read & wrote letters for the rest of the day. Dr. McKee called in the evening. I had a letter from Mother—in New York & well—and telegrams from Father at Yuma & at Maricopa on his way back. The Sisters called also.

Tuesday 2nd. Telegram from Father saying he would be back on Thursday morning—dated Phoenix 2. I went across to Mrs. Churchill's in the morning & asked her to dinner. Reading & sewing day. Mrs. Churchill dined & spent the evening with me. Weather still threatening; my cold troublesome still. . . .

Thursday 4th. We were all up early & watching for Father, but he didn't come by either stage, so I knew he must be coming by private team & gave up watching as I couldn't guess the hour he would come in. He did get in at 12½, having come round by way of Wickenburg sharing the expenses of a team & buggy with a gentleman who is traveling about in the territory. He had a satisfactory talk with the gravel gentleman & telegraphed for leave to East. His next move depends on the answer his telegram meets with. He had a nice visit in Yuma & went over the prison, etc. Thor was wild with joy over his return. In the afternoon came two telegrams from Mother—of the 3rd & 4th—saying in substance "that Furnace" would advance forty thousand to complete purchase of "Library" & furnish working capital, on condition of his receiving one fourth & the milling contracts being completed. Father answered at once congratulating [her] on her success & saying everything would be completed on the Judge's return on Saturday. The good news of these despatches rested Father very much, for he was very tired with his journey. Mrs. Thibodo called.

Friday 5th. Father spent the day answering the letters which had accumulated during his absence. I went across to see Mrs. Churchill in the morning & finding her quite ill went on down to the Hospital to get Sister Mary to see to her as Dr. Ainsworth is out at the "Tiger" where there has been an accident. I went in a moment to see Mrs. Lewis & called again on Mrs. C. in the afternoon finding her somewhat better & Sister Mary with her besides a lot of ladies calling. The local line was out of order so the telegram Father took down for Mother last night didn't get off till 3 p.m. today. The Judge got back about 7 p.m., giving us a thorough surprise as we didn't think they could reach here before tomorrow, but by making long drives—one night till 2 a.m.!—they made the 143 miles between Wednesday afternoon & 6 p.m. today & that without injury to their team of horses. Of course, the Judge was very glad over Mother's telegrams & Mr. Blake calling in, all preliminaries for the milling contract were settled at once—said contract to be mailed Monday when Mr. Blake returns from the "Peck." The Judge staid on a while talking over his & Father's late trips to the north & south of the Territory.

Saturday 6th. The Judge came up early & with him Father arranged all the telegrams to be sent to Mother & to Mr. Maynard—from whom the Judge had telegrams the same in substance as Mother's. All the conditions asked for at the other end were complied with here. In the afternoon I went across to see Mrs. Churchill, who is better, & found several ladies calling on her; then I went on up & made a short visit on Mrs. Buffum & Mrs. Ogier. Judge Silent breakfasted & dined with us, staying on after dinner for a big business talk which branched off into the late stage robberies here & the far worse days of almost terrorism in California during Vasquez's time & his taking by Adams.[20] Col. Price[21] & Capt. Palfrey,[22] U.S.A. called in the afternoon. . . .

Monday 8th. Father worked at official business & letters & saw people. The Judge breakfasted & dined with us; he & Father succeeded in getting the "milling contract" completed today but too late for the afternoon mail as both Capt. Eagan & Mr. Blake are of the "cudchewing" genus & have to talk a long time before they act. Telegrams were sent to Mother & to Mr. Maynard to let them know the contract was obtained. Father took a short walk before dinner. A storm wind blew a rough gale all day & far on into the night.

Tuesday 9th. Pleasant letters from Mother who is well again—from Frank who has reached his Fort & likes it—& from Dr. Jameson telling me about his summer outing up into Scotland on a bicycle, all well with him. Father busy with official work & Genl. Wilcox called. Judge Silent brought up at breakfast time the news that no extension beyond the 16th would be given on the Silver Belt as it is turning out so rich the owners want to work it themselves. This made a quick telegram to Mother necessary & I volunteered to take it out to the Post as both Father & the Judge are pushed with work; which I did, also calling on Mrs. G. R. Smith, Mrs. Fred Smith

& Mrs. Martin. Mrs. La Motte walked back across the field trail with me to the edge of the town. I stopped in for a few moments at Mrs. Churchill's who is better. Father took a little walk with Thor. The Judge dined with us; both he & Father are low in their minds over the probable loss of the Belt, and we are all worried at having to send hurrying telegrams to Mother. The day was cold with a north breeze from the San Francisco mts., which look really grand in their present snowclad condition.

Wednesday 10th. I staid in & did scraps; Mrs. W. Bashford & Miss Bashford[23] & Mrs. Churchill called; also Lt. F. A. Smith & Lt. Story of Washington, who is on an inspecting tour of military telegraph lines. The Judge breakfasted with us & came up again in the evening when Father & he had a long talk over Mother's answering telegrams which foreshadow the loss of the Belt—time too hastened—but say the success of the "Prince" & its consequences "compensate"—also that leave for Father just now is against the law & can't be granted, though Washington authorities would like to; also that she is in direct telegraphic communication with Livingston on the gravel question. They were on the whole pleased with the telegrams & took a cheerful view of things, though the Judge was tired with the day in court & Father with a day of official scrap work, which I had made him break at 3½ & go for a long tramp on the hills with Thor. . . .

Friday 12th. The chief interest of the day was about Father's going or not going East on the gravel business—telegrams thick & urgent from Palmer, but as leave can't be obtained it would have to be resignation which can hardly be on uncertainties; talked it over fully with the Judge & sent telegram to Mother on the subject. The Judge was with us at breakfast & dinner & staid on a while in the evening, maturing plans for future work. Father walked over to the Post in the morning, about Globe City's arms. Weather cold for here.

Saturday 13th. Nice letters from Sally in New York & McLean in Shanghai. Genl. Wilcox & Col. Biddle called. Father was busy with letters & official work, but went out for his walk with Thor at 4. Mrs. St. James, Col. & Mrs. La Motte called in the afternoon. The Judge breakfasted & dined with us—very busy in court, even having a night sitting. Telegraphic answer came from Mother on the gravel question saying Father wasn't needed there; that it could be carried in time if Mr. Livingston put in an immediate appearance; & information that the Prince "was progressing rightly;" but a registered letter of the 29th from her which came today contained a clause from which both Father & I inferred a possible failure,

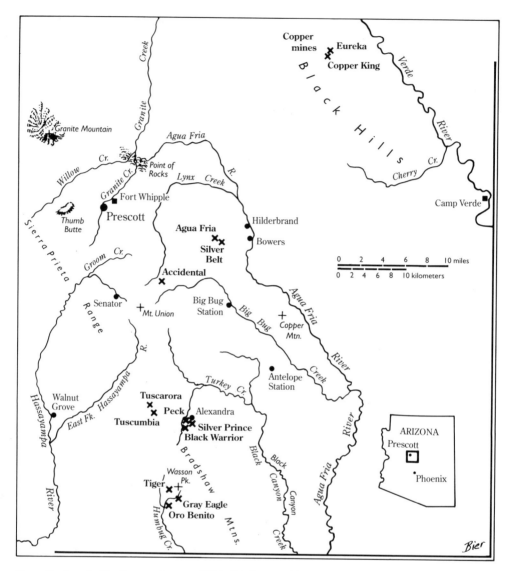

Map of mines in the Prescott area, 1881. (By James Bier.)

which disquieted us. We didn't tell the Judge; if we are right it's too late for help, if wrong there is no use in adding to his worries. Many have called on official business during the week. . . .

Monday 15th. Father answered letters & did official business till about 3 when he went for a long tramp on the hills with Thor. The Judge dined & breakfasted with us; he had court all day & evening, but took time to telegraph Mother a sinews of war telegram in the afternoon (voluntarily & only told us afterwards) & later he had a despatch from Mother asking for a power of attorney from him—the last by a slip having the synonym for "Silver Prince" & therefore no use; which telegram the Judge wrote out & Father went to the office with it in the evening hour & staid till he saw it off. Dr. McKee called in the evening. In the afternoon I called on Mrs. Lewis, Mrs. Smith of Chicago, Mrs. Adams & Mrs. Churchill. Weather lovely.

Tuesday 16th. Father was busy at writing work till 3 when he went out with Thor. The Judge breakfasted with us & discussed a telegram from Mother, which came in the afternoon & looks toward a final settlement of the "Prince." The answer to it he & Father drew up together after dinner & Father took it to the office as the Judge had to go back into court. Col. Martin called in the afternoon & asked me to drive with him which I was pleased to do as I do get so tired of the village. He has a comfortable [. . .] & free travelling bays—we drove out on the stage road & back by the Fort covering quite a distance in the hour we were gone. Then I called on Mrs. Hargrave, Mrs. Wollenberg & Mrs. Thibodo. The weather was lovely & softly warm like a dry April day in the East. Nice letters from Mother, Dec. 1, so long in coming because registered.

Wednesday 17th. Father's morning was busy in the usual way. I went out to try on a dress at the dressmakers. The Judge at breakfast had to tell of a cash offer which has been made for the "Grey [Gray] Eagle," which he fears will take the mine from us & also of a rumor that Mr. Bean is starting out to be met by Eastern capitalists who with him will visit the Tonto Basin, which is Father's reliance for future operations. Both of them were deeply worried & Father more so than I have seen him since the burning of Hale's factory in N. Y. as he feared that through the slowness of action in N. Y. everything he & the Judge has worked up & brought into notice here would slip into other hands & we left to recommence from the bedrock up. The Judge had to return to court. Father tried to work but had to give it up & take to the hills before 3, telling me not to wait dinner for him as he wouldn't come in till he was tired down. I was really frightened for him fearing a coup de sang [apoplectic stroke]. The Judge came up to dinner able to report that Bean's outfit had gone the wrong road for Tonto & was supposed to have gone to meet & bring in here his "capitalists," which relieved Father very much when he came in which he did as we were finishing dinner. The Judge staid on till time for court to open in evening session & we settled to try for a quiet evening when a telegram came from Mother thanking us for what the Judge sent through Laidlaw,[24] then saying "if surprised remember Salem witch, this absolutely necessary, ultimately advantageous, Mont[25] admirable," which we take it is to prepare us for some disagreeable surprise under which we are to be silent. This freshly troubled Father, but not like the prospect of losing the Tonto Basin mines did. It has been a hard day on both Father & the Judge, but harder on Father. I only hope Mother isn't having its counterpart in N. Y. I had a pleasant letter from Frank, Missoula 4th, today.

Thursday 18th. Usual routine in the morning for Father; the Judge came up to breakfast & we showed him last night's telegram & another which had just come in regard to "references for Shipman & Napoleon" which twisted our brains, didn't exactly please the Judge & left us as much in the dark as before: an answer was sent. Father wrote letters, then took his walk with Thor. The Judge had no court in the evening so he staid on quite a while with us, & starting with the order "Pour le mérit[e]" [Positive matters], we talked of everything except business, & had a pleasant little break in our usual talking routine—in spite of the [difficulties] we all feel we are in. Weather threatening again.

Friday 19th. Good long letters from [Mother], 4th & 8th, hopeful about business & herself well; also a pleasant letter from Mr. Evans in Washington. Just the usual day; Father busy with official papers & taking a little walk with Thor; the Judge breakfasting & dining with us; no court in the evening; no telegrams. Mr. Anderson lengthened one of his official interviews with Father into a "social call" on me. Weather lowering & night very windy.

Saturday 20th. Usual routine; the Judge staid on a little after dinner, talking hunting in the Rocky Mts.; both are trying to keep off business which is a tension on them now; the Judge's court gives him a change & lift, but Father has only his solitary walks on the mountain side for a help. High wind all night—through the night very heavy rain & a gale.

Sunday 21st. Father wrote some official things; didn't take his usual walk as the hills are too soft with last night's rain. The Judge breakfasted with us—both he & Father were in a "let down" state of mind. No letters. In the evening came a telegram from Mother saying she could sell the Black Warrior at once if she had necessary "power" & wanting "bonds for everything"—so Father took it down to the Court House & with the Judge wrote out the answer, to be sent tomorrow. Wind continued all day, heavy frost at night.

Monday 22nd. No letters. Father sent off answer to Mother's telegram. Seeing in the "Bulletin" the notice of Senator Farley's bill[26] for a third judicial district in California, we decided to try for it for Judge Silent though of course there can be but a small chance as many others must be entered already, though the bill is in the Judiciary Com. & no action can be taken on [it] till after Jan. 5th. Father wrote fully to Mother as a beginning step. The Judge breakfasted & dined with us, staying on a while in the evening as there was no court. Dr. McKee called to ask me to go with him to hear the Pinafore on Xmas Eve. Father was busy on official things, but took a short walk with Thor. The day was cold & in the evening the clouds closed in & from about 9 on it snowed heavily.

Tuesday 23rd. A washout on the S.P.R.R. made a break in the mails so we had neither letters nor papers. Father did indoor work & was "down town" several times also. The Judge was with us at breakfast & dinner—he is busy with the Tiger case[27] now & will have an argument on it in chambers this evening which together with the heavy cold he has taken may stop his going to the Masonic ball. Father went at nine o'clock & came back at ten, spending the rest of the evening in lamenting that he had to go & that he had gone. I waited up & gave him some hot tea when he got back. Day really cold. Thermometer fell to 10° *below* in the night.

Xmas Eve. An hour after sunrise the mercury still marked 8° *below* zero— such cold hasn't been known here for fourteen years. Our chief work through the day was to keep the house from being too cold to sit still in; which wasn't easy as it is only thin boards lined with cotton & papering. Father did a lot of official writing & took a tramp with Thor into the hills but found it heavy walking. The Judge breakfasted & dined with us. There was no thaw all day though the sun shone brilliantly.

Christmas Day. Part of a mail came in—but nothing for us—& one passenger who had to be lifted out & thawed at Dicksons—as the driver said "he hadn't enough clothes on to clean out a gun." He was one of the actors in the Pinafore troupe. The telegraph lines are down & have been for two days—the washout in Cala. The Judge breakfasted with us & staid quite a while afterwards, talking over plans for us at Santa Cruz (if business gives us a lift) & telling us of the beauty of the coast country right there—Father knows it of course but I don't. Father only wrote to Mother & took the rest of the day as a holiday, reading & resting & in the evening acting as my substitute & going with Dr. McKee to the "Pinafore" & quite enjoying it. He got back at eleven & after a cup of hot tea, retired. I spent the day very quietly au coin du feu [by the fireside] in the parlor, getting over the aftermath of a furious headache I had all last night; pleased with the prospects of a quiet sunny little house by the seaside which the Judge's talk in the morning had given shape to. Mrs. Churchill sent me over a pretty bunch of mignonette & german ivy in bloom, which was all the more of a real Xmas greeting as she is almost the only lady in town who saved her flowers last night. Mr. Churchill brought them over. The day was almost quite as cold as yesterday & the night very cold too, but luckily no wind.

Friday 26th. The event of the day was a telegram from Mother dated 24th saying "Everything right now. Happy completed Xmas. Dear love to you both." It arrived at one o'clock & the Judge had gone back to his room but we knew court didn't open till 1½ so we sent it down to him that he might share our thankful content without waiting for it till dinner time. In the evening hour Father sent off an answering despatch to Mother which the Judge took down to spare Father's going out in the drizzle. We knew Mother would telegraph so as to reach us on Xmas Day giving us the best news she could, but the lines being down we couldn't get it till later; we were quite as glad for her happiness at accomplishing this big stroke of business as for ourselves. I had a nice letter of the 15th from Charley, evidently looking on success as sure & saying they were all well & comfortable. A misty day, with drizzle towards night.

Saturday 27th. Another break to the through mails, so no eastern letters. Father busy over letters & official papers. The Judge up at breakfast & dinner, very busy with the ending of the Tiger damages case & the impanelling the jury for the Miles case.[28] Mrs. Churchill made a short call in the afternoon. The drizzle changed to a soaking rain by one & lasted so on all through the afternoon & night! The court bailiff came up for the Judge who had already left after dinner, the jury in the Tiger case having found.[29] Towards 7 o'clock the Judge came back with a telegram for Father which he had offered Miss McClintock to bring up, the rain stopping her; it was from Col. Lamont, 27th, saying "All closed here. Papers forwarded to San Francisco. Furnace obligated to pay over money in Prescott on or before Jan. 10. Silent to pass title," which quite settled our minds on some details which had been puzzling & worrying Father & the Judge. They discussed it & its fruits with great content & the Judge staid on quite a while talking over different [points] & letting his "stall" at the "Pinafore" stay empty. The papers being sent to Francisco means for Mrs. Shillaber's signature.

Sunday 28th. The heavy pouring rain continued all day & night with one brief interval when there was a splendid rainbow to the north which instead of disappearing behind the hills at its two ends lay out over the hillsides & pine trees in the loveliest effects of misty coloring & lasted nearly thirty minutes; in the night there were some snow squalls & a short time when the clouds drew off & the stars shone out superbly. In spite of the soaking rain Judge Silent was several times at the house during the day & evening—to write telegrams & hear parts from Mother's letters, registered & open mail—& breakfasted with us. Father wrote some letters, but didn't do much work. (Mr. Otis himself brought up Mother's registered letters & Mr. Sherman called by & took our return registered letters to spare Father's going out in the rain, as registering has to be done personally on Sundays or the letters don't get off till next day). Nice long letters from [. . .] today & a Xmas letter from Nell. There were one or two leaks in the house & the storeroom was afloat.

Monday 29th. . . . Father telegraphed Mother about copper in the evening.

Tuesday 30th. No stage came in as the Hass[a]yampa creek is too high for them to cross it & the telegraph line is down also, so we were quite shut off & don't know how long it will last. Father saw people & did scraps in the morning; in the afternoon official business & letters. I went out & did some shopping in the morning & also went to see Mrs. Lewis, Mrs. Churchill, Mrs. Buffum & Mrs. St. James who has been quite ill. Judge Silent took breakfast & dinner with us, staying on after dinner & talking over with Father their favorite m[ining] plan & things growing out of it. No falling weather & a slight thaw; all the trees are snowed over & make quite a New England effect & the snow is several inches deep, but of an icily slushy variety.

Wednesday 31st. No mail came in, but one was sent out; telegraph line down. Father had about the usual routine of people to see & business letters to write. Judge Silent was too busy to come up for breakfast but dined with us & staid on a while arranging for tomorrow's visiting. I went out early in the day & did a little shopping—it was still easy walking then as the ground was frozen, but through the day it thawed—& the mud was deep. Mary was slightly on the rampage in the evening, whilst the Judge was still with us & it bothered Father who so seldom comes into contact with small household worries that they annoy him when he does. As her rampage was confined to the kitchen region I "made believe hard" that I didn't hear as otherwise I should have had to take notice. As for Judge Silent's hearing it of course I had rather he hadn't but he is a "family man himself" & knows what a servant is. Besides he is too nice himself for such an incident to find lodgement in his mind. Talking over all the gains of the year & the almost quite ratified conclusion of the "Silver Prince" matter & the large plans which flowing from it he & the Judge have formed, straightened Father out, but I was tired by it all & had a nuit blanche [sleepless night] in consequence. The old year & the new were rung out & in & lots of firing & crackers at midnight.

Chapter 6

Mineral Wealth on Every Hand

January 1–March 18, 1880

New Year's Day 1880. Up early & saw that everything was ready for visitors before 10, though visiting begins late here & this year there won't be much as the mud make[s] it hard work getting about & there are only two carriages, one of which the Judge managed to secure for Father, himself & Mr. Lewis for 2½ hours in the afternoon. The Judge joined us at 12 & we had a picnic breakfast—solid hot things as usual but eaten like at a supper party. Then the calling began, with Genl. Wilcox & continued scatteringly through the day till a little after 5. Only about 25 in all & each made really little visits, expressing their regrets that Mother & Frank were absent & sending messages to them. *[Lily lists the visitors: Judge Silent, Genl. Wilcox, Col. Biddle, Lt. Wilcox, Dr. McKee, Col. Martin, Col. Weeks, Maj. Fowler, Lieut. J. A. Smith, Lieut. Wotherspoon, Mr. Otis, Mr. Churchill, Mr. Cordis, Mr. Lewis, Mr. Hall, Mr. Peck, Mr. Goldwater, Mr. S. Goldwater, Maj. Dake, Mr. Anderson, Mr. Sherman, Mr. A. C. Burmister, Mr. Clark, Mr. W. Bashford, Mr. Foster.]* In between visits I had time for some articles in "Littell" special while the "Pinafore" matinee was going on as nearly all the gentlemen took advantage of their freedom from business to go to it. I only had english bread & butter, coffee (hot with real cream), several kinds of cake & eggnog with real cream & hardly any one took anything, the officers saying "you know we *have to* at the other houses." I wore Sally's dress, which Father & the Judge consider a success. Father, with Judge Silent & Mr. Lewis, partly in a carriage & partly on foot, called at 41 houses—some having as many as four ladies in them, many two, & including *all* the Post. Only Mrs. Noyes & Mrs. Brooks were obliged to be deferred as they couldn't keep the carriage, it having other engagements & they live beyond walking distance. This was doing a big lot, specially for Father & they couldn't have accomplished it but that many houses & *all* Nob Hill hung out their baskets. We had our dinner comfortably at the table at 5½, the Judge with us. Then he went off for a

General Orlando B. Willcox.
(Courtesy of the National Archives, Washington, D.C.)

little mixed work & rest before the theatre, to which he was going. Father & I settled down by the parlor fire till a moderately early bedtime. No mail; no telegraph—the break in the latter is in the mountains & the mules of the repairers mired down to their girths before they reached the spot so they had to return & repack for man transportation of all their stuff needed for repairs. Bernard Vogt came early in the morning to thank Father for his pardon, which Father had granted at the request of all leading citizens here & which went into effect this day.[1]

Friday 2nd. Father was tired with too much visiting, wet feet & the nuit blanche yesterday's frequent cups of coffee had given, so he rested & read pretty much through the day. The Judge was with us as usual at meal times—he also had a nuit blanche which he had turned to account study-ing up a case & he had a very busy day in court. I sorted over last year's letters to me & housekeeping papers, making maison nette [tidy] for the coming year. Mild thawing day.

Saturday 3rd. Father went back to work at usual office routine. The Judge with us as usual—he is nearly tired out with this long term. Two telegrams came in relation to our business; one from Violet saying she had mailed power of att. to S. Lewis & one direct to Mr. Lewis from Furnace asking how to transfer the money—both of which look to a speedy conclusion of the matter. I didn't feel well—only wrote to Frank & went to bed as soon as I decently could. A California & territorial mail got in today.

Sunday 4th. An Eastern mail came in; we had long registered business letters from Mother of the 15 & 17 to Judge Silent & to Father & an open mail one of the 22 to me: she was well. Father & the Judge took a long talk over business after breakfast. Father wrote to Mother & the rest of the day chiefly talked over business to me—faute de mieux [for want of something better]—for the details of what has been done haven't come yet & he & the Judge don't take clear comfort in having to be in a haze about things. The Judge came in for a while during the evening. Still thawing & mud!

Monday 5th. Father wrote a lot of letters, but no mail came in or went out. Judge Silent was with us as usual; he had no court as the Supreme Court met this morning, but had to be adjourned till tomorrow on account of the non-arrival of Judges French & Porter, which gave our Judge a change of work for the day. In the afternoon I went to see Mrs. Smith of Chicago—out—& Mrs. Lewis & Mrs. Churchill, both in. Weather beginning to threaten again. Miss Wilcox stopped in & made quite a visit while her father was busy in the town—morning.

Tuesday 6th. Nice letters from Mother of the 22 & 24; from Sally of the 23 & from Frank of the 18th, 20th, & 24th. Mother was feeling all the relief of concluded business & was happy & content in spite of a fresh heavy cold; the rest were all well, Frank enjoying himself though it was 23° below zero at midday at his post & promising to be colder still. In a letter from Mr. Palmer to Father he quoted a telegram from Livingston which said (in among business things) "Mrs. F has been very ill but is recovering"— which though we know Mother had a bad cold & suppose it was that made us anxious & troubled us. The Judge was with us as usual—he thinks of buying one of the seats in the new mining board in New York & Father approves of the idea. Stages came in today bringing 34 mail bags & some passengers—Judges French & Porter among others so the Supreme Court will really begin tomorrow. I went in the evening with the Churchills to see the "Dr. of Alcantura," not very badly given & it was amusing to a mild extent. The mud was deep & tough & nearly pulled my overshoes off, for the thawing weather continues. Seeing how run down Father is getting the Judge sent up a lot of nice claret & sherry today & the little Father took at dinner did lift him.

Wednesday 7th. Nice Xmas letter from Mother written Christmas night. She had staid in town fearing to take her cold out in the snow & rain but Charley & Sally had gone down to Nell's to spend the day & stay over night which they certainly wouldn't have done if she had been "very ill," so I was made easier in my mind. Father wrote some letters but didn't do much work as he is still feeling not well. Another business telegram from Mrs. Shillaber came saying she & her husband had passed a deed & mailed it here. The Judge was with us at breakfast & dinner, staying on a while & talking over things—he is resting up a little. Father called on Judge French in the evening. Thawing & threatening.

Thursday 8th. A copy of the deed about the "Silver Prince" enclosed in a letter of instructions from R. Raymond came to Mr. Lewis, who brought them to the Judge—he, Judge S., was very dissatisfied with the position it left Mrs. Shillaber in & for her sake inclined to throw the whole thing up— though willing enough to take the implied risks for himself. This was the situation at breakfast, but he said he would wait the arrival of Mrs. S's letters & would have Lewis telegraph "Deeds from Videt on the way"—in substance so as to hurry them up in New York; of course the Judge was everyway nice about it, but the prospect of all this waiting counting for nothing told on Father who is not at all well—then we are anxious about Mother though we feel sure some of the children would have telegraphed us if she had been really ill. Mrs. Buffum, Mrs. Churchill & Mrs. Smith called during the afternoon. I made Father take Thor & go for a tramp in spite of the mud & he was late in getting back for dinner, but healthily tired & slept well. Judge Silent & I had a little talk over things while we were waiting dinner for Father. He sees too how tired Father is getting & tries to manage things for him & thinks maybe we'd best move across to the Weber place so that he can have more outing than is possible from this house. The Judge is so nice & I can trust him so thoroughly that it rested me to talk with him, but this day was another mauvais quart d'heure [unpleasant experience]. Father was freshened by his walk & we had rather a pleasant dinner, keeping miles away from business. Maj. Dake, Judge Porter & Mr. Rowell[2] of Cala. called in the evening. Some showers in the morning, then cleared.

Friday 9th. The "Silver Prince" business fast coming to a conclusion. Telegrams today to the Judge & to Mr. Lewis—to the latter depositing the money. The Judge breakfasted with us & was in & out, but dined with the Lewises & went with them to the Theatre. He telegraphed Col. Lamont asking how Mother was. Father was busy with people indoors till 3½ when he & Thor went out on the hills. I went out visiting in the afternoon & meeting Mrs. Lewis & [Mrs.] Churchill at Miss Kethroe's where we had gone to tell her goodbye as she leaves next week—we made the rest of our round together, nearly everyone out so we scored 7 visits & when I got in, I found some ladies had called here. Mrs. Lewis came up after dinner & asked me to go with them to the theatre, which I did—a crowded house for Miss [Pauline] Markham's benefit. We sat among people we knew; somewhat entertaining but too long. Both Father & the Judge are glad things are drawing to a close & are anxious to get it all finished & let Mother know it is done.

Saturday 10th. Letters from Mother on 29th saying [she] had had a sharp attack of bronchitis but was better, so our minds were relieved; from Frank telling me of his Xmas Eve festivities & the soldiers whisky row & enclosing a perfect photograph of himself. Father had his usual day's work & walk with Thor; he is feeling rather better. The Judge was with us at breakfast & dinner, tired out & not well. Nothing new in business. I drove out with Mrs. Lewis & Mrs. Churchill in the afternoon & made several visits at the Post, including Mrs. Smith's baby[3] & Mrs. Wainwright[4] who is charmingly pretty; we also called on the Blakes. In the evening I went with the Churchills, Smiths of Chicago & Mrs. Lewis to hear "Pinafore" which I quite liked. Weather very pleasant, Granite cr[eek] running a good stream & the roads drying.

Sunday 11th. I had a quiet home Sunday writing to Mother & to Frank. Father wrote a few letters then went for a long walk & to watch the eclipse, which we saw perfectly well as there was the usual cloudless sky; it was a little over three quarters of an eclipse here & the horns of the sun's crescent were squared; the light effects during the eclipse were interesting & made sometimes the effect of the pale electric lights over the village & hills, a decided blue tinge in it. Judge Silent breakfasted with us. Mrs. Shillaber's deeds arrived & the Judge expects to conclude the whole matter in a few days, which gives both to Father & to him great content & heart for new work. Judge French called in the afternoon—les jours se succedent, mais ne se ressemblent pas [judges succeed one another and are not alike]. Father went across to see Mr. Churchill in the evening. Clear, cool weather.

Monday 12th. Father saw people on official business & wrote some letters. Judge Silent was with us at breakfast & dinner, very busy with Supreme Court, District Court, & the Silver Prince. First intimation from Judge French that he would like to change districts, which would suit us exactly. Mrs. Buffum & Mrs. Ogier called in the afternoon. No home letters, but good business telegram of 11th from Col. Lamont ending "Mrs. Fremont well—success great medicine."

Tuesday 13th. Nell's birthday. Father was chiefly busy on territorial matters through the day & took a long walk with Thor in the afternoon. Judge Silent was with us as usual at breakfast & dinner & came up in the evening with Mr. Rowell for a business [chat] with Father—over a special mining property. I wrote to Nell [and] in the afternoon I went across the creek & made several visits, meeting Miss Wilcox at Mrs. F. Baker's. The middle of the day very warm, rest cold. The Supreme Court adjourned today to meet again at Tucson on the 26th.

Wednesday 14th. Father had the usual routine, only less people & more "papelles" [papers]. The Judge was with us as usual—nothing new in business. I went out in the afternoon for a round of visits but turning in to see Mrs. Lewis a moment I found she had intended to spend the afternoon with me, so I only attended to some housekeeping things & stopped in again for Mrs. L. (finding Mrs. Cartter[5] with her who asked to have it considered a visit at our house too as she had meant to come on there). Mrs. Lewis staid with me till near 5, talking & seeing & quite enjoying the view from our bay window. Father had his usual long walk.

Thursday 15th. Father was busy with people in the morning. When the Judge came up to breakfast, he told us the "Prince" business would be concluded in the afternoon. I made a lot of visits in the afternoon—everybody in. Father took a long walk with Thor. Judge French was to have dined with us, but received letters which obliged him to leave in the evening stage. When our Judge came up to dinner he reported the "Prince" all finished & telegrams to that effect sent to Mother by himself & to Mr. Hewitt[6] by himself & Mr. Lewis jointly. We were very glad to have it completed. In the evening Father, the Judge & I went to "Pinafore," Miss Carpenter[7] as Josephine & Pauline Markham as Rolf [Ralph]. It was right well given & we were quite entertained; the Lewises & Churchills sat by us. On our way home the Judge turned in with us & staid a little while talking it over. Of course we should have been pleased with anything with the background of the success of the "Prince." Mary went too, so we left Thor in charge of the house. Weather bright & pleasant.

Friday 16th. Letter from Mother. She was well but out of spirits. Father was tired & out of sorts; the Judge sick with overwork & a bad headache, so breakfast wasn't very gay; dinner was better as Father came in freshened from his walk & the Judge's head ached less. Father was busy on Territorial work through the day. Mrs. Curtis[8] & Mrs. Wollenberg called in the afternoon. . . .

Sunday 18th. . . . The Judge breakfasted with us & developed his plan for Father's going east in Feby. . . .

Monday 19th. People were coming in all morning to see Father on territorial & mining business. The Judge came up to breakfast, looking & feeling so far from well that I begged him to see Dr. Ainsworth which he did & then sent him up to me. I hadn't intended to call him in but I think it is just as well for this cough has taken a sharp grip on my chest & keeps me awake at nights. Father wrote some letters but he was feeling "hipped" at the enforced state of inactivity he is in & the afternoon was lovely so I made him go out for a walk which he at last did under condition that he might stay as long as he pleased & not have to come in for dinner, which bit of wild dissipation I agreed to. He did not come in till after 6 brightened & healthily tired at dinner which the Judge & I took without waiting for Father as he had asked. We talked over the Tucson plan & I asked the Judge to bring Mrs. Silent down to spend March with us there if we make the move. Mr. Hardy of Mineral Park called in the evening & staid over two hours. Weather lovely.

Tuesday 20th. Father staid in all day seeing people & attending to last things in connection with the Judge's leaving. The Judge breakfasted & dined with us & at dinner told us that *Mrs. Fitch* was going down in his party by private team, Mr. F. having just told him of it. All the arrangements are made & the Judge doesn't yet see how he can get out of it, though he doesn't like it much more than he & Father did last year when the Fitches tried the same thing when Father was going inside in a govt. ambulance.

There chances to be a vacant seat in the Judge's wagon this time so there is no refusing. The Judge staid on a little while talking over last business things with Father; then Father stepped across to see Mr. Churchill taking with him Thor who took advantage of the dark to carry out an idea he has been after for some days & ran off with the yellow dog we called "Pariah" & staid out all night, which we didn't wonder for it must be fine fun hunting cottontails up on the hills these moonlit, frosty nights. Dr. McKee called in the evening; Mrs. Levy[9] in the afternoon. I was out for a while in the afternoon & stopped in to see Mrs. Lewis & Mrs. Churchill. Fine day.

Wednesday 21st January. Father's birthday. Father saw some people & then walked over to the Post to see about an ambulance for the Tonto Basin. While he was out more people called & the Judge coming in for some papers told me he wasn't going 'till tomorrow's stage. Unexpected press of work forces him to stay this afternoon & lose the time necessary for travelling by private conveyance, so the Fitches will have to go down alone, if they go! The bond for the Grey Eagle, running three months from today, was executed in Col. Lamont's name & put in bank—as escrow—a certificate of deposit being mailed to Mother & a telegram notifying her sent, too.[10] I feel lazy from my cough, which is better, & only did some odds & ends. The Judge breakfasted & dined with us, staying on a while after each & telling us goodbye when he left in the evening. Father wrote letters in the afternoon. Thor came home about 9 p.m., having several nips taken out of him—a badly "black eye"—& looking generally "overnightly." He had evidently been in some fights & I daresay given as well as taken.

Thursday 22nd. Saw the Black Cañon stage start at 7 a.m. & waved good-bye to the Judge as it stopped to pick up one other passenger at the hotel. Father was busy indoors in the morning & walked out to the Post in the afternoon, where he arranged the details for his start next week with Col. Weeks & called on Dr. McKee. Mrs. Weeks made me a long visit in the morning telling me of Fanny's singular letter to Mother & showing me Mother's answer & asking me what I had heard of the matter (which was nothing at all). She seemed all shaken & worn out by this freak of Fanny's which she says has "overwhelmed" her & Col. Weeks. I was very sorry for her & told her I would bring her anything I received concerning it. The part that interests us was a singular letter from Fanny, which no girl could have written unprompted, accusing Mother of interfering to "interrupt her marriage" with a Mr. Farrow of whom we didn't know—& to try to keep her for Frank! She a child of fourteen (& en outre [moreover] no ways specially desirable). What a lot of mischief those young miss[es] do get into. Father had an interesting talk with a Tonto Basin miner in the evening. I called on Mrs. Buffum, Mrs. Ogier & Mrs. Churchill in the afternoon & feeling very tired with my cold turned in early. Threatening north wind.

Friday 23rd. Father not feeling very well, but he wrote a lot of letters. Mrs. Ellis called in the afternoon. Mr. Haskell called in the evening & gave us a very interesting account of his bringing in the Chirica [Chiricahua] Indians (100 in number) back from Upper Mexico to the San Carlos reservation. They were very wild & took him five months to do it. Everyone thought it impossible he should succeed. Day cold.

Saturday 24th. Two letters from Mother—one to each of us—still very anxious as to the "Prince" settlement, but otherwise well, dated 12 & 13. Father wasn't well & only wrote letters. He is anxious about whether the proposed advance to be made to Mother contingently on the full completion of "Prince" papers will be made or not & so telegraphed to Mother. Day chilly, though sunny. . . .

Monday 26th. A letter of the 15th from Mother to me; she was well in health, but desperately anxious about the termination of the business of the "Silver Prince," which was concluded at noon that day & a telegram sent her at once, so by that night she was out of suspense. Father walked across to the Fort in the morning & settled with Col. Weeks to start about 9 on Thursday; the rest of the day he attended to business & wrote letters, which letters he is heartily sick of doing. In the evening [we] had a telegram from Mother saying "Advance solidly promised, will see Mont & telegraph again," so Father's mind was relieved on that score. I went out for a while in the afternoon & borrowed some novels from Mrs. Lewis, wanting something trashy to read. Thor was away most of the day but spent the night in "dog tired." The threatening weather culminated in a cold snowstorm during the night.

Tuesday 27th. Letter of 16th (noon) from Mother, our telegram had not yet reached her so she was still very anxious, but it must have reached her before night & ought to [have] on the 15th as we know all the lines were up. There were good points about the "retiring matter" and about Black Point in her letter. Father saw some people on Territorial business, wrote letters & did lots of things preparatory to starting off. I had a lazy novel reading day. It snowed lightly in squalls through the day & was windy & cold & in the night the heaviest snowstorm of the season set in.

Wednesday 28th (Charlemagne). Snow a foot deep when we first looked out & drifted heavily. Busy through the day in looking after things for Father's trip. In the afternoon a telegraphic consultation was held between Father & Col. Weeks & it was decided on account of the heavy & (via Black Cañon) unbroken roads, to defer his starting tomorrow. Father was busy all day over odds & ends & letters. It snowed all day & fitfully through the night—by far the deepest snow we had here since our coming.

Thursday 29th. Storm over, leaving 18 inches of snow on a level here in the valley—the heaviest ever seen here by whites. Mr. Buffum, who got back from the East yesterday, stopped by with a long full letter Mother had taken advantage by so safe a way of sending & which gave us full details of many things. He said both Mother & Sally were right well when he saw them on the 10th. The stage didn't get in till 4 & brought almost no mail. Father went on with the usual routine. The sun was warm & much of the snow melted, but still left more than a foot; the night was intensely cold. Some people were in & out on official business through the day.

Friday 30th. At 4 a.m. 17° *below* zero & the whole day was clear & cold. Towards morning of Saturday it moderated & began to snow again. Usual routine of the day. Stage in at 4 p.m. brought a letter from Col. Lamont, satisfied by the telegraphic announcement that the Prince business was concluded.

Saturday 31st. Snowed all day till after dark, adding about 6 inches to what had already fallen. A letter from Mother written after the Judge's telegram of the 15th had put her mind at rest about the "Prince"—letter delayed by "N. Y. City, N. Y. being written on the envelope instead of Arizona" which some kindly clerk had afterwards added. That shows how preoccupied Mother was. Same routine as usual with us. Everything dead still in the village—everybody snowbound. . . .

Monday 2nd. Father went down to the telegraph office early & met there despatches from the Judge—at Maricopa—saying he would go on to Yuma while Father was coming down & also some good news about placing the Eureka copper mine, which made some business for Father with Mr. Richards & which he answered satisfactorily to the Judge. Also he telegraphed to Col. Weeks & found he could have an ambulance tomorrow at 10, so we were busy through the day fixing up last things. Both Father & I went to Mrs. Thorne's funeral in the afternoon. The services were at her house & were attended by almost everyone in town, though the depth of the snow & bitter north wind made going out risky for the women. Many went over to the graveyard but I was afraid of it & came home. Her death is a sad one as she leaves five little children, the youngest only two weeks old. I found her at home when I called on the 15th ult. & she was then looking very well, but was taken ill right after the birth of the baby. Mr. Thorne was making money fast from the Silver Belt mine & she was looking forward to a visit to her people in N. Y. this summer. She was a pleasant little woman & took no comfort in her husband's trade—he keeps the chief faro & gambling place in the village, but is nevertheless a good citizen. The afternoon was bitterly cold with storm wind from the north.

Tuesday 3rd. Up early & busy more or less with Father's start till 10 when the ambulance—a light one, four strong dark mules & Essig to drive—came around. Father had very light luggage, principally blankets & quilts, so they will travel light & in spite of the snow & heavy roads expect to make Maricopa in four days. There the Judge will meet him & their programme is a touch in through the Pinal & Globe districts & that way into the Tonto Basin—their objective point—& back here by the 20th, maybe. I am heartily glad for Father to have an outing as he is tired out with desk work & Prescott; he & the Judge will have a resting trip together. Mr. Anderson came in before Father left & took charge of some official scraps. Mr. Gosper has been a week in town, but has not yet called. I moved over into Father's room—to give my room a rest & to concentrate the stove work. In the evening I wrote to Dr. Jameson. The night was bitterly cold.

Wednesday 4th. Cheerful letter from Mother (23 ult.) saying they were going to move into a little furnished house, rented by the month (106. E. 25) where they can keep everything down to a much more reasonable rate than at a hotel & far more comfortable. In connection with the "Prince" she wrote Mr. Raymond would be here about the 20th Feby. Mr. Foster called to ask Father to join with Genl. Wilcox in being honorary manager of a new masked ball to be given on the 27th, & was very much surprised to find he had gone out of town. I had just finished writing to Mother at N. Y. & to Father at Maricopa when Genl. Wilcox with the two Mrs. Smiths & Mr. Haskell driving a horse four-in-hand to the Genl's sleigh stopped by & took me with them—a pleasant change from the house. The snow is already soft on the roads so the horses had pretty heavy pulling for a turn out is impossible on account of stumps & stones. The stage only got in so that mail was delivered at 4, which gave me only just time to dot down the items of Mother's letter for Father & catch the

5 o'clock outgoing mail. It thawed heavily all day but was again extremely cold during the night. A telegram yesterday from the Judge says "Tonto frozen up & streams too high for crossing." Shall repeat it to Father tomorrow.

Thursday 5th. My day was spent in reparative surgery on an old dress & evening in writing to McLean. No letters came. Had a telegram from Father saying they had "made Phoenix in good condition." Also one from Col. Lamont, dated 5th, full of good business points, urging Father's & the Judge's presence here to meet Raymond & Alexander[11]—on the 18th & 20th they are to arrive—& telegraphing "one thousand through Laidlaw, more to follow by mail"—which relieves Father of all money anxieties both here & for Mother. I repeated the telegram at once to Father in Phoenix.

Friday 6th. Day began with the receipt of Father's telegraphic acknowledgment "of your Lamont telegram; will go on to Maricopa & meet Judge tomorrow" dated 5th, so that's all right. No eastern letters in the mail, but a long one from Judge Silent to Father, dated Yuma & posted Maricopa which—con permisso—I read & found to contain the initial notes of lots more of active business. Mrs. Hargrave called in the afternoon. Mr. Lewis & Mr. Larkin[12] were in on business. Dr. McKee & Mr. Haskell made me a pleasant little visit in the evening. I sent Mother a telegram telling her "Lamont's telegram overtook Father yesterday. Laidlaw received, thanks. All Well." Sewing & letter writing made the bone of my day. Zero at 7½ a.m., but thawed through the day.

Saturday 7th. . . . Miss Dunning[13] called. . . .

Sunday 8th. Read & wrote. Telegraphed "Laidlaw received; all well; nothing new" to Father at Maricopa. In the evening, Mr. Thorne came in to ask Mother's N. Y. address as he is going on for mining work "& it may be for our mutual benefit." He owns the Silver Belt. Thawed all day & wasn't as cold as it lately has been at night.

Monday 9th. . . . Gave Chung holiday as it was Chinese New Year—he didn't ask it at all. . . .

Tuesday 10th. Telegram from Father (Phoenix yesterday) saying he & the Judge would be here "Thursday noon"; also a letter from him, Maricopa 8th, saying the Judge had finished up thoroughly our part of the "Yonkers" business[14] & would join him that evening. Mr. Thorne, Gov. Powers with him, called to get Mother's last address. Mr. Lewis called in the evening partly on business. Chung was on duty again & Mary off as I gave the whole day for Maggie's wedding[15] which began with mass at 10 & ended with a dance in the evening, Mary getting back tired & highly pleased at midnight. Squalls of snow & hail all day & hail through the night.

Wednesday 11th. Letters from Mother—just moved into their rented house—& from Nell, all well. A splendid mountain "tourmente" [blizzard] which lasted till 4 p.m. & left about 8 inches of snow on the level. I could do little except watch it whirling by—the streets were dead, no one going out who could stay in. Night not very cold.

Thursday 12th. Father & the Judge arrived 2:45, cold & very hungry, but otherwise quite well & pleased with the results of their journey though they couldn't do what they set out for. The Judge had obtained a 60 days bond on the Neahr mill & mines[16] on the Colorado—a day north of Yuma— and the papers had been sent on to N. Y. This is a valuable & big property that they have for some months past been hoping to get control of. Yesterday's storm made the stages four hours behind so I knew they could [not] get in at noon. They came in today from Big Bug. The Judge came back to dinner—his trip has done him good. I read over to Father the mail which has accumulated in his absence, & we talked it over. Not very cold.

Friday 13th. Father was down town & out at the Fort during the day. The Judge opened court & finding the lawyers not ready adjourned it to the 18th; then he was busy with some copper people who came up from Tucson to look into the Richards' mine—so busy that he got no breakfast at all. Twice he brought them up to see Father (they staid 2 whole hours in the evening); also the Judge & Father had a long business talk in the afternoon & the Judge bonded a lot of small mines in the neighborhood as Mr. Lamont's letter received this morning asked them to do. Mrs. Lewis came in to see me in the afternoon. Day only chilly, nights still cold & the coasting enjoyed by lots of young people down the hill back of our house, so we have the benefit of all the gay sounds.

Saturday 14th. A whole lot of people came in through the morning & afternoon to see Father on business. The Judge breakfasted & dined with us. He & Father both angry at Col. Biddle's having chipped in & carried off the copper people for his mine[17]—it was a "spongah twick." Nice letter from Frank who is having fine deer hunting—on snow shoes—& lots of work, too. Mildish weather.

Sunday 15th. Thoroughly good business & total rehabilitation letter from Mother; also nice one from Charley; & from McLean, way up some Chinese river. His letter was dated Jany. 6th so it came quickly. Father was very much pleased by Mother's letter. He worked at letters & papers through the day. The Judge took breakfast with us & came up again in the evening—more new business plans! Not a cold day. . . .

Tuesday 17th. Mr. Raymond & Mr. Rutherford[18] got in by the morning stage. They took dinner & breakfast with us, staying on after each. The town is quite excited over "Prof. Raymond's" coming up to this northern section of the Territory & proposes giving him a "banquet" in the theatre. Of course, it will be a lift for Yavapai [County] if he speaks well of it. Judge Silent took breakfast with us & came in for a while both before dinner & later on in the evening, dining with the Lewises & devoting his day chiefly to & for "Prof." R. Miss Wilcox called & asked me to dinner for tomorrow. I couldn't go on account of efforts [i.e., entertaining Raymond and Rutherford].

Wednesday 18th. Father was very busy answering mail. The Judge, Dr. Raymond & Mr. Rutherford took breakfast & dinner with us—the two latter staying on after dinner when Dr. R. talked over a number of interesting scientific things with Father; Mr. Rutherford tired about [. . .] & went off to write letters. Soon after the Judge came in evidently intending to show Father something & hurry off again, but Dr. R. was in full swing on the law of storms & didn't leave till a quarter to eleven when the Judge brought out two important business telegrams from Mother & Col. Lamont, which he & Father discussed & by 11 he left. Day mild & soft. I went out early to see Mrs. Buffum on a bit of business & stopped in to see Mrs. Churchill on my way back. In the afternoon Mrs. Buffum came in to see me—about the extras put into this house—all pleasantly arranged for.

Thursday 19th. Father was chiefly busy with indoor work; the Judge, Dr. Raymond & Mr. Rutherford took breakfast & dinner with us, staying on a while after each meal. Judge Silent returned after evening telegraph hours with a telegram from Mother in answer to one he sent this morning & which answer pleased him & Father as it told them "Yonkers" was all right. They had been somewhat uneasy over one of last night's despatches as they feared it meant a hitch in the "Yonkers" negociations. Thawing & mild.

February 20th. The Judge was in & out during the morning. They all breakfasted down on the Plaza after the stage got in with Mr. Alexander, which it did late after 10 & at 1 the four set off on horseback for the "Prince" mine, expecting to get there some time tomorrow. Father went out to the Fort about "Yonkers" map in the morning; & in the afternoon went down to Mr. Blake's on "Peck" negociation. I had nice letters from Sally & from Fanny Dart. Day very mild & thawing profusely—some signs of a coming storm. . . .

Monday 23rd. Pleasant, contented toned letter from Mother. Father was rather too much on the strain as to what Raymond would say about the "Prince" to settle to the usual routine. I wrote lots of letters & Mr. Churchill came in to discuss details of arrangement for the "Banquet." Judge Silent got in at 8, having ridden through today in spite of four feet drifts & bad road generally. He staid a while telling us that Raymond approved of the Prince & confirmed Maynard's report of it; & also telling us of other business points in connection with the group of mines in the Peck District. Then he went off to see that the others got a good supper at Thorne's; it was a hard ride back & he was tired (somewhat from the people he had been with too, I think).

Tuesday 24th. Dr. Raymond & Mr. Rutherford breakfasted with us; Mr. Alexander & some others called during the day. Judge Silent was in more than once & "took a hasty plate of soup" in the evening while discussing with Father the necessity of our accepting [the] situation & letting the Hewitt-Raymond-Alexander set buy the Peck, Tuscumbia & Black Warrior to combine them into a company—Silent & Frémont each to have a fourth—but no combination will that outside trio allow with Lamont (of course the money part of that can be fixed out of the Frémonts' interest), but it made Father very angry & only force majeure [overwhelming circumstances] makes him accept. Father & I dined alone. At 8 p.m. Father went up to the "Banquet" where he is to preside & receive. He didn't get back till 3 a.m. as almost each man spoke. It was a success; all the officers were guests. If we don't accept their proposition they will either outbid us—as time on those mines is too short for concerted action with N. Y.—or dropping the whole concern go off & damning with faint praise put off all successful ventures in this section for a long time to come—as "Prof."

Raymond's opinion floats or sinks enterprises—& we can't give the time for a reaction, which with time the mines would win for themselves. It's a disagreeable situation to be placed in, but not the first we've had to accept & make the best of. The Banquet was a success.

Wednesday 25th. The Judge, Dr. Raymond, Mr. Alexander & Mr. Rutherford all breakfasted with us, but we had a quiet dinner with only the Judge, who was in & out on business through the day. I called on Mrs. Lewis & on Mrs. Thibodo. Mr. Sherman called by request about Miss Shearer. I fought one of my bad headaches thro' the night.

Thursday 26th. People were in & out all day, some on business: Mr. Ross to show his divorce papers from Mrs. R. No. 2 who keeps writing letters at him through Father; Mr. Sherman to ask Father to come up at 2 & introduce Dr. Raymond to the school children, which Father did & R. R. made a pleasant speech to them; Gen. Wilcox also was present & spoke; Mr. Churchill to talk over with Father the charges brought against our Judge Silent in Washington (instituted by Capt. Eagan we think)[19] & which appeared in the associated news column of this day S. F. Chronicle; of course false & we know directly from Mr. Rogers, private sect. to the President, that it is all right for the Judge there, but it made us mad all the same. Genl. Wilcox came in about the conflicts likely to arise between the prospectors & the Supis [Havasupai] in the Cañon country;[20] Mrs. Kelly, Mrs. Weaver[21] & Miss Stevens [Stephens] called on me. The Judge, Dr. Raymond, Mr. Alexander & Mr. Rutherford all took breakfast & dinner with us, staying a while after each; Mr. R. R. & Mr. A. saying adieu when they left in the evening as they start East via the Black Cañon tomorrow morning. Then Mr. DeLong,[22] now residing in Tucson, but properly the Judge's teacher, made us an evening visit. All day I was fighting one of my worst headaches & sent for Dr. Ainsworth who renewed my medicine, which had given out & which pulled me thro' dinner & the evening.

Friday 27th. Dr. Raymond & Mr. Alexander left by the Black Cañon stage at 7 a.m.—the Judge saw them off; then came over here early & had a long business talk with Father & they got ready & sent off telegrams to Mother telling her about the arrangements here. After the rest of the business was over, the Judge told Father how advantageous offers had been made him to go into a business connection down in Tucson with some men he knew & how the need to realize money would force him into accepting them if he didn't soon see a surer foundation for rapid work under Lamont than he now saw—as time was an element he had to take into consideration. He did not say so but the inference clearly was that he would be acting on his own account solely down there, which is only fair & right, but it made us very low in our minds to think of losing his business help. His friendship we feel too sure of to think a business change of bases could affect it, but no one can replace him & we should feel his loss horribly up here. It made the whole day mauvais quart d'heure [another unpleasant day] to me. Father of course being a man sees his way out of things as I can't. Dr. DeLong breakfasted with us & the Judge too. The remnants of my headache made me useless all day. The Judge & Mr. Rutherford dined with us, the Judge staying on a while with us & talking over this report of charges made against him at Washington. Mr. Churchill called. Father had his usual routine of day. Father had a French cablegram through from Paris today—from Dr. [Lavin?] saying he could put two million francs into Father's business inside of three months. Father responded.

Saturday 28th. Father had important letters to write—both to Mother & Col. Lamont explaining all this necessary transaction with Mr. Alexander—& other letters too. The Judge took breakfast & dinner with us; Mr. Rutherford dined with us. After dinner the Judge staid on for a time talking over with Father the steps to be taken against the charge made at Washington—by Capt. Eagan it is said—& also "bits" of business to be looked after while he is away at the Prince. Mr. Sherman called during the afternoon.

Sunday 29th. I had a telegram of 28th from Mother saying "Splendid boy born Thursday. Everybody well. Named for our General;" so Sally is all right which is a relief to us. I went right down to the telegraph office with my congratulating answer. On my way back [I] stopped in to tell Mrs. Lewis & she asked us to dine there today. Father had a nice indoors letter from Mother in this morning's mail. We went down to the Lewises at 4. & had a pleasant family dinner with them. I staid on a while after as Mrs. Bean came in. Judge Silent left for the Prince this morning & will hardly be back before the end of the week. He took Mr. Rutherford with him. Weather mild.

March 1st Monday. Father was out down town & saw Mr. Marion[23] & Mr. Churchill at home on this business of charges against our Judge; also did other business & in the afternoon took Thor [for] a trudge on the hills, which are nearly dry now. In the afternoon I walked out to the Fort & called on Mrs. La Motte & Mrs. Weeks & turned in a moment to see Mrs. Martin's baby [Ethel]. In the evening Mr. Churchill & Dr. McKee called.

Weather warm again. A business telegram from Mother to the Judge had a tag that they were "all well."

Tuesday 2nd. . . . Mr. Churchill came in—on Judge Silent's business—in the evening.

Wednesday 3rd. I did some little shopping in the morning & called on Mrs. [Amos M.] Smith—up from Smithville for a few days—& on Mrs. Churchill; Mrs. Thibodo called here in the afternoon. Father was busy over Territorial letters till 4 when he went out on the hills till dinner. Judge Silent got in soon after 7, having ridden in from Alexandra since noon. He staid a while telling Father about the Prince & getting the news of what had gone on here in his absence. A threatening grey day & furious wind all night.

Thursday 4th. Father worked away at indoor things—including endorsing the citizens' & bar's petition to the President protesting against the charges preferred against Judge Silent & which Mr. Churchill brought up & sent off enclosed to Mr. Rogers. At 4 Father went off for his tramp with Thor. Judge Silent came up early, long before dinner, & we had a good long talk together over business matters & after dinner, he staid on talking with Father—a letter with Mr. Lewis who came in when telegraph hours were over. The Judge was at breakfast too. He has got the bonds on the Tuscumbia & B. Warrior & effected the purchase of both, if only Mr. Alexander comes up to time with the money, which he is under business agreement to do, but until it is paid over we all feel a little anxious. I went up to see Mrs. Buffum & Mrs. Ogier; while I was out Mrs. Lewis & Mrs. St. James called; after I came in, Mrs. Adams called. Weather lowering but not windy. Nice home letter from Mother by the mail.

Friday 5th. Usual morning's routine. A telegram came at noon from Lamont about the agreement with Alexander—against it—which gave Father & the Judge an opportunity for talking over business & which they answered explicitly & adhering to said agreement. I sent off the telegram from the Fort as the village office is more than ever leaky now that Mr. Gosper is back. I rode out with Mrs. Lewis & Mrs. Churchill to Whipple where we called on Mrs. Martin, Mrs Biddle & Mrs. Wainwright—all in— & Mrs. Fred Smith, out; then back to the S.E. corner of the village & called on Mrs. Cartter—out—& Mrs. Allen—in—& Mrs. Aram, in. Father after finishing up his letter had been bullied by Thor into going out. The Judge staid on quite a time after dinner talking over with Father the pros

& cons of his—Father's going east on a short leave & trying to fuse all sides so that our business should work solidly & quickly to points.

Saturday 6th. Father worked at Territorial business all morning. After breakfast he & the Judge made out a long telegram, 367 words, to be sent night rates from Maricopa, getting there in a registered letter to the operator; telling Col. Lamont the exact situation & the necessity for prompt action. I made a few visits in the afternoon—everybody out. Bishop [George] Lake—Mormon from Brigham City, Apache Co.—took dinner with us. Father had asked him when he called in the morning; he is here to try & settle the timber questions for his neighborhood as the Land Office reading of the statutes is blocking their using even enough timber for house building. He had many interesting points to tell us about their settlements, & was himself a type [of] industrious pioneer of the better class. He staid on a while into the evening talking with Father. The Judge was busy & left right after dinner. Weather springlike.

Sunday 7th. The Judge was in & out several times thro' the day, breakfasted with us & came in again after telegraph hours; later still a satisfactory telegram about Yonkers came from Mother—brought in by an orderly & saying that Eagan was attacking Father & the Judge anonymously in Washington but had been routed. Father took the telegram down to the Court House & talked it over with the Judge. Mr. Churchill came in twice during the day & evening to see Father.

Monday 8th. Long & good letters from Mother of the 23 & 26, all right with them except Charley is having a very painful time down with sciatica. The Judge was in early & he & Father shaped an urgent telegram about the necessary [$]15,000 which the Judge took across to the Post & sent off from there. He was with us at dinner & breakfast & came in again after telegraph hours. A Mr. [Augustine W.] Ferrin, editor of a Rep. paper in the interior of N. Y., was brought by Mr. Gosper—first time the latter has been in the house since he returned in Jany.—to see Father in the morning & Father asked him—Mr. F.—to dinner & he came. Mrs. Weeks called in the morning. I did a little shopping & made 2 visits in the afternoon. Father was very busy on Territorial work all day. He also sent a telegraphic request for 30 days leave to Schurz via Maricopa. The winds have commenced.

Tuesday 9th. The motif of the day was waiting answers to the urgent telegrams sent east—& as McClintock was rowing all day with Maricopa

& getting no messages through the Judge walked out to the Post after dinner to see if the operator there could get Maricopa which he did & found there were no despatches for us at Maricopa. At 9, after [a] very disagreeable meeting with the Black Warrior owners, the Judge came up & sat till 11, discussing the situation with Father. Neither of them can understand why no answers came to the request for 15,000, either a "can" or a "cannot." In between times Father did a lot of work preparatory to his possible leaving for the East & I made him go out for a walk in the afternoon. I did some shopping & trying on of dresses in the morning—letters & sewing in the afternoon. The days just now are wearingly anxious on us all & I fear on Mother, too, though she can hardly understand how fine the situation is, which for want of Col. Lamont's answering action we seem about to lose—though everything in regard to it has been fully telegraphed them.

Wednesday 10th. The Judge came out at 8 o'clock with a telegram from Mother (which reached here last night but wasn't delivered) & which said they in N. Y. believed the money had been paid here, but as it hasn't & as the last hour of grace on the Black Warrior (the key of the situation & on which hinges all our present plans) is up at midnight of this day & no more time obtainable, Father framed a more imperative [telegram] than he liked to send but one which was demanded by the critical nature of the situation, telling Mont that Father & the Judge being on the spot understood the situation better than he in N. Y. could & that he asked for an immediate telegraphic answer as to whether Mont could or couldn't telegraph the 15,000 already three times asked for as "urgent" in the French parlementary sense—& no answer returned. Father took this despatch himself out to the Fort, as we distrust the village office (pour cause) & also another telling them of the last rich assays of Tuscumbia & Black Warrior ores. The Judge was at breakfast & dinner with us. He nearly always comes & it will be shorter to say when he doesn't—& in & out, the last time just before 9 p.m. when he brought up a despatch from Mr. Alexander saying he had paid in the 15,000 to Mr. Lewis's correspondents in San Francisco & Mr. Lewis had a despatch from his firm notifying him, and as these were received just before 9 there was only three hours grace left us! Such "close calls" are very wearing on one. The Judge also had a despatch from Washington telling him "charges preferred against you through Campbell" whom the Judge saved from financial ruin here last year by personally advancing money; which proves Mr. C. as specimen "Hassayampa."[24] Judge Silent left as soon as he had talked things over a little with Father to notify the B[lack] W[arrior] people that the money had arrived inside the time. I took Mrs. Lewis & Mrs. Churchill in Dinsmore's hack to return visits in south Prescott & across the creek. Judge Tweed, passing thro' to Mohave, called in the evening. Letter from Mother in the morning telling what a strong fine baby Sally's is—brown haired & like Charley at that age.

Thursday 11th. Father went over early to the Post with a telegram to let Mother know that the necessary 15,000 had been paid just in time last night; the rest of the day he was busy seeing territorial people & at business letters. The Judge was in & out several times & quite finished up the "Warrior" business—so all that plan is secure, but it was so near a thing that both he & Father were exhaustedly tired & spent. The Judge staid on after dinner telling us of new things he had learned about Capt. Eagan's plans against him & of the indignation felt at them in Mineral Park. The high winds set in this morning & the wires were down by midday— fortunately for us that this didn't come yesterday. I went across to see Mrs. Churchill for a moment—was indoors for the rest of the day. Mrs. Martin & Mrs. Bean called.

Friday 12th. Up early & made Father eat more of a petit dejeuner [breakfast] than he usually does. At 7½ the Judge came up on a good sorrel mule, with a strong but doubtful tempered buckskin for Father & (with their blankets strapped on behind) they started off for the "Prince," "Warrior," & "Tuscumbia." I had a quiet day—resting & reading. The furious gale which began yesterday forenoon continued all last night & until the sunset of today. The wires were down for over twenty-four hours; fortunately for us that this didn't happen before Mr. A's despatch got thro'. . . .

Sunday 14th. Father & the Judge got back at 11½; Father quite tired as his horse had proved a "pounder." The Judge took breakfast with us & staid on a while talking over the points in the letters waiting Father & two telegrams which were also waiting—one from Sect. Schurz granting Father thirty days leave "by direction of the President" & one from Mother in answer to Father's most urgent telegram of the 10, saying that Mont could take no step now without upsetting things & that "apparent inaction" was necessary, but no explicit answer about the 15,000. Quiet reading day in between.

Monday Mar. 15. Two letters from Mother—she was troubled at the arrangement with Mr. Alexander; well herself & so were Sally & the baby— Charley still ill. The Judge brought up & read to us the charges preferred by Mr. Campbell, as Delegate, against him. They are simply a legally phrased version of Capt. Eagan's rhodomontades [sic] about the Peck decisions, the Fitch & Churchill firm, & also that "he has engaged in business & developing mines with John C. Fremont," the whole of which Mr. Campbell states "makes a crying scandal in the town of Prescott!" The Judge read us letters from Mr. Morgan, telling of his instant denial by telegram to·[James T.] Farley, Cala. Senator, of the part assigned to him in Campbell's charges & also a letter from Mr. Fitch copying one he had sent Senator [Newton] Booth of Cala. denying what Campbell charges about his firm. Father still tired from his trip but worked busily at getting papers—territorial—in order, to be left [i.e., when he leaves for New York]. The Judge was with us at breakfast & dinner. I had a big scare in the morning by the burning of my chimney. Fortunately there were a few inches of snow on the roof & it was a dead calm morning. I was nearly dressed—7 a.m.—& had Wilson over at once & he, being landlord, took all precautions & no harm came of it. Our houses here are such shells, it makes one extra scary. Mr. Foster called in the evening—why?

Tuesday 16th. I went out early, did some travelling shopping for Father & tried on a dress & went in to see Mrs. Churchill for a while. Father was busy all through the day & evening about his going & seeing people who called. The Judge was in once or twice besides coming to meals. Dr. Ainsworth at Father's request took a look at Thor. I wonder what he thought at our asking it of him? Squally weather with snow in the night.

Wednesday 17th. Morning was busy with Father's preparations & the Judge's packing of specimens for the office in N. Y. During the day & evening many people called to see Father & tell him bon voyage, including Judge Tucker, Dr. McKee & Dr. Lightfoot,[25] Maj. Dake, Mr. Sherman & Mr. Otis & others. Mr. Buffum, Mrs. Bean & Mrs. Ogier called on me. Judge Silent was in—helping Father get ready in lots of ways, big & little. Snow & hail in squalls; very chilly. The Bar passed resolutions sustaining Judge Silent—a copy to be sent on to Dept. of Justice.

Thursday 18th. Up at 5 & Father had his breakfast soon after six—the Judge with us. Then Mr. Lewis came in. The Black Cañon stage came round at 7 & as Father was quite ready, of course, it got off in a few moments. Mr. St. James & Mr. Hugo Richards were already in it, bound for Gillett [in Maricopa County]. Father expects to make N. Y. on Easter morning & to return over the Mogollons via Santa Fe., which gives him four days more of his leave to stay in N. Y. A registered letter of the 2nd from Mother arrived this morning, all about the shock over signing the Alexander agreement out here had given, which was natural as they had not received the explanatory telegrams. Mrs. Allen called. I had a quiet day; the Judge staid on a while with me after meals, feeling a mite sorry for my being left alone up here. Weather cloudy but not cold. Thor still very sick.

Chapter 7

Judge Silent's Vindication

March 19–June 20, 1880

Friday, March 19th. I spent most of my day in writing letters & looking after Thor who is still very sick. The Judge came up to breakfast & dinner. Letter from Mother of the 8th, very down on account of Dr. Raymond's adverse opinion on the Prince written to Hewitt, whose further action in mining matters is shaken by it.

Saturday 20th. Had a despatch, dated Maricopa 19, from Father who was there all right. I made visits in the morning & afternoon & some ladies called here. I missed them all except Mrs. Churchill. The Judge came up to breakfast & dinner. I had a quiet evening by the parlor fire. Lovely weather, though still cool.

Sunday 21st. Letters from Mother saying Charley was better, Sally & the baby all right; and giving some good business points. The Judge came up to breakfast, but dined of course with the Lewis family. Mrs. L. sent the children up to ask me down, but I excused myself, thinking the Judge had more than enough of Frémonts during the week. The little Lewis girls[1] staid quite a while with me. Thor much better.

Monday 22nd. I sent to the dressmakers in the morning; then to Mrs. Buffum's to ask her & Mrs. Ogier here to breakfast on Wednesday, stopping a moment at Mrs. Lewis & at Mrs. Churchill's to ask them also. The Judge was at breakfast & at dinner, chiefly occupied in getting every paper in order to send on with his answer to the charges made by Campbell against him. . . .

Wednesday 24th. Pleasant letter from Father, Los Angeles, Palm Sunday. He was well & in an ecstasy over the wild flowers & the climate of California. Mrs. Buffum & Mrs. Churchill took breakfast with me to meet Mrs. Ogier—not a lunch, only a hearty Southern breakfast, which they ate with appetite & seemed to like their afternoon, staying on till after four o'clock.

Thursday 25th. Lt. Smith came for me at 11, with pretty buckskin Nelly & their pony carriage, & took me whirling out before the wind to their house where I met Mrs. Wainwright & Miss Gulliver,[2] as well as Mrs. Smith & the baby—a pretty & good little dark haired thing. Spent a pleasant time talking Washington, Japan & San Francisco with them—skipping Prescott entirely—& had a good Fort lunch with fried chicken etc. Mr. Smith brought me in again, in the teeth of a "Washoe zephyr," but Nelly put us thro' so quickly it hardly mattered. Mary had looked out for the Judge at breakfast as I wouldn't let him make a restaurant breakfast two days handrunning. He came up to dinner, too. There was a meeting of Prescott ladies about a stupid party they are going to give, held at Mrs. C. Bashford's this afternoon. I was asked to it, but only after I had accepted Mrs. Smith's lunch invitation, so I fortunately missed it. Stormy all day & snow in the night.

Good Friday. 3 letters from Mother to Father, all more or less troubled about the telegrams which we had to send from here on the 10th; nice ones from Father, at Lathrop; from Frank—Missoula of course—to me. Mother will be all right after she has talked things out with Father. The Judge came up to breakfast & dinner—he is tired with the pain of having to answer charges, feeling as we did about the French suit; & in the afternoon came a telegram from Mother saying she had been to Washington on a letter from Mr. Rogers about the Judge's affair & had succeeded in "staying hasty action; situation serious." I am so glad Father is nearly there—at Omaha today. In the afternoon I went to see Mrs. Churchill & as we were interrupted in discussing the coming party she came down to my house & finished the talk; then after dinner I went to Mrs. Lewis's house for a little while & later in the evening Dr. McKee & Dr. Lightstein [Lightfoot] called here.

Saturday 27th. I went out in the morning to see Mrs. Bean about my share in providing food for the party; the ladies are determined to furnish the supper—& also called on Mother Basil who has come up from Tucson on business connected with the Sisters' school here. Lots of ladies called in the afternoon. After dinner I stepped across to ask the Churchills to dine with me tomorrow & they asked me to dine with them instead. Judge Silent came up to breakfast & to dinner. The uppermost topic with us of course is the charge against him & his answer, with tout ce qui s'ensuit [with everything that followed]; a little too about this ridiculous party which is being managed by the ladies of the Bashford & Parker families who have dropped about twenty families who are usually asked to such things "they not being in our set"! Society distinctions up here! but it is going to make a lot of trouble. Miss Sherman called today to announce her coming marriage on the 8th April. A lovely, still Spring day.

Easter Sunday. I wrote a lot of home letters; took dinner at the Churchills, only themselves [being there]; came home early to be on hand for the telegraph hour as there were some messages the Judge wished sent; he came up just before 7 & after we had simmered them down took them to the office. He was also at breakfast & left with me to read over the original affidavits which make the exhibit to accompany his answer. They are very thorough endorsements of him & certify to the falsehood of the charges brought. I don't see how they could more completely give in their adherence to him than Mohave & Yavapai counties—his District—have. Weather springlike in spite of the wind. No letters through a failure to connect between the R.R. & the stage. Fine services at the Catholic church—no Protestant services as Mr. Adams is away.

Monday 29th. I went out for a while in the morning & called to see Mrs. Lewis & Mrs. Ogier. Had a letter from Nell with two charming photographs of her babies in fancy dress. The Judge was at breakfast & dinner. A telegram came from Mr. Palmer to Father asking when he could go to N. Y. & was answered saying he reached there today. Windy & warm.

Tuesday 30th. Quiet morning. The Judge came up to breakfast & to dinner & gave me his Answer to read over. I had a nice letter from Father at Ogden & from Mother. There was also a very pleasantly reassuring letter from Mr. Rogers about the Judge's case. In the afternoon Mrs. Lewis, Mrs. Smith of Chicago & Mrs. Churchill called & I wrote letters. Windy day. Judge Silent got his Answer, with all its accompanying affidavits, off today.

Wednesday 31st. I was out during the morning & did some shopping. The Judge took breakfast with me, but dined with Mr. Lewis. I went up about 3 to Mrs. Buffum's where I was asked to a high tea. Mrs. Ogier, Mrs. Lewis, Mrs. Churchill & Mrs. A. M. Smith, Mrs. St. James & Mrs. Bean were there besides the Buffums. We ladies chinned till tea—which was a very nice one—& afterwards till near 7 when I made the move homewards on account of the telegraph hours & most of them came away with me. The Judge came up for a while in the evening & sat talking over plans & probabilities—he is let down & tired. Soft Spring day, without wind.

Thursday April 1. Indoors through the day—not doing much. No mail owing to detention of the train by a sandstorm. Judge Silent took breakfast & dinner here & coming back in the evening we walked up & called on Mrs. Ogier & Mrs. Buffum. I had a telegraph—31 Mar.—from Father in N. Y. saying he was keeping Campbell at bay; that the situation was complicated. That Mr. Hewitt & Lamont were acting together in the Alexander matter. Day very windy, but evening delightful; air moist & the sky full of scurrying black cirrous [sic] clouds, so that coming down the plank walk from the school carried me back to last walks on deck before turning in for the night. The Judge shivered & said it was "awfully damp" which shows how Californians & eastern seaboarders take the same weather.

Friday 2nd. Had pleasant letter from Mother, Washington, D.C. Mar. 22. I was out in the morning, scraps in connection with my share of the supper at tonight's party; went in to Mrs. Lewis & Mrs. Churchill for a little while. Judge Silent came up [for] dinner & breakfast & left with me the rest of his Answer & affidavits—copies—to read (at my request). Windy & overcast, with showers on the mountains.

Saturday 3rd. I stepped across & asked Mrs. Smith to dine with me tomorrow, she accepted. The Judge took breakfast with me & was to have dined here but Mr. Lewis begged for him as he was alone. Mrs. Lewis, Mrs. Bean, Mrs. Ogier & Mrs. Buffum dined with me & evidently were pleased with their evening, staying on till after 8 when Mr. Lewis & Judge Silent came in & Mrs. Lewis went home with Mr. L., while the Judge took the Nob Hill ladies to their houses, coming back & staying for a few moments talk over last night's party, etc. with me.

Sunday 4th. Unpleasant letters from Mother & Charley—all written on a misconception of Pen's action in the Alexander agreement business & of Pen himself. I didn't answer to them as Father is there. The Judge came up to breakfast but dined with the Lewises. Mrs. Smith didn't come to dinner—"headache." So had I.

Monday 5th April. Went across to Mrs. Churchill's for a few moments in the morning; in the afternoon walked over to the Post, going by the road & coming back by the trail, & called on Miss Wilcox—at the Verde; Mrs. Martin, ill & not receiving; Mrs. Fowler, out; Mrs. Fred Smith, in; & Mrs. Wainwright, also in. Then when I reached the village as it was still early, I called on all the Burmisters, Bowers, & Bashfords of Nob Hill, seeing only

Mrs. C. Bashford & Miss Lizzie Bashford. Got home, just in time for dinner, having succeeded in tiring myself out physically & so shaking off so[me] of the unpleasantness of yesterday's letters. The Judge took breakfast & dinner with me, staying on a little after dinner. Mr. Sherman called in the evening. Rather windy day.

Tuesday 6th. Seeing Mr. Churchill drive by for the mines I sent over & asked Mrs. C. to dine with me. She accepted, but came over later to say she might not be able to as Mrs. Bean was going to breakfast with her & might expect to stay on to dinner. Mr. Beach called, hunting the Judge to "show him some press despatches just received." Just as Judge Silent & I were sitting down to breakfast, Genl. Wilcox called. Hearing a knock, I sent Mary to excuse me as I was at breakfast but Genl. W. came in saying he would join us which I regretted as with his accepted position as Capt. Eagan's friend I knew the Judge & he couldn't fuse especially as this new despatch, the contents of which were still unknown to me, had come.

Soon the Genl. did lead straight to the subject & the Judge said a few hot words on it which were natural enough to a man who is still in the first hour of knowing that the associated press has been used to spread over the country false charges which it will be days before the contradiction can follow, & specially when speaking about the man who has so used the ass. press; but I was sorry for it & wished the General had come some other time. He only said he "feared Eagan was letting himself be made a catspaw of!!"

I also then learned that in the Despatch Father also is attacked, but as we are always catching it for something or other I don't so much mind & Father's record before the American people is of such long standing & has been so thoroughly overhauled in political campaigns that if in the teeth of what is known about they choose to believe these charges, then they [are] "idjuts" & I don't care for their opinion.

But the Judge is younger, his record is local to parts of California & here & to be thus unjustly introduced to the nation at large is very hard on him. It is a square outrage for these charges to be thus published ten days before his answer can reach the Dept. of Justice to try in this way to manufacture public [opinion] & make a big thing out of what is simply the intention on the part of the San Francisco Peck people to get a fair judge removed & one bonded to them put in his place. As Judge Silent is a sensitive man & one who values his reputation in the old fashioned way all this hurts him—the more [so] that [he] is away from his family & from all his friends of long standing.

Gen. Wilcox had come to ask me to telegraph Father that if the city man appointed to San Carlos was sent there instead of Jeffords[3] or some one who like him understood the Indians two full regts. must be sent here at once ("though where they can be squeezed out of our little army I don't know," he said). He wouldn't take the responsibility of himself telegraphing but said it must be done, as in the event of this city man's coming the Indians would surely break out & probably wipe out the Tombstone & other mining camps before he, with the few troops at his disposal, could be of much use—"it would be infinitely worse than Victoria in New Mexico & stop all mining in this Territory for years to come." He was very urgent & very nervous about it—for, in secret, the Indians generally are restless. Capt. Haskell & one co. to the south; Col. La Motte & two cos. to the N.W. are out quieting them—& these not Apaches.

I ought to add that after the little outspoken feeling on the Judge's part, the breakfast went along smoothly enough for I got the lead & kept it, talking with equal interest—to myself & my hearers I'm sure—of the horrors of an Indian war & the beauties of a properly managed swell Catholic wedding (I gave them bridesmaids dresses & all). In the afternoon I wrote to Father to N. Y. & to Washington & telegraphed him to N. Y. about the Apaches & in answer to a despatch from him asking something about the Accidental[4] mine which I had Maj. Dake attend to with Mr. Blake. There were other scraps to do & the Judge turned in for a few moments too to ask some questions; he came back to dinner at 5 & staid a little afterwards.

I know a good deal of what he is feeling for I can remember with minute distinctness what I felt when riding down in the 8:20 morning train from Tarrytown, the whole full of people who knew I unexpectedly read in the "Herald's" big headlines the ass. Press despatches about the French suit against Father. In the evening I sent off another telegram to Father about these charges & their publication here. It has roused the town for the Judge; & I also wrote to Alexandra asking Mr. Churchill to return. Mrs. Churchill spent the evening with me, she is an uncommonly nice little woman & took just right my running across & asking not to come to dinner. She staid till after 9. I turned in decently early & got to sleep after 1 a.m. A high gale & clouds of dust all day. . . .

Thursday 8th. I was out in the morning & chanced on a really pretty little oxidized silver Paris Dragée box which I filled properly & sent around to Miss Sherman with some very prettily iced cakes I had Chung make for her refreshment table. No Mail. I stepped in a moment each at Mrs. Lewis's & Mrs. Churchill's. The Judge was here at breakfast & dinner; &

at 7 I went with him, the Lewises, the Churchills & the A. M. Smiths to the Church which was very prettily dressed with evergreens & flowers—real—on the altar. All the school children sat in reserve seats at the front, the rest of us anywhere—& the church was packed, everyone going as Miss Sherman is herself a favorite here & Mr. Clark well liked. The bride came in at 8 & the ceremony was smoothly gone through, the babies kindly keeping quiet. After little talks with some of the many people in the church whom we knew, we adjourned to the Churchills till a little past 9 when we walked round to the Shermans, where everything was very nicely got up with Chinese lanterns from the trees as there was no moon—porches enclosed & carpeted, pretty refreshments attended to by the Bashford ladies & by Miss Dunning.

Mrs. Clark herself was looking well in a [. . .] silk tulle relieved by a pattern of old gold & her white veil well put on. Both she & Mr. Clark looked content & happy; the genuine good will of all toward them was evident & created a pleasant atmosphere to be in. Some of the Post people were there, including the Wilcoxes—Miss W. in a short brown woolen walking suit & old brown straw round hat. Everyone else had on their best—a very moderate best with some of course but all had done their part to fête the occasion. The presents were really good & plentiful. When we came back, the Smiths turned in at the Churchills; the Lewises went on to their house & Judge Silent turned in at ours for a little to talk over the evening. I had a new bonnet for the occasion made by Miss Watson[5] & trimmed chiefly with my pet "Fernian" feathers[6]—it was a success, even the Judge saying it was "very nice.". . .

Saturday 10th. I went up to see Mrs. Ogier & Mrs. Buffum in the morning—both sick; & Mrs. Levy called here in the afternoon. The mail brought me letters from Mother, Frank & Mrs. Palmer. Judge Silent staid on a while after meals—he is very much worn & tired. Besides home letters I wrote to Mrs. Silent by the afternoon mail. Mr. Sherman called in the evening. Day almost hot. . . .

Monday 12th. No letters for me, but a satisfying telegram from Father to the Judge about piano[7] & burns & evidently on the eve of leaving for Washington, dated 11th. The Judge took breakfast & dinner here, but hurried off having a suit in chambers & lots of other things. During the day I called on Mrs. Lewis & Mrs. Smith & started to tell Mrs. Ogier goodbye—she leaves by Black Cañon tomorrow—but meeting her with Mrs. Buffum on her way to my house, we all turned in at Mrs. Churchill's & clubbed visits there. Windy.

Tuesday 13th. A furious wind & sand—or rather disintegrated granite—storm raged from about 4 a.m. till past sunset. I thought several times that the house would give way before it; it was cold too so I had to keep low oak fires in the stoves (fortunately ours didn't smoke). Of course I didn't stir out. Judge Silent managed to get up for meals. I had a letter from Mother—Apr. 1—& wrote to her & to Father. The wind made me seasick & fit for nothing. Heavy frost during night. . . .

Thursday 15th. Pleasant letter of the 3 from Mother. I went down to see Mrs. Lewis for a while. Mr. & Mrs. A. M. Smith made a short call in the evening. Judge Silent came up to meals & again about 9 p.m. with a despatch of the 14th from Father in Washington. It was to Mr. Lewis & had just arrived & said in substance that they, the citizens here, need give themselves no further concern as everything was being done. We took it as the initial note of victory & were glad accordingly.

Friday 16th. Judge Silent came up to breakfast & dinner & gave me a letter he had had from Father to read. I went across for a while & sat with Mrs. Churchill in the Fitch house which the Churchills have bought & are busy getting into order. After dinner I went up & made Mrs. Will Bashford a short visit. She has been ordered "inside" by Dr. Ainsworth & goes as soon as she can be moved. Dr. McKee called in the evening. High winds all day & driving clouds.

Saturday 17th. Wrote to Mother. Fussed over closets & drawers. Judge Silent came up to meals. We had a lovely Xmas scene at sunset, about the most effective snow picture I have seen here for as the snow followed a rain everything was coated & the driving rack of grey clouds pierced by the sun lit the whole up with real beauty—which our bay window commanded. . . .

Monday 19th (Charley's 29th birthday). Usual morning. In the afternoon I went across to Mrs. Churchill's where I found Mrs. Bean & where Mrs. Smith joined us, & we all helped Mrs. Churchill sew her dining room carpet. Miss Wilcox, who had been at our house to get me to go driving with her, called & staid quite a time—there was a regular buzz of women's chatter as Mrs. St. James came in too, but we finished the carpet. Besides coming up to meals the Judge was up for a moment at 4, Miss McClintock having told him I had a telegram [from] Father, [dated] N. Y. 17th & which said: "Back from Washington well satisfied; return there next. Tell Judge give no weight to publications. Tell Roland will attend to Indian business. All business well in hand now."

Naturally this telegram gave both Judge Silent & me great satisfaction (Roland means Genl. Wilcox). I let Thor out at about 6 o'clock a.m., as he made signs that he wanted to shoot cats. I was rather worried that he didn't come back but supposed he had gone for a run on the hills with "Pariah" & was quite taken aback when Friedrichs express stopped at the door with Thor tied behind! The Black Cañon stage had stalled five miles out of town & the driver had come back for fresh horses & harness. Friedrichs took out the latter & recognized Thor who was following the stage—to find Frank & Father I suppose as he always had watched that stage since they left. So he brought him back for which I was really grateful.

Tuesday 20th. Morning usual routine at home. In the afternoon, I made a short call on Mrs. Lewis & then up to Mrs. Churchill's where I helped her & Mrs. Smith with the parlor carpet. Finished Mdme. Remusat's Memoirs[8] in the evening. The Judge came up to meals. Glorious pale gold sunset. . . .

Thursday 22nd. Was over at Mrs. Churchill's for a while in the morning. The Judge came up to read me a letter he had had from Mr. Alexander, the substance of which he thought I had best telegraph Father which I did. I heard from Father & from Mother—8th & 9th. Owing to the storm blocked conditions of the railroad these are the first letters I've had in a week. The afternoon was so I had a headache & staid in. Judge Silent came up to meals. Mr. Blake called to receive a letter from Father which had come enclosed to me. Went up to see Mrs. Bean after dinner.

Friday 23rd. Letter of 11th from Mother. Sally not well. I went across to see Mrs. Churchill, but as there was nothing special I could do, I went on up to see Mrs. Buffum; & after breakfast, as there was a stiff breeze only, I sallied out & made *nine* visits—everybody in but two. The Judge came up to breakfast & dinner & brought me a lot of strawberries—came in the morning's *mail* from Wickenburg—they tasted good & fresh.

Saturday 24th. Was at Mrs. Churchill's a good deal through the day.[9] The Judge came up to meals. Just as we were finishing dinner there was an alarm of [some] size on the Nob side of the Plaza & he hurried off, coming back in the evening for two minutes to tell me about it. A chimney caught through carelessness, but as the wind had dropped it was quickly put out, all the town helping.

Sunday 25th. I had a telegram of the 24th N. Y. from Father, saying "Telegram concerning Alexander most opportune. Arranging with Piano. Everything going well." The Judge took breakfast here & came up again to write a despatch which I sent at the evening hour.

Monday 26th. Went over in the afternoon & helped the "Rebeccas" set the supper table at Curtis Hall. Mrs. Churchill & some six others were there; I had volunteered a contribution for the supper, too. In the evening I went to the ball with the Churchills—all the ladies had insisted & as it wasn't "select," like the last, I was afraid my not going might offend them. They had a full house & quite a pretty party. The Martins & Dr. McKee were the only ones from the Post. I got Judge Silent to bring me home before the supper, he returning of course. The Judge came up as usual to meals. Lovely moonlight. Middle of the day more than warm. . . .

Wednesday 28th. Felt tired & staid in—also hoping for a telegram as the bond on the Tuscumbia will be up Saturday so there is another pull of suspense going on & we haven't heard a word about it from the East. Mrs. Lewis & Mrs. Bean called in the afternoon. Judge Silent came up to breakfast & dinner & staid on a little time after the latter. Just at 8, Miss McClintock gave him a despatch for me, which he brought me & after we read it hurried back to get her to send off the answer at once, as it was from Father asking the "latest hour" on the Tuscumbia; after some trouble he got her to send it off & then came up & told me it had gone, staying a few minutes to discuss our present business situation & its outlook.

Thursday 29th. The first eastern mail in five days got in this morning. It has been blocked by the snow in the Sierras & by it I had letters from Mother, Washington 14, [from] Father, N. Y. 17, from Frank at Missoula & from Nelly at Atlantic City. Father's letter was very encouraging as regards the Judge's case & not discouraging as regards business. Mother's letter was chiefly about the pleasant position she & Father felt they had in Washington. The Judge also had a letter from Father which he shared with me when he came up to breakfast. In the afternoon I called on Mrs. Clark & on Mrs. Lewis, both in—& on Mrs. Aram, out. The Judge came up to dinner also & staid on a bit giving me some business items to add to my Santa Fe letter to Father. Later in the evening he came in for a moment for me to write off a telegram to Father about the Tuscumbia's rich ores. Cloudy & warm day. . . .

Saturday May 1st. Letter of 20th from Father giving good business encouragement. Followed at 11 by a telegram asking to have an extension procured on the Tuscumbia of a fortnight & new deeds made out to "Geo. [W.?] Bower." The Judge went right to work at it & though it looked impossible at first, succeeded before night in obtaining the extension & new deeds for two thirds, but required a spurt of very hard work on his part & an unexpected combination of circumstances working with him to accomplish it. He was up at meals as usual & in the evening with last instructions to me as this business takes him out to the Bradshaw Basin tomorrow.

When I went across to see Mrs. Churchill in the morning I found that I was rather expected to go to the Children's May Party over at Curtis Hall, so I went at one o'clock with Mrs. Churchill & Miss Bashford. All the children of both the Public schools & the Sisters' school were there—& nearly all the mothers & even many gentlemen. The children had a substantial collation to which we contributed a ham & a big cake—the Fort band to play whilst they danced & romped & swung in the trees. They all seemed to enjoy it. I met lots of ladies I knew & went about talking to them. We came away toward four & made Mrs. Buffum a visit. (In the evening there was a party for the older scholars & public generally, to which I didn't think it necessary to go). The day was actually hot & for the first time since last October we had no fire in the house even at night.

Sunday 2nd. I dined at the Churchills. No letters in the morning's mail. The Judge left 5 a.m. for the Prince.

Monday 3rd. I was entirely surprised to see Judge Silent a little before 9 in the morning. He came up to get me to send off a despatch saying "New deeds in bank, no increase in price, etc." & then went right down town again to try a case "in chambers." He got back last night at midnight, having done the whole seventy miles, all rough ones & including the crossing of three mountain ranges, in one day when neither he nor his mule are in training, which isn't bad. So inside forty-eight hours he has worked a business tour de force & obtained an extension on the Tuscumbia which looked impossible at the outset & necessitated this forced march. Now if all is worked as smoothly at the N. Y. end, things in business will take another & and upward start.

I had a pleasant little letter from Mother written on the Putnam, off Stony Point. She was with Charley who was taking supplies to the Light houses up the Hudson. Judge Silent came up to meals & was by no means as tired as he had the right to be. Mrs. Lewis came up in the evening. Day warm. . . .

Wednesday 5th. I was over at Mrs. Churchill's a moment in the morning & in the early evening I went to ask Mrs. Otis, Miss Dunning & Mrs. Wollenberg to dinner here on Friday—all accepted. The Judge came up early to breakfast & brought me a photograph of his house—a real pretty house. He came up to dinner, too.

Thursday 6th May. Had a good business letter of the 24th from Father. Indoors all day except when I went across for a moment to see Mrs. Churchill about lunch for the travellers tomorrow. The Judge came up in the early morning & cleaned Mr. Cordis's gun & took it back to him—it felt like the hall at Pocaho to see again a man working at a gun all in pieces. He was up to breakfast & dinner, staying a little to give me my A.D.C. [aide-de-camp] instructions how to manage in his absence (of over two weeks probably) & who to see if telegrams requiring action came; & getting in return instructions from me not to shirk eating at the proper hours & to be sure & bring me the prettiest wild flowers they saw. Yesterday morning he brought me in a great bunch of white-scarlet ones with sage green leaves when he came in from his morning ride, on which Thor had refused to accompany him, & which I mixed with those Harry Thibodo had brought me Sunday, so that the parlor was all brightened by their "chere presence." Cool enough for a fire in the evening for there has been a high wind for the last two days.

Friday 7th. Judge Silent & Mr. Churchill got off at 4¾ a.m., in a double C. spring buggy drawn by a strong pair of brown horses whose powers they tested in their last trip to Mohave. They expect to reach Mineral Park Sunday afternoon by making long drives. Pleasant letter from Mother, postmarked 26th but evidently written a day or two earlier.

Went across for a while to Mrs. Churchill's in the morning & met Miss Bashford there & asked her & Mrs. Burmister to dine with me Monday. She accepted for both. Mrs. Churchill, Mrs. Otis, Miss Dunning & Mrs. Wollenberg dined with me; staying on till 9, talking & gay all the time & seeming to enjoy themselves. Mrs. Carpenter's funeral took place today, many of the ladies going, fixing what flowers they could get. She was "Buttercup" here last winter & left a girl baby only nine days old, which is to be taken to her people. She died at the Hospital where Dr. Ainsworth & Sister Mary had charge of her, so everything possible was done for her.[10] Had a letter from McLean at Shanghai.

Saturday 8th. Went out on some errands, including asking Mrs. St. James, Mrs. Lewis & Mrs. Smith of Chicago to dine here Monday. They all accepted; also asked Mr. & Mrs. Lewis to a family dinner here today but they refused; so I went over & asked Mrs. Churchill to come & share some sweetbreads & asparagus a rancher had brought me in. Sewed in the intervals of visitors. Mrs. Rodenberg, Mrs. Burmister & Miss Bashford, Col. & Mrs. La Motte all calling—the last two full of questions about the neighborhood of Dresden as he is ordered to Carlsbad [in Austria-Hungary] on sick leave. After dinner Mrs. Lewis & Mrs. Smith, then Dr. McKee called—they leaving pretty early, but he staying on [till] his usual time. I asked him to dine here Wednesday as he leaves in about ten days. After he left, Mrs. Churchill & I settled the list for a few more dinners & lunches—sorting the ladies—& she showed me a new afghan stitch. Mary & Thor saw her home 9½. The day was right hot.

Sunday 9th. Went up in the morning to ask the Buffums here to meet Dr. McKee on Wednesday—stayed a while helping Mrs. Buffum settle her fireplace fixings into place. I dined with Mrs. Lewis, coming home at 7.

Monday 10th. Went over to Mrs. Churchill's for a while in the morning. Mrs. Burmister, Miss Bashford, Mrs. Lewis, Mrs. Chicago Smith & Mrs. St. James dined with me, staying on till after eight. The dinner went off smoothly.

Tuesday 11th. I changed things round in the house & did scraps. Mrs. Martin called in the morning with her baby—a fine girl blonde. In the afternoon I went across to Mrs. Churchill's where I staid a while & met Mrs. Lewis, Mrs. Levy, Miss Wilcox & Mrs. Fr. Smith—the last two had been at my house before coming across to Mrs. Churchill's, Mrs. Smith wanting to show me how her baby—a brunette—had improved. In the evening Mrs. Wells & Miss Banghart[11] called. Windy. Dr. McKee called & asked me to dine with him on Saturday.

Wednesday 12th. Went out & did a little shopping—fixed things in the house. Dr. McKee, Mrs. Churchill & Mrs. Buffum came to dinner at 5. Mr. Buffum failed at the last moment on account of some large orders from the Little Colorado which needed to be attended to at once. I don't think Dr. McKee was very much bored; the others were amused. Mrs. Buffum had a really good Paris gown on, olive green & old gold brocade.

Thursday 13th. Letter of 1st from Mother; she was at the Everett [hotel in New York City] & said "situation cleared now & business going well," but no points, no details. Sally was up in the Catskill Mts. & doing well. This is

Margaret Bashford Burmister and her son Robert, c. 1877.
(Courtesy of the Sharlot Hall Museum/Library Archives, Prescott, Ariz.,
photo #PO 223p.)

the first time I've heard [from Mother] in five days. Went over to Mrs. Churchill's for a moment in the morning & she asked me to dinner. Mrs. Clark & Mrs. Otis called in the afternoon. Had a quietly pleasant dinner with Mrs. C. & afterwards we walked down to Goldwaters & chose the worsteds for an afghan I'm crotcheting. I came in by 7. Mr. Lewis called. I reported to Judge Silent about business this morning.

Friday 14th May. Had a letter from Sally, May 3, up in the Catskills, both she & the baby were well. Also a nice letter from the Judge—Mineral Park 12th—giving me some points to report on to Father & saying he expected to be back here next Friday. Fussed around rearranging the storeroom. Today the extended bond on the Tuscumbia expires & I can't help being somewhat anxious as neither by letter or telegram do I hear a word from the owners to again extend the time. Quiet indoor morning & in the afternoon I made ten visits—on foot—with Mrs. Churchill & on both sides of the creek; & I asked five ladies to lunch here Monday. Pleasant weather.

Saturday 15th. Quiet indoors day. Mrs. Thibodo & Mrs. Ellis called in the afternoon. Mrs. Churchill brought me a pretty little bunch of flowers to wear at Dr. McKee's dinner to which I drove—ambulance—with Mr. & Mrs. Lewis & Mrs. Bean at six o'clock—the hour for dinner but the doctor's cook, he told me, got on the rampage because Miss Wilcox made some suggestions & didn't let us have dinner till 7¾. When it came it was well cooked & *nine* courses. Miss W. had arranged a beautiful centre piece of gorgeous wild flowers which she had sent mounted orderlies out to gather. They were really a pleasure to look at. I didn't mind waiting for dinner as there were several society small talkers present (& as I had taken the precaution of five o'clock tea & solid bread & butter at home, having heard that Dr. McKee's "Mary" had a temper I thought she would probably be unpunctual) so the time slipped along easily for me, but poor Dr. McKee & Dr. Ainsworth, too, were on thorns visibly as it was their dine[r] d'adieu [farewell dinner] & things going crooked seemed a bigger thing to them than it would to a woman. In fact I think all the women present were rather amused at seeing the perplexities of the two autocratic doctors when it came to confronting their cook & managing their bachelor household.

Col. & Mrs. Martin, Miss Wilcox, Mrs. Fr. Smith, Lt. Palfrey, the Lewises, Mrs. Bean & I were the guests. Dr. McKee took me in. We all, except the exasperated hosts, had an amusing time; & as the mules reared & nearly upset the ambulance when we village folks started home, Dr. Ainsworth drove in with us & saw us each safely deposited at our doors—11 p.m. Stingingly cold night.

In the morning a telegram from Father of the 14th came saying "Business successful, but delay in Tuscumbia caused by Alexander claiming benefit of extension"—so I sent [to] Mr. Lewis first, then Mr. Buffum & Mr. Gobin[12] & after some talk they agreed to wait till Tuesday for the money to come, which I telegraph[ed] Father at 1 p.m., thinking he might manage it as the extension under which Alex. claimed—without a shadow of a right—had lapsed. At any rate it was the best I could do. . . .

Monday 17th (Frank's 25th birthday). I was up early & arranged a lot of wild flowers Harry Thibodo had brought me late yesterday. Wrote to Frank; to Sally & to Judge Silent. Saw Mr. Gosper who called about Globe City's requisition for arms. At 11½ the ladies I had asked to lunch arrived—Mrs. Kelly, Miss Stevens [Stephens], young Mrs. Rush, Mrs. Wells & Mrs. Churchill. They were a harmonious set so everything went off smoothly & pleasantly. Mrs. Churchill & I arranged to go wild violet hunting with Mrs. K & her sister tomorrow morning. Just as the last of the ladies was leaving, Mr. Rutherford called. He came in from the Prince on account of a touch of mountain fever & has been staying for some days at the Sisters' Hospital & taking lunches out at the Wilcoxes, so he isn't fearfully ill.

After dinner Mrs. Lewis & Mrs. Churchill called to say that Mrs. Lewis had taken the barouche, which has returned from Tucson, for tomorrow afternoon to make visits at the Post—that they expected me to go with them & to write & put off our violet excursion till Wednesday mg. I sent off a letter to Mother via Santa Fe. Miss Dunning called in the evening & made me quite a visit. Harry Thibodo brought me in a magnificent [stalk] of heavy scented white lily-shaped flowers with about 30 flowers on it. I had a nice letter from Frank & two from Mother. . . .

Wednesday 19th. Went in the morning with Mrs. Churchill, Mrs. Kelly & Miss Stephens for a violet hunt up a rocky creek with water, which Thor made the most of. Had a pleasant time though tired some with the 3 mile walk. Dined at Mrs. C., meeting Mr. & Mrs. A. M. Smith. Had a very nice letter from Judge Silent in the evening mail from Mohave. Fine sunset.

Thursday 20th May. I went up to ask after Miss Dunning, who was taken ill in school yesterday, & staid a while with Mrs. Churchill on coming down the hill. Mrs. Churchill dined & spent the evening with me. The event, public, of the day was Mr. Gough's funeral; he dropped dead Tuesday evening.[13] As he was well known here having been head clerk at Hdqts. since the times of Genl. Crook & the Apache war, was an Odd Fellow & a Mason & was liked, everyone turned out. The shops without exception were closed during the two hours of the funeral; all the Masons & Odd Fellows walked, the Post sent a good ambulance—hearse—about thirty vehicles followed & the Post band led the procession, playing really well. . . .

Saturday 22nd. I was out for a little in the morning, asking after Miss Dunning & stopping for a small clack with Mrs. Churchill & in the evening I staid a while on the Churchill's porch. Rest of the day indoors, where it is pleasantly cool though in the sun very hot. . . .

Tuesday 25th. Went over & asked Mrs. Churchill to breakfast with me, then went down & called on Mrs. Lewis. Mrs. C. came to breakfast & we sewed on some toilet covers of hers till 2¾ when we saw Mr. Churchill drive by in the buggy. Of course she went right home. Judge Silent came up at 5, tired from his journey & from the douche of disagreeable things which had been poured over him since his arrival, but on the whole benefited by the two weeks in Mineral Park & pleased at the way all Mohave Co[unty] behaved to him. He staid a bit after dinner & came back later in the evening & staid a decent time, talking over his journey north, flowers etc. Dr. McKee called also in the evening & Mrs. Churchill & Mrs. Smith each stepped across & gave me some wild flowers.

Wednesday 26th. Had a nice letter from Mother. The Judge come up to meals—with his Prescott face on—& after dinner he staid on a while into Mrs. Buffum's visit. We had a good telegram from Father in the afternoon saying the Judge's case had been thoroughly investigated by the authorities who were writing an answer to an extra point raised—that he was entirely satisfied with the condition of the affair & would telegraph about business "soon;" this N. Y. 25th, but he had evidently been in Washington. I made four visits in the neighborhood & was back in time to see the two Mrs. Rush[es],[14] the elder of whom came to say goodbye as she is "going inside" for a while. Some others called while I was out, & after dinner, Mrs. Buffum, who staid on all evening, & Mrs. Kelly & her sister called. Ice last night & the morning so cold I had a fire in the parlor. I had a really bad headache.

Thursday 27th. Was out a while in the morning & called on Mrs. Lewis; rest of the day pottered about indoors tired from my headache. Mrs.

Raible[15] called in the afternoon. Judge Silent came up to breakfast & to dinner, staying on a right decent time after each—it's very nice to have him back again—& returning in the evening to introduce a Mr. Stevenson [Stephenson],[16] who was in the Judge's office in San Jose once upon a time & who after a trial of Phoenix is changing up to Mineral Park where he will be partner of Mr. A. E. Davis.[17] As they were leaving I chanced to ask Mr. Stevenson if he was provided against the cold night ride in the buckboard & finding he was not offered him some of our "travelling quilts," which he will come for in the morning. Weather still cool.

Friday 28th. Pleasant letter of 17th from Mother. Mr. Stevenson came early for the quilts & made a short call. Mrs. St. James called in the afternoon. Judge Silent came up to meals, but being busy over his answer to the last Eagan-Campbell attack didn't stay on. Both the Judge & I were a little stirred by these last papers & the village is very much. . . .

Sunday 30th. Note of 18th from Mother—she had made all arrangements to spend the summer at the Pavillion, New Brighton—Charley & Sally with her—which will be very nice for Nelly. Of business she only said it "was going solidly well." How I do wish she [would] risk the mails to give me some details. The Judge took breakfast with me, but dined of course with the Lewises.

Monday 31st (Mother's birthday). I was busy all day, going out early to see the dressmaker & do a little fruitless shopping; then sending round some nameless little trees which arrived by express for Father—no letter, no directions with them, but coming from Washington via Tucson. No one knows what they are, but all are glad to get them & I have to distribute them as we have no yard. Then the Judge came up with his reply for me to copy as he had a stunning headache & yet wanted to get it off by this day's mail. I had it finished by 2½ when he came up for it, showing me another letter he had sent on to the Atty. Genl. with it—& stopping a moment to talk with Mrs. Churchill who had come over to spend the afternoon with me & show me how to put my afghan together.

In the evening I called on the Burmisters—out—Mrs. Buffum, Mrs. Smith & Mrs. Lewis—in all—& was home before dark. The Judge came up to meals, hurrying back after breakfast. Just as we finished dinner Mr. Lewis brought "Jacques"[18] to look at the little trees & took the Judge off with him for a smoke on his porch. "Of course" I wrote to Mother. The morning's mail brought me a note from Frank—21st at Deer Lodge, M[ontana] T[erritory], where he was waiting further telegraphic orders before starting off on a hunt after deserters through the mining camps. Weather cool & pleasant indoors, but beginning to get hot in the sun.

Tuesday June 1st. Nice letter of 21st from Mother in Washington, D. C., saying that everything there was "most satisfactory" about the Judge & would be "all right" when his 2nd answer got there, "the case having been thoroughly studied to his great advantage." She was too hurried to give details. She & Father were to stop a day over in Phila. with Alexander pere [Sr.] & she says "business is all working well." Dr. Morton & his wife—just married—were at the "Arlington" [hotel]. Judge Silent came up to give me a telegram about the Tuscumbia to send off just as I received the mail, so I had the pleasure of sharing my good news with him as I read it.

Busy sewing & attending to those little plants—several people came for them & I sent lots away, too. Judge Silent came up to meals & staid on a while after each. In the [afternoon] Miss Dunning, Mrs. Smith, Mrs. Churchill & Mrs. Lewis called, Mrs. Lewis spending the evening with me. Hot day outdoors but pleasant in the house. The local papers are having vigorous articles against both Campbell & Eagan.

Wednesday 2nd. Unpleasant telegram of 1st from Father, saying in substance that the retrieved business situation was probably destroyed by Penn's answering Grey's telegraphic request to know if the Tuscumbia was still for sale; that Piano's action hinged largely on business & asking [for] an immediate answer "yes or no," if he could rely on no communication from here except through him & to answer halfrate. I sent it down to the Judge & when he came up to breakfast we arranged & sent off the answer—of course in my name: "Yes. Your request will be strictly complied with." This will reach them tomorrow & yesterday's explanatory telegram about Grey's request they must already have. I know so little of what is doing in our business east that I can form no opinion.

Mrs. Churchill spent the afternoon with me working on Frank's afghan. Just after dinner Col. & Mrs. La Motte & their boys stopped by & asked me to go driving with them which I did—way out the Mohave road & saw lots of pretty wild flowers, specially the caroubier colored cactus. Got home before 8 & soon after, Judge Silent, who had taken breakfast & dinner here of course, called, chiefly to see if the La Mottes had said anything about my going to the ball at the Post tomorrow for by some odd chance no invitation has come to me & one to Father only came late Monday night & in view of the circulation through town of the Campbell-Eagan pamphlet with Eagan's pettily personal attack on Father this is an "awkward incident."

I have said nothing about it & shall get off an excuse tomorrow & not speak of it till after the ball as it might make an unpleasant feeling amongst our friends & among Judge Silent's as he also has received none though everyone else in the Court House received theirs last Friday morning. Everyone in town is asked except just us two & all the cards ask "please reply" so it ought to have been noticed when no reply came from either of us. The Judge staid on & spent the evening with me. I had a pleasant time in spite of the background of unpleasant business situation & doubts as to the issue in Washington which are of course very present to both of us, but which we kept clear of. The day was the hottest we have had this year, but not uncomfortable in the house. The evening & night deliciously cool.

Thursday 3rd. I was over at Mrs. Churchill's twice during the day & on the last time told her I wasn't going to the party & why. She was astonished & I fancy Mr. Churchill told Col. Martin for he dashed up to the house on horseback just after rehearsal, asked why they had no "reply" & when I answered because I'd had no invitation [he] said it was some outrageous mistake & made full apologies saying he would come for me himself if I couldn't get ready to go late with the Churchills. It was already nearly 8— & cornering where I had to be huffy or go, which latter of course I then did, going with the Churchills at 10 & returning with them at 2 a.m. Everybody was there & it was a successful party.

Col. Price took me in to supper where I sat with Miss Wilcox & Grace— just back from school & "toujours Grace" [she is still the same old Grace]. Genl. W. came up & spoke to me when I came in but not again, as under the circumstances of Capt. Eagan's pamphlet & its circulation here in town he should have been particularly careful to do. I didn't dance & felt thoroughly hors de mon milieu [out of place]. Just before I left Dr. McKee in talking to me asked "why isn't Silent here"—so I told him & left him a bewildered & angry man.

Judge Silent came up to meals & again for a little while in the evening before I went out to the Post; (in the morning I sent a business telegram to Father about a week's extension which has been obtained on the Black Warrior & later received two on business—things for us to do & forward from here—from Father dated 3 & received 4th for which date I mean this).

Friday 4th. I sent off & received the telegrams which I put wrongly under yesterday's date. The "wind" of the last two days culminated in a roaring sandstorm which only dropped with the sun. I was tired with the party & the wind & tired out with business for the situation is very trying &

strained here & the telegrams from the East are no help. Judge Silent came up to meals, but hardly staid any. I spent the afternoon with Mrs. Lewis. There was a performance at the theatre in the evening to which I sent Mary. Night cool & resting. . . .

Sunday 6th. Quiet morning. Judge Silent came up to breakfast & staid a little while after talking over the present aspect of business—that is, what we know of it and the report in the Phoenix "Herald" from Washington that Father was to resign & go into mining in N. Y. & the portée [impact] of both things. I haven't the slightest inkling as to whether there is or is not any foundation for the "Herald" report. At 4, I went up to Mrs. Bean's where I had [a] quietly agreeable dinner with her & her three pretty girls & Dr. Ainsworth. I came home at 7, stopping a bit at the different porches which were all more or less filled a la Sunday evening. Dr. McKee called to say goodbye, as he leaves on Tuesday morning.

Monday 7th. I went across to Mrs. Churchill's for a while in the morning, the rest of the day sewed & wrote to Frank till 4, when Mrs. Smith & towards 5 came Mr. Smith & Mrs. Bowers—all of whom I had asked to dine with me—& when the Judge joined us we had dinner, which went off smoothly. Soon after it, the gentlemen went down town to learn what news there was from the Chicago convention. The ladies staid on till after 8. Judge Silent came up for a few minutes after 9—Miss McClintock having staid late in the office—to give me the latest Chicago news. He had been up at breakfast of course; Court began today. The wind blew all day, almost a gale.

Tuesday 8th. No California mail & the telegraph down—so we "in outer dark remain." The Judge came up to breakfast & to dinner. Mrs. Churchill was in for a while. The rest of the day I worked on Frank's afghan & wrote letters. Both the condition of the Judge's case & our own business matters are—at this end at least—in such a state of tension that I can't settle to reading.

Wednesday 9th. Letters of the 27 & 28 from Mother—everyone well & she "contented about business." Also a letter of the 29th from Frank who was back at Fort Missoula, having caught the deserters he had been sent after. I saw Mrs. Churchill for a moment, then went down on the "piazza"—as Mary insists in calling it—for a bit of shopping; rest of the day sewed & made lamp shades for the Churchills & for us. Mrs. Smith came in a moment to ask me to go with her & some others tomorrow to make our party calls at the Post—of course I said yes.

Judge Silent came up to meals, very tired & worn, for hearing nothing from Father either on business or on his affaire leaves him unable to answer the hosts of questions that pour in on him now [that] the last extension on the "Warrior" is closing in; & Mr. Estill reporting every-where in town that he has received a telegram from Eagan telling him that Devens[19] assures Eagan that on the 20th "Judge Silent will be given the option of resigning or being dismissed." It hardly seems possible that the Atty. Genl. can have said such a thing before the last papers he asked for from Judge Silent have even arrived in Washington, but Mr. Estill asserts it positively & it raised a fresh storm for the Judge so that his friends decided to telegraph Father—officially—through Mr. Lewis, asking him to look into it & report. Naturally all this adds to the disagreeable sus-pense the Judge is in & makes a very trying situation & the village is too small & too quiet to afford any change.

The news of [James A.] Garfield's nomination got here this morning. There is a very decided sense of satisfaction that the third term project was balked, but not a ray of enthusiasm for Garfield who is accepted as "doing well enough." The high winds have blown day & night for over three days now, making the cool mountain climate one reads of, so that light woolen dresses & one half the doors & windows closed are comfort-able.

Thursday 10th. Indoor morning. Went with Mrs. Smith, Mrs. Lewis & Mrs. Churchill, in spite of the sandstorm, to make our party calls at the Post. Called on everyone of the garrison ladies including Mrs. Dr. Smith[20] & found Mrs. Buffum & Mrs. Bean doing the same. Naturally in such weather they were all in; *[one line unreadable].* In the early evening I called on Mrs. Buffum, Mrs. Bowers, Mrs. Burmister & Miss [Lizzie] Bashford & stopped in a moment on Mrs. Churchill's porch as I came in. Judge Silent came up to meals—a little less worn than yesterday, but still very tired—being busy with court he didn't stop any. The gale which has blown for the last four days & two nights was a ferocious sandstorm today & blew itself out by sunset leaving us a quiet & very cool night. Business telegram from Father, 9th, saying he was trying [to] harmonize things & hoped to send good telegram soon.

Friday 11th. Letter from Father of the 26th & one of the 29th from Mother, both cheerful as to business, but for the future only—also Father is confident about the favorable verdict in the Judge's case; also a pleasant letter of the 15th May from McLean at Shanghai. Indoors morning; in the afternoon, I made four visits, including Mrs. Alexander[21] & Mrs. Houghtelin.[22] Judge Silent came up to meals, but hardly staid any.

The Grand Jury brought in its report last night &, amongst other things, passed very strong resolutions endorsing Judge Silent & condemning the Eagan-Campbell pamphlet as "meriting the contempt of all just men." As this jury was composed of all the leading substantial citizens here, & examined witnesses in the matter, its resolutions are worth having. I spent part of the evening on Mrs. Churchill's porch. There was no wind. This was the last day of the extension granted on the "Warrior" so we watched anxiously for a telegram, but none came.

Saturday 12th. I spent part of the morning & afternoon in helping Mrs. Churchill make a Queen Anne table to hold her illustrated books & magazines & in sorting the latter. In the evening I went down to Mrs. Lewis's for a while. Campbell's telegraph (printed in the democratic paper) "by request" against the Judge & the "Prince Mine" riled me, though the same paper had a strong editorial in favor of the Grand Jury's action on Judge Silent's case. The Judge came up to meals, & staid a tiny bit after dinner. . . .

Monday 14th. I was indoors all day with the exception of a short visit to Mrs. Lewis in the evening. Mrs. Levy & Mrs. Churchill called here. The Judge came up to meals but barely staid long enough to eat them, as "cases" & "juries out" were on his mind. I had letters from Father, June 2 & 3, all on business & from Sally June 2nd, all baby & with the photo of little Jack who is a very nice looking baby indeed.

Tuesday 15th. Nice long letter from Dr. Jameson, written at Portsmouth, May 25th (Queen's birthday). He has been having a lovely time off with Prince Edward of Saxe-Weimar who has been reviewing Volunteers & staying round in great charming country houses—in one of which the Doctor had the good luck to have the Duke of Cambridge for a patient. Edie has passed her examination at the [. . .] school & goes up to Cambridge in the Fall! Indoor morning finishing small afghan for Jack. In the afternoon went to Mrs. Churchill's for a moment, then on to Mrs. Wollenberg's where I "spent the afternoon," getting home at 4 to find a telegram from Father, dated Washington 14th, saying the Judge's case would be concluded on the arrival of his papers which were hourly expected & asking exact name, etc. of Mr. Murphy's brother[23] that he might finish that up at the War Dept. Judge Silent came up as usual & staid on a bit after dinner.

In the evening Mrs. Lewis, Mrs. Coles Bashford, Mrs. Buffum, Mr. and Mrs. Churchill & Mr. Haskell called, the latter only back yesterday from the Southern Indians & San Francisco, & wanting to see me about "Yonkers" which he thinks he can place in London, wanting Father to retain his interest in it. Also Mr. Murphy was in & out several times on his brother's business. The day was hot out of doors but comfortable inside. Mr. Richardson[24] called about the Gray Eagle. . . .

Thursday 17th. Short letter of 5th from Mother, on business. Indoor day for me on account of the heat & headache, but in the evening went across to the Churchill porch for half an hour. Mr. Haskell called during the day for a moment in connection with the Neahr business & Mrs. Buffum & her niece called in the evening. I had a telegram from Father in Washington, 16th, asking to have the fact [of] the Eagan telegram about the Judge's removal proved as he denies it, saying that the Judge's last letter was "satisfactory" & "the delay will be brief now."

The Judge came up to breakfast & to dinner, telling me of Dr. A's clean bill of health verdict, and again in the evening for a few moments to tell me of the splendidly rich strike in the "lowest tunnel" of the "Prince," which proves all & more than all, that Father & he have claimed for the mine. This news was telegraphed Father to N. Y. The flag was flying from the Court House & from many private buildings & the band from the Fort played on the Plaza from 7 to 9 p.m. in honor of Bunker Hill. A good day.

Friday 18th. Nice letter of the 6th from Fanny Dart at Northampton, Mass. Three months today since Father left! The Judge came up to meals & staid on a little while. Last night's primary Democratic meeting went for Hugo Richards as against Campbell. After dinner I went across & called on Mrs. Smith, coming back to receive a visit from Mrs. Burmister, Miss Bashford, Mrs. Lewis & Mrs. Churchill. While they were still here I saw Miss McClintock coming our way & knew the telegram must be important or she wouldn't come up so late—8—with it herself, so I went & met her at the gate & read it on the steps before turning in again. "Attorney Genl. has today mailed letter to Silent dismissing case against him & thoroughly sustaining the Judge. This Official. Fremont, Washington, 18th June." At which reading I was thoroughly glad.

As soon as the ladies left I hunted up Mary & sent her to the Court

House with the telegram, but she crossed the Judge on the way up so brought it back & I had the unexpected & very good pleasure of being the one to tell him—& of course gave him the telegram. The news he decided to tell only to a few tonight, making it public tomorrow. He staid a bit talking it over with me, each in our way happy & grateful at the verdict—& I specially glad that Father could do so much to bring it about. Of course, we could have fought on & conquered in the end since clear right was on Judge Silent's side, but this is quicker & the endorsement of one's own Department is better than its condemnation, even when the latter is wrongfully given. The strain has been long enough anyway, ever since the last part of February.

The Judge went back down to the Lewises where he had already promised to spend the evening. Later Mrs. Churchill stopped in on her way home from the Lewises & I told her, con permisso [with permission], & we exchanged congratulations. I didn't turn in till near 12 & had a perfect nuit blanche hearing every hour strike from the C[ourt] H[ouse] clock, but lying awake through sheer, thorough rejoicing content don't come so often but that one can easily stand it. Name & honor come so far before everything else that I hated the idea of the slur a Dept. condemnation might leave against the Judge, for people generally can't—& don't stop to see if such a verdict is justly given but accept [it] without questioning.

The day was extremely hot; the night cool, moonlight & clouds contending, & the first shower of the season coming towards morning. I let Thor go on a moonlight hunt with some of his favorites, so he had a good time, too.

Saturday 19th June. Morning quiet—wrote to Mother & to Frank. Judge Silent came up to breakfast & to dinner, staying only a moment after each as he was very busy & had court too. At 6 this morning, the "Miner" had extras out with the news of Judge Silent's vindication; & when I looked down the street the flags were flying from Democratic & Republican buildings alike—for this affair has been taken up on a broad basis both of the rights of a Territory to *some* voice in her government & a determination that Arizona shan't have "Nevada Judges;" & personally our Judge is popular in his district & everyone knows his droiture [uprightness] of character & how thoroughly he has done his legal work up here & they resent warmly this totally unfounded attack upon him. I received two more telegrams from Mother 19th & still in Washington confirming Father's despatch of yesterday.

The Judge came up for a moment in the afternoon to share a congratulatory telegram he had received from "the Frémonts" & I gave him

Mother's. He also told me there would be a serenade given him at the Court House & to Father (represented by the house & by me) here & probably to Mr. Churchill as he was so very sharply attacked in Eagan's pamphlet, so I went out & asked Mrs. Buffum, Mrs. Lewis and Mrs. Churchill—each of whom has been consistently & outspokenly for the Judge & for us through this controversy—to come down & receive the serenade & serenaders with me. Mrs. C. couldn't as she had to be on duty at home, but the others did & Mattie Evans came with her aunt [Rebecca Evans Buffum].

As the dusk fell the Court House bell rang out a peal, the anvils answered from Capitol Hill, keeping it up quite a time while the band played & splendid bonfires on the Plaza lit the whole town. The Judge spoke from the Court House steps, taking of course the large view of the subject; and was followed by Judge Rush, but I'll clip that from Monday's papers. The front of the Court House was all lit with Chinese lanterns & all the lights inside lit & the great big Court House flag still hung draped over the Judge's chambers where it had hung all day, & the Plaza was full. On leaving the Court House the band & a small portion of the crowd marched up to the Churchills where Mr. C. spoke a few words to them & then they came down to our house, serenaded, cheered Father, then Mother, then Grandfather [Benton].

The Judge, who had joined us after his serenade was over, responded in a few words in Father's behalf & asked them in—only cakes & claret. They came & such a number! But things behaved widow's cruse[25] fashion & lasted; there being plenty [of] wine left but not a crumb of cake. Mrs. Buffum went into the dining room with me & helped me do the honors, the Judge with us of course. Both the crowd & the band evidently liked being asked in. After they left Judge Silent went down town & soon after Mrs. Lewis left with Mr. Lewis, Mr. Churchill & Mr. Smith who had turned in for a moment. Mrs. Buffum staid on a while.

The band did more small serenading—to the two papers & one or two other places. The crowd was gay & had "a wee drappy in its ee,"[26] but everything went with perfect smoothness & there was no drawback at all for each one was determined it should go off rightly, & by a little past eleven the town was dead quiet & remained so all through the night.

The Democratic County convention was held today & of Yavapai's forty delegates only *two* went for Campbell & those were beholden to him, one his clerk now, the other was till lately. The convention went for Hugo Richards. The Eagan set said our telegram was a bogus one we had pretended to receive in order to influence the Convention! It did come in very appropriately. There was a Republican meeting which had been previously called for this evening & which its chairman, Probate Judge Hargrave, tried to keep to its work but they just laughed at him & adjourned. The morning's mail had brought in a great lot more of the Campbell-Eagan pamphlet with fresh affidavits tacked on from Hargrave, Blake & Hobart[27] each sustaining some special point in Eagan's statement. But in spite of all their efforts, Yavapai & Mohave counties—the Judge's District—have repudiated Campbell & outspokenly on the ground that he has misrepresented them in this matter & that they believe in Judge Silent. Man sagt [They say] that the Judge spoke well this evening. I could only hear the cheering with which he was received & repeatedly interrupted.

Sunday 20th. A good letter of the 9th from Mother, with a contented & hopeful ring all through it. The Judge came up at breakfast & staid on a decent little while after, resting in our bay window which makes a cool & sheltered "refuge" now the green blinds are up, and talking over with me our big triumph—with occasional side shoots & "skate tracks" to the small ones which follow in its wake. The rest of the day was just a still contented one to me. The day was cool indoors, piles of beautiful cumulus clouds & one heavy shower in the afternoon; a fine gold-brown sunset followed by glorious moonlight with cloudy effects on Granite Mt.

Judge Silent came up after telegraph hours with Mother's despatch of the 19th giving the full official text of Atty-Genl. Deven's letter sustaining the Judge & dismissing the case. Naturally he staid on a bit as we were both glad, satisfied & relieved at its thoroughness. The Judge both wrote and telegraphed his thanks to Father & to Mother today.

Chapter 8

Territorial Politics

June 21–November 21, 1880

Monday [June] 21st [1880]. Indoors morning, not settled down into routine yet. Mrs. Churchill came over for a little to talk over Saturday's events & in the afternoon I went with her to call on Mrs. Hargrave on whom I haven't called since early March because of their stand in this case, but now we've conquered I called, but she was out. We made some other visits & did a little shopping. Judge Silent came up to meals & staid a bit though Court is still sitting; & came up again in the evening. The moonlight is so lovely that even from our window, it is enjoyable & then our household is so dead quiet, with even Thor out, that I suppose it's a rest to him after the steady interruptions at his chambers day & evening. And he knows how pleased la casa y toda que tiene [the house and everything that is in it] always is to have him. Coolish day & cool night. I wrote Mother via Santa Fe a fullish account of Saturday & what went on here, enclosing the report in this evening's papers.

Tuesday 22nd. Sewing morning & in in the afternoon. Mrs. Churchill came over & made the tassels for Jack's afghan. In the early evening I called on Mrs. Dake. Judge Silent came up to meals, staying a decent little while after dinner; & later in the evening he brought me up some deliciously juicy oranges which are trebly good in this fruitless town at the end of a hot day. But the night was cool & the moonlight lovely. I had a nice letter of the 10th from Mother, telling me of the birth of Nell's 3rd boy on the 9th & of Dr. & Mrs. Morton's departure for Europe on "their wedding journey," and speaking contentedly of business.

Wednesday 23rd. Genl. Wilcox & Grace called at 9:20 a.m.! "as they were driving by." Luckily as I'm rather an early bird the house was en tenue [tidy] for the day. As they left Mrs. Churchill came & staid the morning & we finished up the tassels. In the afternoon I finished the afghan & had a call from Mrs. Weaver. Judge Silent came up to meals & staid on decently

"Bird's-Eye View of Prescott, A.T., Looking North East." After C. J. Dyer. Chromolithograph, c. 1885. (Courtesy of the Amon Carter Museum, Fort Worth, Tex., photo #1968.45.)

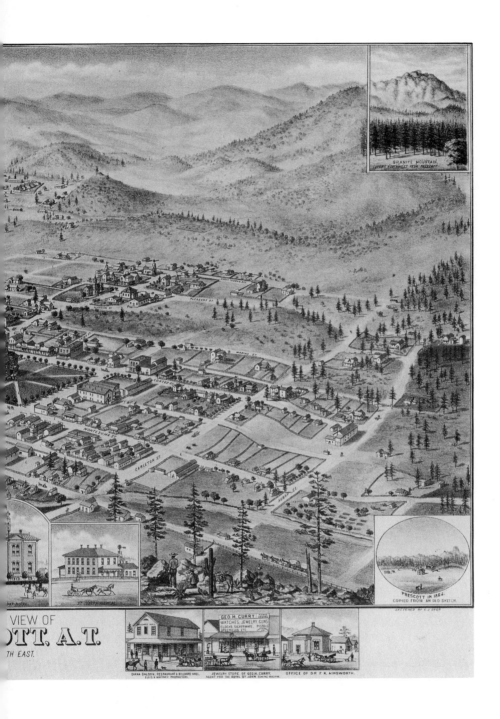

GRANITE MOUNTAIN,
SEVEN MILES NORTHWEST FROM PRESCOTT.

PRESCOTT IN 1864.
COPIED FROM AN OLD SKETCH.

SKETCHED BY C.J. DYER

VIEW OF
OTT, A.T.
TH EAST.

DIANA SALOON, RESTAURANT & BILLIARD HALL,
ELLIS & WHITNEY PROPRIETORS.

GEO. H. CURRY
WATCHES, JEWELRY, GUNS,
CLOCKS, SILVERWARE, PISTOLS,
SPECTACLES, ETC.

JEWELRY STORE OF GEO. H. CURRY,
AGENT FOR THE ROYAL ST. JOHN SEWING MACHINE.

OFFICE OF DR. F. K. AINSWORTH.

after them. Very hot afternoon, but morning & night pleasant & glorious moonlight. A quiet day.

Thursday 24th June. Mrs. Churchill spent part of the morning with me, working over worsteds, & told me of yesterday's unpleasant disagreement between Mr. Lewis & Mr. Churchill. I went down for a moment before breakfast & showed Jack's afghan to Mrs. Lewis. In the afternoon packed & sent it off by mail & did a bit of scraps. Had Dr. Morton's wedding reception cards this morning.

Judge Silent came up as usual, staying on a while after each meal for we have lots to talk over yet, & neither of us have even worn the edge off our great satisfaction & content at the result in Washington. Later in the evening the Judge turned in again, making a regulation "evening call," during which we talked over the future of Southern California, the sound of the guns firing for Hancock's nomination,[1] which reverberated finely from Thumb Butte & Granite Mt., & of the practising for the concert. I had a very pleasant evening. Afternoon fatiguingly hot, but morning & night cool.

Friday 25th. At home all day, doing scraps & writing letters. In the early evening called on Mrs. Bean & on Mrs. C. Bashford, and stopped a moment on Mrs. Churchill's porch. The Judge came up as usual but had barely time to eat as they are busy in Court. He turned in again for a little in the evening after telegraph hours. I'm watching now to hear of Father's start westward. One week tonight since we got the good news. Some fatiguing heat this afternoon but very cool night.

Saturday 26th. Quiet indoor morning. The Judge came up to breakfast & dinner, still busy in Court. I spent part of the afternoon at Mrs. Lewis— horrid to have to go out of the darkened & partly cool house into the hot glare of an afternoon here, but the rest of the women don't mind it & can't understand my doing so. I was home in time to receive some ladies who were "out calling" in spite of the heat, which lasted on into the evening later than usual though we had our customary cool night. Judge Silent came up in the evening & we "skate-tracked" off into the Santa Cruz Mts., & away from Prescott generally. It was a specially still night as all the men of the town were at the Republican & Democratic Club meetings. The stars were glorious & the sky crowded full of them. The Judge sent me up a whole lot of Cal. cherries, apricots, & peaches which came in [by] express today. The cherries took me back to Pocaho.

Sunday 27th. Letter of 16th from Mother in Washington. Everything was going rightly for the Judge, but she was overtired & not very well & anxious about Sally's health. The Judge came up to breakfast, but hurried off again to answer congratulatory letters. Mrs. Lewis came up for a while in the early evening, during the time the Judge & Mr. Lewis were out walking with the children. They brought in lots of wild flowers & the Judge sent me up a big bunch of them by Emmy Lewis, coming up later himself for a tiny while as Mrs. Lewis had told him I wasn't looking well. I was very tired with the hot afternoon & made somewhat anxious by Mother's letter. Lt. Smith and Lt. Haskell called.

Monday 28th. Two nice business letters of the 17th from Father in New York, which pleased the Judge when he came up to breakfast. They gave hopes for Yonkers & spoke encouragingly of some other matters. The Judge was at dinner, too, but busy with Court & lots of other things & hurried off. I was over at Mrs. Churchill's for some time in the morning; indoors all the rest of the day. Very hot afternoon.

Tuesday 29th. Went over early & told Mrs. Thibodo goodbye. They go to Idaho. Judge Silent came up to breakfast & to dinner. Shared with him scraps from Mother's letter, 18th in Washington, & from two from Father of the same date in New York. Afternoon chiefly wrote long letters to Mother & to Father. In the early evening I called on Mrs. Ellis, the Sisters, & Mrs. Churchill. Later the Judge came up for a while. It was the warmest evening yet hardly a breath of breeze even in our bay window where the air currents meet, but the night was cool enough.

Wednesday 30th. Letter from Frank, Missoula 16th. He was well & just starting to Helena with a batch of prisoners. Letter from Mother, Washington 19th, glad over our victory in the Silent affaire & giving me lots of details though she was tired out & had been made sick by the Eagan-Jones procured delay of twelve hours in sending off the decision,[2] which they made a last effort to have rescinded—& that after Mother's despatch had gone, sent on a certainty of the Atty. Genl's letter having been mailed. Of course, it made her sick. Also Judge Silent sent me up by Chung the official decision from Devens which he had received in the morning's mail—a day sooner than we had expected it.

I had two letters of the 19th from Father, N. Y., acknowledging the telegrams about the strike in the "Prince" & pleased about the "victory for Silent;" so the mail was a very good one. I went out with Mr. Churchill in the morning & called on Mrs. Lewis & Mrs. Levy; in the evening I called on Mrs. St. James & on Mrs. Buffum. The Judge came up to breakfast & dinner, staying on a bit. The Democratic convention in Phoenix nominated Oury[3] of Tucson as their candidate for delegate—Campbell not getting a single vote. Miss Wilcox & Mrs. Lt. Smith called while I was out. Not quite so hot as yesterday.

Thursday, July 1st. Indoors all day, reading up in "Littell." Mrs. Churchill came over for a little while. Mrs. Wells & Mrs. Hargrave called in full tenue [dress]! The Judge came up to meals & took me to the concert, where we sat near the Lewis colony. Some of the singing was real good; there was a very full house. Mrs. Buffum sent me some splendid California cherries which Mr. B. had just brought from Yuma.

Friday 2nd. Usual day & in the early evening called on Mrs. Otis & Miss Dunning. When I got in [I] found a lot of tissue flowers Mrs. Ellis had left for me—from Brookside. The Judge was up at meals & for one moment in the evening for me to write a telegram—about the Prince—& about the outside offers for the Warrior & Tuscumbia.

Saturday 3rd (Dr. Morton's birthday). Quiet indoor day, sewing & reading. Judge Silent came up to meals, & again in the evening to get the quiet he can't have in his rooms as he was having nearly as bad a headache as those we women get up here. Cool all day in the house but everyone complained of the heat out of doors.

Sunday 4th July. Flags flying everywhere. The Judge came up to breakfast. I had a quiet day indoors till 4½ when I went across to the Churchills where I dined & staid till near 8 o'clock. Mrs. Bean dined there also & some others came up on the porch afterwards (including Judge Silent who later in the evening came across to our house for a while). Everyone else was used up by the heat of the day, but I had not minded it in our house. There were piles of clouds all day & three rolls of thunder & the night was cool. Village perfectly quiet all day.

Monday, 5th. Kept as the Fourth, with picnics—to one of which I sent Mary—& a ball & salutes from the Fort. The sunrise one re-echoed superbly from the hills. The Judge went to the Hassayampa picnic & so only came up to dinner & again for a while in the evening. Starlight & stars beautiful. I had a quiet day indoors.

Tuesday, 6th. Quiet indoors day. Mrs. Lewis, then Mrs. Churchill & Mrs. Smith called in the early evening. Judge Silent came up to breakfast & to dinner, staying on a while after the latter, reading "Littell;" & in the evening he brought me up a business telegram, chiefly about Mr. Rutherford's letters not supporting our accounts of the strike in the "Prince" & asking us to telegraph "details." The Judge staid on a little discussing ways & means of sending them a verified telegram. Weather still promising rain.

Wednesday 7th. A letter from Mother—the first in seven days—everyone well; she was at New Brighton. Indoor day. The Judge came up to meals & staid a mite after them. We sent off a telegram to Father answering one received last night from him asking more information about the late strike in the Prince. So did Mr. Buffum. Fine clouds all day & the rain set in about 3 p.m. & continued at intervals on into the night. The damp air was delicious. . . .

Friday 9th. I went across twice during the day to Mrs. Churchill's as she isn't well; in the afternoon Mrs. Dr. Smith & Grace Wilcox called & in the evening Mrs. La Motte dropped by & took me for an hour's drive among the hills. Judge Silent came up to breakfast looking right ill, so when he didn't come up to dinner, I got anxious about him & sent first Chung then Mary down to the Court House & found he had called in Dr. Ainsworth & was ordered to lie still till Monday morning, which disposes of tomorrow's court. Messengers are unsatisfactory; I didn't learn half of what I wanted.

Saturday 10th. Sent for Dr. Ainsworth, on the pretext of my headache medicine, which did need renewing, & saw him about 12. He told me the Judge had dysentery & that he was going to try the East Indian remedy, as it was a bad case, but he thought strong treatment would bring [him] through & that he would stop in tomorrow & tell me how he progressed.[4] I told him to use our house as an annex to the Court House & he said he would; & might move the Judge up to Father's room when he got stronger. Mary & I worked through all the afternoon getting Father's room in fresh order.

Both Mary & Chung were down at the Court House on errands & in the evening I heard through Dr. Lincoln that there was a faint improvement. I went to see both Mrs. Lewis & Mrs. Churchill for a little while in the early evening. It was hard work but I had to. Mr. Lewis came in to see me; he could only give an outside report of the Judge as Dr. Ainsworth has forbidden Mr. Long,[5] who has charge of him, to let any one at all in. But Mr. Churchill ran the blockade & came up at our house at 10 when he told me he thought the Judge was dying, "killed by doctoring." Fortunately, Dr. Ainsworth had told me a little of what the effects of his treatment would be & I could recognize it in some of the symptoms Mr. C. related & I knew too that he disbelieves in all doctors & hates Dr. Ainsworth & I had Dr. Lincoln's little word of encouragement, so I tried hard to be sensible, but it was a miserable & long night.

Sunday 11th. I went down at 7 to Dr. Lincoln's to see what news he had of the Judge—found the drugstore closed & had to knock up the little clerk—only to find Dr. L[incoln] had gone for a day's hunting! I staid in all [day] waiting for Dr. Ainsworth who never came higher than the Lewis's house. Long was up for beef tea & Mary & Chung were down there frequently. She saw the Judge once for a moment & said he was looking "awful sick." All the reports through the day were very disheartening; Mr. Churchill brought in one with a little hope in it late in the afternoon.

Finally, I couldn't stand the waiting any longer but took Mary & went down to the C. H. where I waited in the hall for Mr. Long to come on the south porch where my voice couldn't reach the Judge, who mustn't see anyone at all, Dr. A. says. There I got the latest news—slightly better & Mr. Long's promise to come for me instantly if there was the least relapse & to keep me informed. I also arranged about the rice soup & other things. I think Mr. Long will keep his word better than Dr. Ainsworth has & that's a little comfort, but waiting with no work to do for the one who is in danger is heart wearying work. I had one of my worse headaches all day but I couldn't take my medicine as it stupifies [sic] & puts me to sleep & I wanted to be on hand if I were needed, so had to face the music there, too. It troubles me so much too that I don't know what the Judge wants done about telling his family. There's no use telegraphing for his wife; in the five days it would take her to get here, he may be past all danger—in the other case I know he would not want her to have the anguish of such a journey.

Monday 12th. Chung came up at 7. "Judge little better & wants tea," which made a big lift. Letters came from Mother which required a lot of writing & copying; she was getting over the effect of her last stay in Washington. The letters referred back to things she & Father thought hadn't been done & thanks not sent. They were done & sent but miscarried in both mails & telegrams: all of which I answered to. Later in the day I had a telegram from her (10th) saying "thank Judge for good letter. Am quite well. Afghan lovely." So part of the "thanks" had reached. The Judge was enough better to send me up a business telegram to forward. I met Dr. Ainsworth at Mrs. Lewis's & he told me he hadn't understood I wanted to see him yesterday or he would have called. I went out on the side walk with him & had a little talk about the Judge's case with him; he said the Judge was quiet for the day.

I went out in the afternoon & bade Miss Wilcox goodbye as she leaves Thursday—not to return—taking the boys & probably Grace with her. She was her very nicest to me & gave me a pretty Chinese bowl with a plant in it as a reminder. I also turned in for a moment at Mrs. Churchill's. Had a business telegram from Father & wrote to Dr. Ainsworth asking if it wasn't imprudent to let the Judge touch business. He came up & said it was—that we might try it in a day or so but not now; also he promised me he would have me sent for at once if Judge Silent should become *seriously* worse, but he didn't have any such anticipations about him, which I was vastly relieved to hear him say, especially as the Judge isn't near as well tonight as he was this morning. Mr. Long also came up with the latest news & a business message from the Judge. After they had left & the last things had been sent down to the Court House, I found out how completely tired out I was & staid still till bedtime. Judge Silent has his forty days leave from the Atty. Genl., granted by a telegram, to which he sent me up this morning.

Tuesday 13th. Was busy attending to things for the Judge who was ordered feeding up today. He is visibly better though still utterly prostrate, Mr. Long told me. No one whatever allowed inside his door but the doctor & the nurse; they don't count Chung so [they] let him take in his food & each time he reports to me how the Judge looks. The last report at 8 p.m. was still a good one. I staid in all day. Wrote to Mother of course.

Wednesday 14th. I went down to see Mrs. Lewis in the morning as she has been ill; Mrs. Churchill called in the afternoon & Mrs. Wollenberg made me quite a long visit in the early evening. The rest of the day was chiefly spent in seeing [that] things went down on time & rightly to the Judge & in fighting an inclination to get sick myself. I had a cheerful home letter from Mother. Chung brought me up a little note from the Judge who continues to improve. I had some scraps of business to look after, too. Hot out of doors, but cool in the house. Last report at night still favorable.

Thursday 15th. Indoor day, looking after the dinettes for the Judge, who continues to improve though very weak.

Friday 16th. Had to refuse a lunch invitation to Mrs. Lewis as I didn't feel well enough to go out. The Judge was driven up to our house about 11 & staid till just 5. Intensely weak & very thin, but clearly & visibly getting well. I made him lie down all I could & gave him things to read, neither talking much to him nor letting him talk; he had two little naps & at my insistence was driven back to the Court House. He had actually intended walking down! not yet realizing how weak he is. I rather think he played truant to the Dr. in coming up here today, but he said he just couldn't stand his room any longer & at the worst it can only retard his recovery a little. Va sans dire [Goes without saying] I was glad to see him again. We had one heavy shower in the afternoon. In the evening I went for a moment each to Mrs. Churchill & to Mrs. Lewis.

Saturday 17th. Indoor day for me. Mrs. Churchill & then Mrs. Aram called in the afternoon; Mrs. Lewis in the evening. The Judge wasn't so well today—only weakened from overexertion yesterday—& staid down at the Court House, but opened Court & adjourned it to Sept. 27. I had a little note from him in the evening, saying he was better—I had sent to ask. Dr. Ainsworth stopped here a moment in the morning thinking the Judge had stopped over night with us. Beautiful orange tinted "pluie de Danaë" [Danaë's rain][6] sunset & grand cloud masses all day, with some slight showers.

Sunday 18th. The "month's mind" of the good decision in the Judge's case. I had a letter from Mother enclosed in a notelet from Charley, all well. The Judge walked up just before breakfast & staid till 3½, when he took the short cut down to the Court House, as he was too tired to feel up to stopping at the Lewises. While he was here I made him rest on the sofa & read newspapers. He is still very weak but mending visibly. There was some rain during the day, which was a quiet homelike one, very different from last Sunday's anxiety.

Monday 19th. A lovely grey day with almost constant soft rain, grand cloud effects over Granite [Mt.] & a fine orange sunset. I went down for a moment in the morning to make Mrs. Lewis the Judge's excuses for not having stopped there yesterday. She was a little stiff about it, so he stopped there himself a moment on his way down from breakfast, for he walked up to both breakfast & dinner, staying on a while after each, resting on the sofa & reading "Tribunes" while I worked away at Frank's afghan, leaving him right still. He lost 25 pounds in the few days of his illness & is still very weak & needing building up—ordered to cat 6 times a day, so what he doesn't take here, Chung carries down to the C. H. for him.

Tuesday 20th July. Indoors except for a short call on Mrs. Churchill. Several drizzles & a grey day with a fine yellow, pink & grey sunset. Judge Silent came up to his 9, 12 & 5 o'clock "lunches"—staying a little after each. He has decided to leave on Friday reaching Los Angeles on Monday & there Mrs. Silent will meet him. When he first came up he told me of Judge French's request—written this time—asking him to change districts for the Fall and Winter terms with him. He gave no reason in his letter for asking the exchange but the Tucson Bar knowing him sent the Judge a copy of their petition wherein they, taking advantage of a little leave of absence Judge French has, had asked him to request Associate Justice Silent to hold Court for him in Tucson this Fall & Winter. Also the Judge had several private letters telling him about it. Coming as it does just after all these "charges" business, it is a triumph for our Judge to be asked to take the Chief Justice court by the united Bar. Also the Law Journal has as its opening item an account of Judge Silent's complete vindication in which it rejoices for the sake of the character of the Bench, as well as personally [for] Judge Silent. No letters or telegrams from home.

Wednesday 21st. The Judge came up to his three meals staying a few minutes after each. He is getting tired on top of his weakness by the work the lawyers are crowding on him. Dr. Ainsworth says he must get off Friday. Mrs. Lewis, then Mrs. Churchill, called in the evening. Fine sunset, triple rainbow, gorgeously clear, splendid full moon.

Thursday 22nd. Nice letter from Frank who was back at Missoula from Helena where he had had a charming time. Several contradictory business telegrams from Father & from Grey to the Judge, to Mr. Lewis & to me came in about noon. They all united in asking the Judge to stay, which Dr. Ainsworth positively forbids. The weighing pros & cons, dislike of vexing Father, & all the business work he had to do in connection with it all & the money (20,000 [dollars]) [that] was telegraphed into Mr. Lewis's bank to [a]wait [the] letter from Grey nearly broke the Judge down. He was up at our house for four of his lunches, resting a little each time & talking over the situation with me. Finally Dr. A.'s orders & his own recognition of how perfectly unfit he was in his present weak condition to cope with business made him decide to leave tomorrow and manage by telegraph, in which decision I concurred.

Friday 23rd. Up early, packed the Judge's lunch basket & sent it & his petit dejeuner [breakfast] down by Chung at 6 a.m. with an auf wieder-sehen note. Chung brought me back a goodbye note from the Judge—also saying he felt somewhat rested by the night & thought he could manage the journey without much difficulty. It's a hard one for a man in his state of health to make, but better than staying here. I watched the Black Cañon stage round the corner out of town, exchanging my adieu waves with the Judge. I'm very glad to have him go, but it does leave me pretty lonesome for he has looked out for me so considerably since Father left. Nice letters from Mother & from Nell.

Saturday 24th. Nice letter of 13 from Mother, & a tiny note from Judge at Big Bug—40 miles out, saying he had got so far in comparative comfort. Mr. Lewis brought me up a despatch he had received from Father in accord with Grey & which I at once repeated to Judge Silent at Phoenix. Mrs. Smith called in the evening. Threatening weather with light show-ers—glorious yellow sunset & perfect double rainbow.

Sunday 25th. Good business telegram from Father, showing accord with Grey & ending "well satisfied," dated 24th. I saw Mr. Lewis in the morning & Mr. Buffum in the evening about this. Mr. B. was just in from the Prince & gives fine account: "ore richer than any *ever* taken from the Peck." I had also a telegram of the 24th from the Judge saying "Quite well & not much tired" and something about business at Maricopa. Also a letter, 14th, from Mother. Mrs. Buffum made me a pleasant long visit in the afternoon. Wonderful sheet & zigzag lightning in evening.

Monday 26th. Nice letter from Mother, 15th, holding out prospect of some plan which will give us "a permanent pied-a-terre [cottage] in Los An-geles." Wouldn't I like that! & a nice little note from the Judge written Saturday morning at Phoenix. He wasn't very much tired, felt better from the time he struck the lower altitude & was going to rest a few hours before going on through to Maricopa, which yesterday's telegram shows he reached all right. I made calls on the Sisters, Mrs. Alexander, Mrs. Levy & Mrs. Lewis in the morning & on Mrs. Churchill in the evening. Mrs. La Motte stopped by & asked me to drive, but I excused myself. . . .

Wednesday 28th. Nice letters: from Charley, 17th; from Mother, 17th & chiefly about some lawns for me & other women's things; from Judge Silent, Sunday morning at Maricopa. He says he has no ill effects from the journey. Mr. Long called to get the last news from the Judge. I had shared Saturday's Maricopa telegram with him. Mr. Churchill called, about young R[utherford]'s gambling. And Mrs. Churchill came across with some flowers; in the evening Mrs. Lewis came in for a while.

Thursday July 29th. Mrs. Levy, Mrs. Buffum & Mrs. Curtis called. Mr. Churchill was in & out concerning Mr. Rutherford's gambling. I sent Mary to the ice cream festival, & going to bed early had fallen asleep when about 10, I was awakened by cry of "fire." When I saw it was by Goldwaters I dressed & began packing up, aided by Mary & by Chung, who reported at once. We got everything ready to be moved out on to Capitol hill; the church emptied instantly & the men had a desperate fight for an hour before they got the fire under control; there wasn't the least breeze or all this part of town would have gone. Three buildings, one a feed & oil storehouse, went; others were wrecked & the Goldwaters barely saved their fine brick building, which made the bulwark for all of us to the north of it. The Cordises caught several times.

It was hard work fighting the fire with the old-fashioned "bucket line," for all water supply & that line leading to wells nearly dry. Our landlord came here towards twelve ½ & said things were safe, so towards one Mary & I laid down. The big blazing cinders were dropping everywhere during the first part of the fire, & as all the houses are tinderboxes it is a wonder more didn't catch, but nearly every roof had a man on it putting out the cinders as they fell. Everyone worked really well. Of course it frightened me, for having been twice burned out I know how it is myself![7]

Friday 30th. Up early & put things to rights—rest of the day was tired & lazy after last night's scare. In the evening called on Mrs. Lewis, Mrs. Buffum & Mrs. Churchill. Mr. Lewis said he expected the whole block to go last night & so did most of the other property owners. The mail brought me a nice letter from Mother, 19th, N. Y.; & one from the Judge at Los Angeles, 27th, "feeling right well again." Mrs. Silent & "one of the little girls" had met [him] there. . . .

Monday 2nd. Letter from Mother, & the "Fool's Errand" from the Judge.[8] Mrs. Lewis took breakfast here. I was at Mrs. Churchill's for a moment. Very hot afternoon.

Tuesday 3rd August. Went to a lunch party at Mrs. Wollenberg's—seven ladies. After dinner Mr. Buffum turned in & told me the Warrior-Tuscumbia sale to our parties was "satisfactorily concluded," the money paid over & the deeds in escrow. The facts I at once telegraphed on to Father & to

Judge Silent. Later Mr. Lewis came in giving me his account of the negociations, & away after 9 o'clock, when I had settled to a quiet read of the "Fool," Mr. Churchill came in white mad considering himself slighted—angry with us all & venomous against the Judge. I heard that the whole negociation for the B.W. was nearly broken off by Mr. C.'s way of taking things. Weather very hot.

Wednesday 4th. Mrs. Bean & Mrs. Churchill took breakfast with me & staid on into the afternoon. Mrs. A. M. Smith, Mrs. N. [B.] Bowers & Miss Bashford called in the evening. Mr. Richardson came in about the Grey Eagle.

Thursday 5th. Quiet indoor day. Called on Mrs. Bowers & Mrs. C. Bashford, & Mrs. Buffum in the early evening. Finished the "Fool's Errand" at night—it seemed real. Very hot day. . . .

Saturday 7th. In the morning I went down & sat a while with Mrs. Lewis, who isn't well, & in the evening the La Mottes stopped by & took me for a drive. Rest of the day letter writing & afghan. Weather still hot. Clouds in beautiful masses, but no rain here, though it seemed to fall N. & E. of us. . . .

Tuesday 10th. Light showers in the afternoon, splendid grey clouds & one ripping clap of thunder such as I've never heard before. It seemed to tear clouds & air asunder. Mother Monica & Mother St. Jean; Mrs. Wollenberg; Mrs. Buffum & her niece all called during the morning—then Grace Wilcox (why?) turned in & breakfasted with me & staid till after 2! Quelle mouche a piqué le Genl? [Whatever has gotten into the General?] In the evening I went down to the Hospital & bade Mother St. Jean adieu. The notices in the local papers about Father's not being well—mentioned in connection with his speaking at public meetings East—have bothered me, but Mother's letters say he is "tired with the heat," & his telegram of the 1st said "all well here," so it can't be anything serious.

Wednesday 11th. Nice home letter from Mother. Mr. Lewis came in to tell me that Capt. Eagan & his set were after the Judge again, but keeping dark. I reported the fact to Mother & he to Judge Silent. Reading & sewing day. Lots of little showers & a beautiful lunar rainbow about 9 p.m., which I stood out in the rain watching. . . .

Friday 13th. Home letter from Mother telling of Jack's and Belmore's christening on the 1st & that Sally & Charley had chosen me for Jack's

Godmother—Nell standing proxy & Father & Col. Anderson being God-fathers. It was very good in the children & I hope I'll be able to be of use to the little man. I was out for a little shopping in the early morning. Mrs. Buffum & Mrs. Churchill called during the day. Mrs. Smith & Mrs. Lewis in the evening. Damp & grey day. . . .

Tuesday, 17th. Nice letter 6th from Mother with lots about both business & politics—including Garfield's cordial ways to Father. Mrs. Buffum spent the morning with me. It rained, real soft eastern rain, nearly all the afternoon.

Wednesday, 18th. Very nice letter of 6th & 7th from Father & Mother, "Los Angeles no mirage," & things going really well. Sewing & writing indoor day. Mrs. Beach called in the afternoon, Mrs. Bean & Mrs. Lewis in the evening. Heaviest showers of the season this afternoon—could hear the creek run.

Thursday 19th. Mary busy at the theatre all day with final preparations for the ice-cream & dancing "festival" for the Catholic church & towards which the Protestants all helped willingly & which came off under a full moon in the evening. Was a complete financial success; crowded & everyone enjoying themselves—a good natured lark—*mixed* of course; piles of nicely dressed children. I went with the Lewises & came away early with the Churchills. Mary has been the Mrs. Townsend of the affair & like her is worn out. Usual indoor day, with a short visit across at Mrs. C's. No rain & glorious moon & Jupiter. . . .

Saturday 21st. Mr. Murphy called to tell me about his brother & also told me that Knowles had been telegraphed from N. Y. that the Prince com-[pany] had concluded a big contract for ore crushing at the Bradshaw Mill. Mrs. Churchill took breakfast with me & spent the afternoon. Mrs. Bashford called; & in the evening I called on Mrs. Lewis. Clouds but no rain.

Sunday 22nd. Mr. [Jules] Deraches, the curé, called, to thank me for what I had done in helping on the party for his church benefit & was storm bound by the rain & hail so we had quite a talk over Paris & the Commune. It was the biggest rain storm we've seen here & after the fury of it was over it still kept on some hours in a gentler way. The creek ran bank full & when the clouds lifted we saw the hills to the southeast all snow clad & it lay through the night. The weather changed to late Fall. I dined with Mrs. Churchill, meeting the Smiths there. Came home early.

Monday 23rd. Nice letters from Mother & Frank. I went out twice, calling on Mrs. W. Bashford & Miss Watson. Mrs. Wollenberg, Mrs. J. G. Campbell, who staid two hours telling me about her troubles & her mines, then Mr. Richardson of the Gray Eagle called in the afternoon. Mrs. Churchill dined & spent the evening with me, & Mrs. A. M. Smith came across in the evening, too.

Tuesday 24th. I went up to Mrs. Buffum's in the morning to arrange to go to the Ainsworth party tomorrow, where I have to put in an appearance. In the afternoon, I drove to the Post & made seven visits, including Grace W. as I found she was to leave for school in the morning—& then made 3 more in town. Found Genl. Wilcox & Grace had called in my absence & Grace returned later to say goodbye, bringing Miss Stevens with her. Mr. Lewis called in the evening. Only a few light showers during the day—a beautiful flame colored sunset.

Wednesday 25th. Mrs. Buffum was in for a moment. Dr. Ainsworth called to take leave. Mrs. Smith & Mrs. Churchill took breakfast with me. I went with the Buffums to the Ainsworth party—quite a pretty affair—coming back soon after 10. Dr. A. refused all consideration for his services, saying "no officer of the army could take pay for anything done for Genl. Frémont's family."

Wednesday 26th August. Quiet morning till noon when I heard little Charley Wollenberg's cry, "Albert is dead!" as he ran down to the Plaza for his father, & saw all the men pour down Cortez St. I went at once to their house & on down to Mrs. Alexander's near whose house the accident happened & into which the child was carried. I saw Mrs. Levy & Mr. Ellis—everyone in town had gathered up, for the child was a pet all over the town & the parents are liked, too. He was trying, with some other boys, to ride on the front of the trailway of an ox team heavily loaded with wood for the Post. He must have slipped & fallen, both wheels passed over his chest. Mercifully death was instant.

By the way all outsiders feel it we can get a glimpse into the awful blow it is to the parents—& she is a sweet natured, home keeping little woman. I turned in for a moment each at Mrs. Churchill's & Mrs. Smith's to let them know that the poor little fellow was spared the agony of a lingering death. Mary went off at 6 a.m. with three of the Sisters—in a wagon loaned them by Brannen—for a day's outing down to Maggie Hiltenbrand's ranch in the Agua Fria Valley. She got back at 8 p.m., having very much enjoyed herself.

Friday 27th. Went with Mrs. Churchill at 2 p.m. to little Albert's funeral, first at the house then across to the Masonic burying ground. Every lady & nearly every man in town was there. All the women were in black if they could possibly manage it, many of us melting in our winter things. The Post ambulances were late so that many [vehicles] had too many [passengers]. Mr. Goldwater gave Mrs. C & me a lift in Mr. Head's buggy. The services at the grave were in Hebrew & read by Goldwater, & Mr. Butler[9] made a short & right appropriate address. Everyone was genuinely sorry. All the stores, except Bashford's, & all the saloons were closed until the funeral was quite over & every one did what they could to show they took part in the Wollenberg's grief. I went in to Mrs. Churchill's for a while.

Saturday 28th. Very nice home & business letter from Mother, 17th. My "things" arrived by express from Mother—lovely things, dresses, shoes, stockings, corsets & ribbons & each dress fitted perfectly. I was delighted—so was Mary, both with my things & with those for her. Mrs. Churchill in the afternoon, & Mrs. Lewis in the evening called to see me & my things. Miss Stevens called on a message about starting an Episcopalian church here. Lovely graded pink to flame colored sunset.

Sunday 29th. Indoor day. Fall weather with almost a frost at night.

Monday 30th. Indoor morning & good long letter from Mother. Afternoon put on one of my new dresses & went visiting with Mrs. Churchill & Mrs. Smith (to Mrs. McClintock,[10] Allen, Cartter, Dake & Buffum & asked the two last to breakfast here on Wednesday). The Lewis children came in for a while in the early evening. Brightly cool, Fall-like day. . . .

Wednesday Sept. 1st. Mrs. Dake, Mrs. Buffum & Mrs. Lewis took breakfast with me & spent part of the afternoon. Dr. Warren called—he is here to see if a Congregationalist church can be started in this town.[11] Coolish day. . . .

Friday 3rd. Mrs. Clark, Mrs. W. Bashford, Mrs. Smith & Mrs. Churchill took breakfast with me & spent part of the afternoon. They all seemed to amuse themselves. Later Mrs. Wainwright & Mrs. Egbert[12] called. In the evening Mrs. Lewis came in for a while. Hot again in the afternoon. . . .

Tuesday 7th. Quiet day. Shower in the afternoon & saw another old gold sunset. Mr. Haskell—just back—called in the evening.

Wednesday 8th. Went down to see Mrs. Wollenberg in the morning—had to come home thro' a shower—& to see Mrs. Smith after dinner. Judge Silent sent me by express a big box of delicious plums which it was a pleasure to handle as well as to eat. I sent some to the Sisters, to Mrs. Churchill, Smith, Buffum, & Wollenberg. . . .

Friday 10th. Mrs. Wollenberg & Ernie came in to see me in the morning & I kept her to breakfast & on into the afternoon. Mr. Lewis called to complain of the Judge's non-arrival as Mr. Churchill did some days ago. Heavy showers all afternoon & on into the evening. Lovely pluie d'or [golden rain] sunset. Granite Mt. looking its very best.

Saturday 11th. Nice long letter from Mother. Mrs. Bean called & asked me to drive with her tomorrow. In the afternoon I went out visiting but was driven in by the rain after calling on Mrs. Beach & Mrs. Hargrave. Not much rain fell in town, but it was a grey afternoon, with thunderstorms in the mts. . . .

Tuesday 14th. I went across to see Mrs. Churchill in the morning & in the afternoon went out for a little & got some views of Prescott. In the afternoon Mrs. A. M. Smith, Mrs. Churchill, Mrs. Lewis, Mrs. La Motte & Mrs. Dr. Smith called. It rained lightly in the morning & very heavily & for a long time in the night. A lovely pink & gold sunset with a broken double rainbow ending in the edge of a white cumulus cloud close beyond which was the moon—half full & bright. . . .

Thursday 16th. Usual indoor day. Went with the Beans to the R. R. meeting in the Court House, at which Mr. Bean spoke—pretty well—& which was crowded.[13]. . .

Saturday 18th. Six months since Father left. Had a letter of Sept. 2 from Mother; no trace as to where it laid over. Went down & spent the morning with Mrs. Wollenberg. Drove over to the Post in the afternoon & made all my visits owing there (7); then, on foot, four more in the village. Full moon—splendid—& so was Jupiter. Lovely weather.

Sunday 19th. Nice letter of 8th from Frank & from Judge Silent, written Yuma, 16th, & posted Maricopa as he was passing thro' to Tucson; there were many points in it. He is almost really well & Father has been asked by the S. Calif. Agr[icultural] Society to make the address of Welcome to the President at their Fair opening Oct. 15. Mr. Lewis called to learn when the Judge was coming & later the curé made me a visit. . . .

Tuesday 21st. Useless from remains of headache, still pretty active. Had stoves put up & all the clean curtains. Mrs. Lewis, Mrs. Levy, Mrs. W. Bashford, & Mrs. Wollenberg called. I divided a big box of pears the Judge sent me with the Lewises. Saw in the evening papers that our Judge's exchange with Judge French has been definitely completed.

Wednesday 22nd. I went up in the morning & asked Mrs. Buffum to take dinner with [me]. I was tired of being alone. Stopped on the way down & called on Mrs. Churchill. Mrs. Buffum did dine with me & spent the evening.

Thursday 23rd. Went with Mrs. Buffum in the morning to call on Mrs. Hamilton of Mineral Park[14] who is passing thro' town going north. In the afternoon went down for a while to Mrs. Wollenberg's. In the evening Mrs. Masterson & Miss McClintock, and then Mr. Lewis called.

Friday 24th. Judge Silent came in on the B. Cañon stage. He came up here at 7 & took coffee with us & staid on till 10, talking over things. He is looking really well again & of course has had a lovely holiday. Letters of the 13th from Mother, Father & from Maggie, all in N. Y. & all well. The Judge came up again to meals, but was busy & tried a case in chambers in the evening. Mrs. Lewis spent the evening with me. It is very nice to have Judge Silent back.

Saturday, 25th. Wrote to mother (about plan of change of base to Tucson, via Santa Fe [mail]), to Frank & to Maggie. Mrs. Wollenberg spent part of the afternoon here & Mrs. Campbell called. Judge Silent came up to breakfast & dinner, staying a little after each meal.

Sunday 26th. Duplicated yesterday's letter to Mother. Judge Silent took breakfast & spent the evening here, dining with the Lewises. He had an altitude headache (& was also homesick). Weather so cool I kept the parlor fire going all day.

Monday 27 Sept. 1880. Indoor morning; I made some visits in the afternoon. Judge Silent came up to breakfast & dinner & staid on a while after dinner. Court met today & his altitude headache continues. Mr. Stephenson of Mineral Park called in the evening. . . .

Wednesday 29th. Indoor morning. Mrs. Churchill called on the Cline subscription business.[15] In the afternoon Mrs. Stahl[16] called, & I made three visits including Mrs. Wollenberg. Judge Silent came up to meals, staying on after dinner when he talked over with me the necessity he feels himself to be under of resigning; both health & other reasons seem to require it. But it is a hard pull on him to make the break in his career. I'm very sorry it has to be, but see in both health & business urgent "reasons why." Still it is hard. It won't be to take effect at once as he will hold the Tucson term & redd up the work there as he promised those lawyers he would & he will send his resignation through Father.

Thursday 30th. Indoor day with letter writing & sewing. Mrs. Beach called. Judge Silent came up as usual but only staid a few moments after dinner (talking Richards copper)[17] as he is very busy getting ready to leave in the morning's buckboard for Mineral Park where court opens Monday. He is fast getting ill again here so I'm glad to have him get off to M. P. where he always feels better.

Friday Oct. 1st. Up early & fixed the Judge's lunch which Chung took down to the Court House. The Judge was too driven to get up PPC, but sent me a packet of letters to send on to Father. Mr. Long has been sick for a few days past & we have been seeing to his food. He is better today. No letters from the east since one of the 14. Indoor day. Mrs. Smith called in the evening.

Saturday 2nd. Letters of the 17, 18 & 20 from Mother, all well & business going well. Quiet morning. Young Mr. Bowen called in the afternoon to hear what I had learned lately from N. Y. "about the consolidation." As I had never heard anything at all, he enlightened me telling me in detail about the arrangement of the three mines & the B[radshaw] B[asin] mill into a stock co[mpany] at 2,000,000 [dollars].[18] He is very much excited over the hitch in the mill contract for working ores, which is en outre [additionally] the company business. I suppose the letters telling me of this con[solidation] have been lost or else there was some good reason for not telling me. Mr. B. says he arrived yesterday.

Sunday 3rd. Letter writing day. Mr. Bowen called in the evening—a continuation of yesterday's talk. He says the con[solidation] was completed 19th August.

Monday 4th. Indoor day, sewing on Frank's afghan. Mr. Lewis called for a moment. Mrs. Churchill spent the evening here.

Tuesday 5th. Quiet morning. Mr. Bowen called a moment to show a notice in the N. Y. "Mining Record" Sept. 18 of the "Silver Prince Con[solidation] M[ining] Co[mpany]." Mrs. Churchill & Mrs. A. M. Smith took breakfast with me & spent part of the afternoon. When they left I went out & called on Mrs. W. Bashford—out—and on Mrs. Burmister & Mrs. Wollenberg—both in. Pleasant weather, but warm.

Wednesday 6th. Two years today since we arrived in this town, during which time I've not been five miles away from the house. Sewing day. Mrs. Wollenberg took breakfast & spent the afternoon with me & Mrs. Otis called. Also Mrs. Fr. Smith to ask me to this evening's concert, from which I excused myself. Then she asked me for the one this day [next] week & as in Prescott it would be absurd to plead a previous engagement, I accepted, but don't intend going as I shan't to any Post entertainment till after Father's return.

Thursday 7th. Sewed lots on Frank's afghan. Mrs. Lewis breakfasted with me & spent the afternoon. Mrs. McCandless[19] called. I dined with the Lewises—a special fine piece of beef being the "motif," but came home early.

Friday 8th. Mr. Murphy called to give me his brother's letters of thanks to Father & Mother & to re-express his own. Mr. Bowen called to talk over the muddled contract & consolidation affair. The rest of the morning was sewing & letter writing. I spent the afternoon & dined with Mrs. Wollenberg, coming home early. Yesterday's jour couverte [sic; stifling weather] culminated today in several showers with thunder & lightning & to the W. of the Mts. a very heavy storm seemed to be raging all day.

Saturday 9th. Quiet indoor day sewing & watching the clouds over the mts. There were some showers in the village & falling weather all day in the Mts. to the S. & W. of town. Mrs. Wollenberg with her Charley[20] came up for a little while in the evening. . . .

Monday 11th. Went up to see Mrs. Churchill in the morning & made some calls in the afternoon. Mrs. Churchill was here a while in the evening. Cold weather & San Francisco Mt[s]. snowclad. Had nice note from the Judge at Mineral Park, Oct. 9. May get back here tomorrow.

Tuesday Oct. 12. Went up to see Mrs. Buffum about the poor German woman & hearing she had a nurse & was taken care of, I staid & made a visit. After I came home, I thought it would be wise to go & see for myself, so I took Thor & walked over into Goose Flat where I found the woman needing almost everything—her baby born dead Saturday night, she all alone as the nurse hadn't come. The neighbors are all kind to her but they are poor & each has lots of small children. The woman is stout hearted & I think will pull thro' & the ladies will take care that she & her children are helped along.[21] After leaving her I went back & told Mrs. Buffum how things really were with her. Mrs. Lewis brought her sewing & spent the afternoon; Mrs. Bean & Mrs. Dake called; & late in the evening Mrs. Churchill came across to let me know she had heard from Mr. C. that they would be back Thursday even[in]g. Some tedious criminal work is detaining them. I half expected the Judge this afternoon & waited dinner for him—only to see the buckboard drive up to the P. O. empty. Mr. Lewis & Mr. Bowen called on business. Cold lasts.

Wednesday 13th. Did a little shopping for the German woman's children in the morning & sewed away at the things most of the day, Mrs. Lewis cutting them out for me in the afternoon. Took lunch and spent the afternoon with Mrs. Lewis, meeting Mrs. Wollenberg, Mrs. Ellis & Mrs. Levy there. Both Mr. Thorne & a Mr. Sims, also a Silver Belt owner, called to ask what news I had about that mine.[22]

Thursday 14th. At home all day, chiefly sewing. Some ladies called in the afternoon. Mrs. Lewis spent part of the evening with me & Mr. Lewis called for a moment on business. Read Busch's book on Bismarck in the evening—interesting not only from the subject treated but on account of all the places round Paris he mentions & which recall old times to me.[23] Mary went down yesterday & today to see the German woman, taking her beef tea, etc. & this afternoon a full suit of new warm clothes for the 6 yr. old girl. Weather moderated.

Friday 15th. Indoor sewing day except when I took a short walk with Thor. Mrs. Wollenberg spent part of the afternoon with me & Mrs. Hargrave called (in a canary colored bunting with lots of bright ribbons). The Judge came in on the Mohave buckboard & came up to dinner soon after—only his own dinette as I was too uncertain as to his coming to wait. He is looking moderately well tho' tired by the travel & last night's cold. We had only a few minutes to talk after dinner when Mr. Lewis came & took the Judge off.

Saturday Oct. 16. Letter from Mother for me & for the Judge—the letter in answer to misapprehensions some meddlers had started in the Judge's mind. Judge Silent only staid a little after meals as he was busy with court & lots of accumulated work. I sewed, took a scrap of a walk up the hill with Thor to look at the San Francisco Mts. already snowclad. Mrs. Levy called & Mrs. Wollenberg came to ask me to dine with them tomorrow, which I accepted as the Judge goes to the Lewises then. A sizeable & very characteristic turnout—running the scale from the Post band in parade to the ranchers on horseback with colts following—was made to welcome the entry of the Rep[ublican] can[didate] for delegate, [Madison W.] Stewart, into town from Mohave, & in the evening there was a torchlight procession, with band & a big meeting over in Curtis Hall. Lots of Ladies went but I didn't care to. Politics so very much en petit [on a smaller scale] don't interest me. The town wasn't quiet again till nearly 3 a.m. Moon & Jupiter kept together all night & at 2 a.m. each was shining as though the other didn't exist. It was a beautiful sight.

Sunday 17th. As it was Sunday Judge Silent only came up to breakfast, dining with the Lewises. I had a quiet indoor day & took dinner at the Wollenbergs where there was only Mr. T. Butler beside[s] the family. They told me of the Eagan interruption incident at last night's meeting. I came home at 6, spent the evening chiefly in writing to Frank.

Monday 18th. (7 months since Father left). Nice letter of the 7th from Mother saying Father would be sure to meet the President in Tucson, & at 4 p.m. a telegram from Father dated N. Y. 16th saying "I leave this evening for Arizona"—which naturally I was very glad to get. The Judge was up to meals but hurried off after each; he called in the evening for a few moments with Mr. Stephenson of Mineral Park. I felt nervous & "low" through the day. Lovely weather in the sunshine.

Tuesday 19th. Indoor morning—made visits in the afternoon. The Judge came up to meals, very busy. Mrs. A. M. Smith called in the evening. Mother's wedding anniversary.

Wednesday 20th (Z.E.K.). I went up to see Mrs. Buffum & Mrs. Churchill in the evening & Mrs. Lewis in the afternoon; sewed the rest of the time. Judge Silent came up as usual, staying & returning for a while later in the evening; almost equally urgent reasons require him to be here & in Tucson next week & he is going to meet Hayes at Maricopa—also by telegrams we see that Father will be just twenty hours too late to meet Hayes, & Alex[ander] sent a very disappointing telegram about mines—so between perplexities & wearing disappointments his head is a hot box & we have need to make a further draft on our Mark Tapleyism [optimism].[24] I had a letter of the 11. from Mother this morning, 8½ days.

Thursday 21st. Letter of the 4 Oct. from Mother, which shows the pleasing irregularity of our mail service. Also a telegram of the 18 from Albany (which means she is with Charley on the Putnam), saying all well & Father started 16 for Tucson. During the day I went across & bade Mrs. A. M. Smith goodbye as they leave tomorrow & down to see Mrs. Wollenberg for a little. Rest of the time indoors. Judge Silent came up to meals & was so very tired that he staid on a while after dinner. He is so wearied that he thinks he won't be up to the journey down to the rail & back starting tomorrow especially as it would oblige his sitting up all this night doing legal work; & yet he wants to meet Hayes. Also the escape from jail in Mineral Park of two of the three desperate highwaymen whose trial & conviction was the case of the last Mohave term, worries him for they are really bad men & both counties were relieved when they were tried, convicted & sentenced.

Along near 9 o'clock the Judge came up again (bringing Mr. Stephenson with him) to tell me that the escaped prisoners had been recaptured, hunted down by the Hualapais—& to show me a telegram which said Hayes "wouldn't reach Maricopa till Monday or Tuesday morning," which gives Father some twenty-four hours ahead of him in the Territory. This double good turn in the chapter of accidents was very welcome to both of us, & freshened Judge S. up so much that he thought by doing a hard day's work tomorrow, he would be able to start Saturday & meet the President & Father at Maricopa, which I hope he can do.

Friday, 22nd. Quiet indoor day. Judge Silent came up to meals & staid on a while after each as Court wasn't sitting today, he having other sorts of legal business to attend to, some of which is of such a nature as to take all his time & prevent his going down to meet Mr. Hayes, which is a real disappointment to him. Venus & Jupiter just superb right after sundown.

Saturday 23rd. Letter of 14th from Mother. Went & asked Mrs. Wollenberg & Mrs. Lewis to spend the afternoon here, which they did. Judge Silent came up as usual & might have staid a little after dinner & rested but that Mr. Lewis came after him. The lovely weather broke in the afternoon with clouds & a cold wind, but the night was mild.

Thursday Oct. 24th. Good letter of 13 from Mother. Saw in the morning's "Bulletin" (S.F., 20th) a notice of the death of the Rev. John Daniel, the

Judge's father-in-law [by his first marriage] who has been more like a father to him & to whom he is thoroughly attached. He must have known it by the telegraph & it is that which has worn him down so in the last few days. Very few people here know they are related so he won't be put through the trial of unfelt condolences. The Judge came up to breakfast, & as he left, seeing I knew it, he spoke a little about Mr. Daniel's death. But he belongs to those who can't speak a real grief that is just fresh upon them, which I understand. We both dined at the Lewises, it being their wedding anniversary (& they not knowing about Mr. Daniels). I came home right after dinner. The rest of my day was indoors & my letter to Mother was forgotten by Chung which I didn't know till the Santa Fe mail was closed—the first time it has happened.

Monday 25th (Springfield).[25] Went out for a little to see Mrs. Lewis & Mrs. Churchill in the morning—rest of the day indoors sewing. Mrs. Wollenberg & Mrs. Ellis called in the afternoon & the La Mottes stopped by to take me driving, but I didn't go ("just dressing for dinner"). The Judge came up to meals, & staid on a while after dinner, coming up again later with telegrams from Father (Maricopa 25) to him & to me, saying he would write from Tucson & asking the earliest day the Judge could meet him there, "very important." We had each telegraphed to him this afternoon to Maricopa; it's very good to have him in the Territory & to know he & the Judge will so soon be together.

Tuesday 26th. Two good letters of the 15 & 16 from Mother—full of cheering business news, which she has risked through the mail, thinking Father will be some time with the Judge in Tucson (as has been planned for this date) & I hearing nothing for a while yet. A very pleasant letter of the 5th from Dr. Jameson, still at Portsmouth. Sewing morning; afternoon wrote to Father & to Mother; went to see Mrs. Lewis & Mrs. Wollenberg; several ladies called here while I was out. The Judge came up to meals & staid a bit after each, talking over future possible plans. Mr. Lewis came & took him off right after dinner, or he might have staid longer. Weather still good.

Wednesday 27th. Letter of the 12 from Mother, rather low in the mind about business, etc., so I'm glad yesterday's cheerful letter of the 16 got here first. Mrs. St. James called in the morning & I went up to see Mrs. Buffum in the afternoon; rest of the day sewing. A report was circulated in town that Father was coming up with Genl. Wilcox. I don't believe it, but telegraphed & tomorrow I shall write, asking Father not to. Judge Silent came up to dinner & again for a while in the evening. I think we were the only ones of the "beau monde" [fashionable society] of Prescott who didn't go to the theatre where the Dramatic Club were giving "Damon & Pythias."

Thursday 28th. Letter writing morning; called on Mrs. Rodenburg in the afternoon & Mrs. Merrill called here. Hot & summer bright out. Judge Silent came up to breakfast & dinner, staying on a mite after the latter—busy today with the ruling about an adjourned term not holding good in this Territory when a term in another county intervenes; & its consequences in the Alexander case—set for this day but now having to go over to the next term—next week. Also lots of B[lack] W[arrior] & T[uscumbia] business. The evening papers had telegrams from Tucson about a public reception given last night to "Gov. Frémont" & largely attended & three more to follow this week to Father & to Genl. Wilcox, at private houses.[26]

Friday 29th. Indoor day—mostly sewing. Judge Silent came up to meals & again for a while in the evening; his day had been very busy including winning an extension of 60 days from the Tuscumbia owners, & also from three of the B. W. owners & sending out to get the consent of the fourth— & most troublesome one. Without that consent the B. W. arrangement falls thro' & there are parties here working for that result, CC [Clark Churchill?] strongly, but they don't know that we are working for an extension, but expect our prospects to fall thro' with a non-payment on Nov. 1, the day time is up on the old arrangement.

Saturday 30th. Letter of 18th from Mother, off Albany—all well on the Putnam. Sewing & letter writing day for me, with some copying for the Judge. Mrs. Wollenberg, Mrs. W. Bashford & Miss Dunning called. The Judge was very tired when he came up to breakfast & staid on quite a little while after it—talking of his home people & of San Jose. He went down again looking a tiny bit rested. At dinner he reported the Black Warrior matter satisfactorily closed & papers in bank; the distribution of the money to take place tonight when there may be some unpleasantness on the part of those whose plans against us have been balked, but there can be no disarrangement of the business. This is a triumph for us & achieved by a tour de force on the Judge's part which has left him very tired & worn.

Sunday 31st. Quiet morning. When the Judge came up to breakfast he told me that as Judge French had arrived by the morning's stage, he would—by working double tides all day & on into the night—be able to get off tomorrow morning; that they had gotten quite through with the

Bl[ack] W[arrior] business last night; & also of Capt. Eagan's request to see him before he left in order to say to him that he believed he had been mistaken. The Judge granted the interview at his room this evening & Mr. Geo. Bowers[27] to be present—an odd turn in affairs! Judge Silent was too hurried to stay long or to return; he dined with the Lewises. In the afternoon I saw to the Judge's lunch for tomorrow & read. Judge French called but "I didn't hear him knock."

Monday 1st Nov. Up at four & had the house good & warm for the Judge when he came up for his breakfast at 6—the restaurant food is so bad I had insisted he should do so that he might start fair. He told me of last night's interview & Capt. E[agan] saying that he was "becoming convinced he had been totally in error in regard to" Judge S. & would when he became quite so make his apology as publicly as he had made the charges—that was the gist of his visit—Geo. Bowers present. The Judge had other scraps to tell me & some "instructions" as I had acted a little as his A.D.C. He stayed on till near stage time, leaving by the Black Cañon, seemingly the only passenger. He will reach Tucson Tuesday at midnight & on Wednesday Father & he can begin their talk, which I wish I could be by to hear. Then he holds a term in Pinal [County] & may have to in Pima [County] before his resignation is acted on. What he does then is still hazy. I am glad for his sake that he is going to be out of this town, but I shall miss him so very much.

In the afternoon I went down for a little to Mrs. Lewis's & found Mrs. Wollenberg there. Judge French turned in there later, so visibly to see me & give me some messages from Father that Mrs. L. was huffed at it. He had been at our house again & heard where I was. The weather trying to spoil itself.

Tuesday 2nd Nov. Even in this far away place the excitement over Election Day ran high but everything was quiet enough, considering the locale, very quiet. Our bay window commanded the approach to the polls so we had a busy scene all through the day as the local & territorial elections are hotly contested, this being the first time party lines have been drawn in the Territory. No returns from the east at 9 when the telegraph office closed. Mrs. Wollenberg & Mrs. Lewis took breakfast here & spent the afternoon with me & Mrs. Bean called. I felt half sick all day—chilled. Had a pleasant letter from Father, 30th.

Wednesday 3rd. Mr. Lewis called early to tell me that New York state had gone Republican, wh[ich] makes things [sure?] for Garfield. As I had a headache I took Thor & went for a walk, stopping a moment at Mrs.

Buffum's. Read & sewed. Mr. Haskell, back this morning from the south, called to tell me he had seen Father in Tucson. I had pleasant letters from Father & from Frank & a nice little telegram from Judge Silent (Maricopa, 2nd). . . .

Friday 5th. Had four letters from Mother posted at New Haven & Bridgeport, Conn. & New Brighton on the 26. She had had a lovely trip on the Putnam with the children & was *quite* well; but when they got back they found orders for Charley to sail on Nov. 5 (today) for Brazil there to join the flagship, which naturally upset them & all their plans. However, they think it will be good for Charley's sciatica to avoid the cold winter & they hope to get him a new station for next summer.

Towards noon I had a telegram from Father (Maricopa, 5) saying he would reach here Sunday morning; so Mary & I did a lot towards getting things in order for him. Genl. Willcox called to tell me "how your Father is enjoying Tucson" & made quite a visit. Now [that] Garfield is surely in I suppose he thinks it just as well to renew friendly relations, but I won't be "picked up again." Mrs. Wollenberg also called & asked [me] to dine with them Sunday, but I excused myself. Sewed a lot on Frank's afghan & wrote him a long letter. Weather getting pretty cool. Nights cold.

Saturday 6th (McLean's birthday). Helped Mary get the house in its best order for Father; wrote McLean; sewed; & at one went to Mrs. Ellis to lunch where I met Mrs. Wollenberg & Mrs. Lewis & staid till near dinner.

Sunday 7th. Up at 4 & had the house well warmed by the time Father got here (6½). He was tired by the journey & chilled to the bone by the long cold night in the mountains, but I made him go to bed & stay there till midday taking his petit dejeuner [breakfast] there & he was almost quite rested before he went to bed for the night. We spent the day talking over things—some very good ones for the future & one real bad one in the near past—& in the packing for Father's backward journey on Tuesday morning. I'm afraid he took the hard journey up here chiefly to see me, but I didn't know in time to do anything to stop him. It wasn't known in town that "the Gov." had arrived so we had our day uninterruptedly to ourselves. Father is looking really well in spite of the hard journey & of all the business worries he has had to breast; he had his "talk" with the Judge & is "*quite* satisfied."

Monday 8th. A year since Frank left. Letters from Mother & from Nelly. Father was intensely busy all day, seeing a stream of people (including Mr.

Gosper 3 times & Mr. Churchill!) who each had their grievances to lay before him; writing Thanksgiving Proc[lamation] & lots of other Territorial work: the people even called while we were at meals. In the evenings the Buffums & Lewises called, knowing he was going tomorrow (Mrs. B. claimed me for Thanksgiving dinner). Then he went down & secured his seat in the morning stage & after he came up again we had a little home talk till an early bedtime.

Father has to go East again after one day's halt in Tucson for finishing talk with Judge Silent (who is pinned down there by court), but counts on being back here on Dec. 20. It is sharp work & fatiguing but holds the possibility—he thinks probability—of such thorough success as to be worth the trouble & the risk of discontent it may make in this part of the Territory. Tucson is pleased just now with him & won't care.

Tuesday 9th. Up very early & had everything ready for Father's 6 o'clock breakfast & start at 7—by the Black Cañon. We had time for some scraps of talk; & Father started feeling well & confident of his success in the coming work. It was a hard journey up here for him to take, but, I think, Territorial affairs needed it which reconciles me to it somewhat; & I was happy to see him, though knowing how short a time he had to stay it seemed like a long goodbye & "last words" are always insufficient. Then, too, I had to act as glossary to the quarrels the people told him each only their own version of, which took time & wasn't pleasant, but I think he was himself more satisfied than if he had returned East directly from Tucson. I moved over into Father's room where I'll stay till his return, & close my room & the parlor which are cold rooms & need lots of wood to warm them, whereas the dining room stove suffices for that room, Father's & Mary's & even then burns but little wood. Settled back into my routine of sewing & letter writing, with scrapy reading. Cold day.

Nov. 10th. Indoor sewing morning. In the afternoon I made ten visits, including some in S. Prescott & some across the creek. Had a telegram from Father at Phoenix saying: "reached here in good order;" so he is over the fatiguing part of the road & reaches Tucson & the Judge tonight at 12.

Thursday, 11th. Sewing indoor day. Mrs. Wollenberg called in the morning & I made her stay to breakfast. Mrs. Biddle & Mrs. Churchill in the afternoon; & in the evening Mr. Foster! ostensibly about a Nat[ional] Pub[lication] com[munication?] which he wanted Father to review, but I think in reality to pump [me] about Father's movements.

Friday 12th. Cheerful toned letter, of the 1st, from Mother with lots about Dr. Morton & his wife. Worked at Frank's afghan as the bone of the day, & made four visits in the afternoon. Weather nipping cold all day & ice nearly two inches thick formed in the night. The "Miner" copied from the "Citizen" of Tucson the notice of the Bar's action in regard to our Judge's resignation, which it gave me great pleasure to see.[28]

Sunday 14th. Quiet home day till 4 when I went to dinner at the Lewis's— only their family & Dr. Ainsworth came. Home early.

Monday 15th Nov. My 38th birthday. Had a pleasant letter from Father, written Tucson, 12 & posted Maricopa, 13th. He started eastward feeling thoroughly well & leaving everything smooth in Tucson. I sent Emmy Lewis down a pretty birthday cake & later in the day she brought me up an "objit" which Mrs. Lewis told me she had insisted on getting for me. Mr. Lewis called for a moment in the evening. Night cold.

Tuesday 16th. Letter from Mother & a goodbye note from Charley, written as they were convoying him down the bay on the Putnam to take the Brazilian mail steamer. He only expects to be gone a few months. Worked on Frank's afghan nearly all day & made Mrs. Wollenberg a visit. Night very cold.

Wednesday 17th. Day extremely cold. I staid in & worked on Frank's afghan. Nice little note from Father, dropped at Los Angeles. . . .

Friday 19th. Had a nice little letter from the Judge, 14th at Florence. Learned that he had written before from Tucson; that hasn't reached me & as it had business in it I'm sorry outsiders got hold of it. I wrote warning the Judge & sent my letter through Mr. Long. . . .

Sunday 21st. A lonesome, homesick day—silly of me but I couldn't help it & a nice letter I had from the Judge only made me want to be near them all the more.

Postscript

March–November 1881

As far as the editor knows, the entry of November 21, 1880, ends Lily Fré-
mont's Prescott diary. Perhaps she continued a daily record, but if so, that
portion either is unlocated or has been destroyed. Her errors in chronology in
recalling her Tucson experiences suggest she abandoned her practice of keep-
ing a diary. Frémont returned to the territory in January 1881; on March 17,
after the conclusion of the sessions of the eleventh legislative assembly, he and
Lily moved from Prescott to Tucson. At the end of March, Frémont again left
for the East. Lily stayed on in Tucson until after her father's resignation of the
territorial governorship. She recounted some of her Tucson experiences and
especially her illness in The Recollections of Elizabeth Benton Frémont,
written with the assistance of I. T. Martin and published in 1912. A short-
ened version of this thirteen-page account follows.

It was in March, 1881, when we left Prescott for Tucson and began again,
as it were, a new life. I had grown to like Prescott and was particularly fond
of its people, the women having been so warm hearted and hospitable that
it was not so very hard to forget that I was many weary miles away from
my home part of the country.

Tucson was about three thousand feet lower than Prescott, and perhaps was then one of the oldest as well as one of the most unsanitary
towns in America. The heavy summer rains drew the poison out of the sun
dried soil, until even the seasoned Americans fell by the wayside, as flowers fall after a blighting storm.

"You will die of the fever in Tucson," I was told when first I mentioned
the plans to move there, a prophecy which came near being fulfilled.
There was but one "vegetable man" in Prescott in those days who had
asparagus for sale—a vegetable of which I was very fond—and when he
learned that we were to leave for other parts, he resolutely refused to
longer supply our table. . . . "Nothing to sell you. You are going to leave
Prescott." . . .

The time at Tucson was filled to overflowing with excitement, one thing succeeding another with lightning like rapidity, though one experience in that town—the blowing up of a powder magazine—almost defies description.[1]

The magazine was situated about a mile from town and at the time of the explosion I was the only member of the family at Tucson, with our faithful Chinese cook [Ah Chung] and a maid [Mary] of all work for my companions.

The great comet of that year had filled the hearts of both whites and Mexicans with fear and dread, even though the scenic effect in the heavens was beautiful to behold. Most of the people slept on what might be termed the sidewalks, and in going to post letters on the Overland Mail, I often passed the rows of sleepers, in company with our dog Thaw [Thor].

The night of the blowing up of the powder magazine, the walks were lined with the sleeping populace. I slept in the corral back of our home, its high walls giving it the seclusion of a private boudoir, and the maid shared this "apartment" with me. A second before the explosion I was wide awake. Above were the shining stars, the comet in its almost supernatural beauty, clear skies and an almost living illustration of "Peace on earth, Good will to men," when lo, with a roar like unto that of a hundred thousand cannons, the town was instantly covered in darkness. The heavens were obscured by an inky pall, which hung not more than ten feet above the people. The soil became covered with a black mist resembling burnt flour and as the glory of the stars was blotted out, the night was filled with the piercing screams of a terrified multitude. Men and women fell instinctively on their knees, beseeching mercy from the Father of all, while here and there could be heard the rushing footsteps of fleeing people—fleeing, they knew not from what or whence!

Viewed in retrospect, the sight was wonderful to behold! The earth blown heavenward, fell again like a black snow covering the ground like a harbinger of death. People forgot about the scorpions and were rushing barefooted hither and thither, feeling in the blackness of the night for friends, and anxious to make peace with foes!

Ten minutes, which seemed like an hour, of unspeakable terror reigned, before the townspeople learned what had caused the trouble, and were assured that the end of the world was not at hand. . . .

Where the magazine had been two minutes before the explosion, there was a great hole in the earth, as if a hundred monsters had mowed to the bottom crust, and there was not a trace of a wall left to show that an adobe had once been there. . . .

The house we occupied at Tucson was noticeable mainly for its very

The restored Sosa-Carrillo-Frémont house in Tucson.
(Courtesy of the Arizona Historical Society, Tucson, photo #59635.)

long rooms, and it contained a "sacred parlor," as I used to call it, because the owners of the house never thought of using what was their best room.

The hallway was really the living room. The door was left open all night but closed during the day, in order to keep the room in habitable condition. It was known as a cool room—exceptionally cool—so cool in fact, that its thermometer never registered much higher than 97 or 100 degrees in the coolest part of the day, when the hall was thought to be delightfully cool. Towards evening, it was like a bake oven and had to be abandoned for the corral behind the house.

I can remember using the "sacred parlor" just once during my stay at Tucson. Archbishop Salpointe came to pay a little visit and I ushered him into the best room in the house. The piano was there and a Prussian soldier from Fort Lowell, who happened to be a fine musician, was in the room tuning the instrument. Soon we were joined by two nuns from the nearby hospital, and we were deeply interested in a tale the Archbishop was telling us concerning his experience in the wilds, when the front door burst open and a man, a stranger to me, called out:

"Miss Frémont, Garfield has been shot and is dying!"[2] . . .

Scarcely had the excitement over the fate of the martyred president died away ere a cloudburst came, lest life and living in Tucson might grow to be monotonous! The summer rains last for six weeks in that town, and before the cloudburst, four inches of rain fell in less than three-quarters of an hour, quite a respectable rain even for Tucson.

Across the street from our home was an adobe house that had been newly painted and furnished throughout. I looked that way and saw a flood of muddy water running through its immaculate interior. The town itself was all but submerged, the streets a perfect sheet of water.

Adjoining the ill-fated house of our neighbor was another adobe to which a bride had been brought from New York but two days before. As the walls of the adobe cracked and ran together again like so much ginger bread, a wagon drove up to carry away the hysterical bride, so thoroughly frightened that she was only able to emit a series of piercing screams! . . .

Our house was not affected by the water. It was built on the higher side of the street, and there was a doorway underneath the hall made for just such emergencies, with a way to let the water out, rather than up and into the house. I had a Mexican break open this doorway with an axe, the poor fellow worked up to his knees in water, and the hundred foot lot surrounding the place looked like a miniature lake after he had finished his task.

Our Chinese was as faithful during that cloudburst and as valuable as he had been in every emergency which he met with us during our life in the new country. His first thought was ever for our safety and welfare, and I am glad of an opportunity to say a good word for the son of an abused race, for after his years of service with our family, he merited full well the words:

"Well done, thou good and faithful servant!"

The great danger threatened by a cloudburst in Tucson may not be realized by people of to-day until it is known that in those days a ton or more of earth was thrown over every cactus roof in order to keep the adobes cool, and with incessant rain much less than with a cloudburst, there was always the danger of the roof falling in and the earth smothering the occupants of the house.[3]

After the cloudburst, Tucson was shut off from the outside world for fully two weeks, no mail coming in and no food supplies, parts of the newly made railroad from Yuma to Tucson having been washed away in the twinkling of an eye. During that time, I kept house with no butter, no eggs, very little milk. The town depended upon the water from a spring which was peddled around from house to house. I did manage to obtain some Chinese sugar and to exist, after a fashion.

Butter was a luxury which I scarcely ever tasted during that time at Tucson; it had to be shipped in from California and there were then no refrigerator cars. In crossing the desert the jars of butter were melted into liquid oil, and as ice was twenty cents a pound in Tucson, only the enormously rich could afford to boast always of a plentiful supply.

After the excitement of the cloudburst had worn away, I was awakened one night by the clatter of horses' feet and the pitiful cries of a woman:

"He has been bitten by a rattlesnake. For God's sake, get a doctor quick," the cry filled with all the agony of a despairing mother's broken heart.

The mother was hurrying her six-year-old son to the Mexican family next door, crying for help as she tenderly lifted the little sufferer out of the rude wagon. She lived on a ranch a few miles out of the town, and the trip could not be made in the heat of the day, hence the wild night ride.

The little lad had gone to the well bare-footed, at sundown, stepped on a rattlesnake and was instantly bitten in the heel by the poisonous reptile. The mother picked up the fatally wounded child, her mother heart telling her that he was in the grip of Death.

As the mother reached our door, a man of the town happened to be riding by on horse back. Like the wind he was off for a physician, but before he had arrived the soul of the little one had hearkened to the call of its Maker and only the agonized cries of the bereft mother broke the silence of the night.[4]

Tucson, filled with the many similar experiences that will remain with me forever, brought its own share of suffering to me. For weeks, I lingered between life and death, fast in the grip of typhoid fever. I had reached the point where the physicians told me I had better arrange my property affairs and make known any wishes I might have in regard to my funeral. Cheerful news for a sick woman miles removed from kindred, but I sent for Judge Charles Silent, now of Los Angeles, and did truly make my last will and testament.[5]

That I was near unto death may best be understood in the light of an experience of that sick room. My maid had been leaving a glass of water and a cracker beside my bed—real evidences of solicitude in Tucson—and the cracker had tempted a rat, when it failed to tempt me. One night when alone in the room I felt a hard lump in the back of my heavy hair. I tossed from side to side in an effort to find a spot free from what I thought were tangles, when I found that the tangles must be removed before I could rest. Accordingly I put my hand in my hair. Horrors! A rat was entangled in its meshes and vainly trying to extricate itself. Too ill to be mindful of the danger, too ill even to feel a pang of fright, I helped the rat free himself from the tresses, and fell into a dreamless sleep.[6]

My father at that time was in New York working for the territory and for himself, as men have a habit of doing now and then. He was purchasing arms for Arizona, as the Indians were growing more desperate and defiant, and at times he was trying to float an Arizona copper mine upon which he held a six months' option.[7] He tried to convince the New York financiers that the "Jerome" copper mine was a fortune maker, but they would not listen to him and credited his enthusiasm to his zeal for opening the western country. He lost his option and years later Senator [William A.] Clark of Montana obtained the "Jerome," now known as the Clark mines, and the source of perhaps the greatest share of the Clark millions.

Just as I was recovering from the fever, I was sitting in the corral back of our house when the report came to me that Fort Apache nearby had been wiped out and that all the officers were killed. All at that fort were friends of mine and the news was freighted with distress for me. On the morrow, however, I learned that the report was exaggerated, and that the officers had successfully beaten off the attack, which was picturesque in the extreme.

The old Indian chief led the attack on the fort, rode into the corral at Fort Apache when it was filled with officers and men, and threw up his spear, whirling it and catching it as it fell—a signal of defiance such as was used in the border raids of Scotland. His bravery went for naught and the white men saved the day against the courageous red men of the plains.[8]

The paper that brought the news of the safety of the men at the fort, however, brought other dismal news to me, the news of the burning of Mor[r]ell's warehouse in New York City.[9] It was the first warehouse built in the upper part of the city and the residents made a practice of storing their priceless treasures there when they left the city.

When leaving New York we had stored at Mor[r]ell's, all those belongings that we considered too precious to take with us to the west—and now all was in flames![10]

Small wonder that the fever lingered and that I was finally sent home to New York to recuperate.[11]

Appendix

The following letter from Elizabeth Benton Frémont to Ella Haskell Browne, Prescott, 9 December 1878, is in the Frémont Papers, Bancroft Library. The main portion of the letter is in typescript; the notes to the floor plan in EBF's handwriting. The floor plan has been made from her original drawing.

Dear Nelly,

We have made our move & are beginning to feel settled in our new house; we moved in on the day after Thanksgiving having to do things very suddenly as our landlady changed her mind & only gave a few days notice of her coming, so we had to move before our house was ready for us & were only camped in it for the first week, papering & carpeting going on after we came in; in repapering our new landlord let Mother choose the paperings so they are pretty & match; the whole house is sweetly clean having been done over à neuf for us, & I think we shall be right comfortable in it. I enclose [for] you a plan of the house, which though out of [scale] will enable you to follow our letters & to place us rightly in our rooms. The view from the bay window in the parlor is very fine: to the east the Fitches cottage on the corner diagonally across from us, with their mule deer "Bessie" walking about in her paddock, & above it Mr. Churchill's little octagon red brick house with its tall central chimney from which the thin blue smoke is sharply outlined against the sky, with these is one very sym[m]etrical & tall pine back of which for the past week there has been a coolly brilliant full moon; to the north our view is somewhat blocked by two cottages but to the northwest & west we have a really beautiful view ranging from the rugged grandeur of Granite Mt. along the line of intervening pine covered hills to Thumb Butte, which rises a sheer columnar mass of rock from the top of an already tall mountain—right behind it the sun sets & when there are clouds "the effects" are wonderfully beautiful. In the immediate foreground one block below us the Plaza begins & it is the business centre of the town; we overlook one side of it & one of the streets which leads off towards a busy part of the Territory—

the Camp Verde & Santa Fé road—so that we see all sorts of teams from the "prairie schooner" with its twenty, or more, mules down through many gradations to the solitary miner going out on a prospecting tour & driving before him his one burro with its heavy pack. My window has an even more extended mountain view to the West & slightly southward. To come inside the house Mother's room & mine are papered of a warm brown with fall leaves on it, & we are to have curtains of a brown grounded chintz which has oats, daffadowndillies & narcissus on it—Mother's to be lined, mine only bound, with a soft dark red cottony stuff—so you see they are all well matched. The parlor is papered with a good New York looking red & gold papering & has a carpet of a red ground with small bunches of flowers—reds, yellows, brown & purples—on it, not exactly modern East-lake but pretty & very convenient for muddy feet,—the furniture in the parlor is very solid with large comfortable chairs & looks very well in the red of the room though you will be horrified to hear that it is horsehair & rosewood; but it is a good stuff for this dusty town & possible to keep clean: we are going to have a big centre table round & with a red cover & some book shelves & when our "objects" are properly scattered about the whole will have a right homelike effect. We have put muslin blinds—with big spots—against the windows eastern fashion & mean later on to have a curtain across the bay window. The dining room is chiefly in oak colors & having a window to the east is a cheerful bright breakfast room. Frank's room is of the warm grey & red order, with oak furniture; Mother's furniture is walnut; mine & Mary's are cottage sets of the make belief oak kind; all of us have comfortable beds—even to Thor who has his own comforter in a corner of my room. Mother likes this house very much & is very well.

Father has gone north to look into the condition of the Hualapais & Mohave Indians & will be absent two weeks, he took Frank with him & is also accompanied by Judge Silent, judge of this district, & by Mr. Churchill—one of the first lawyers here; they went off very comfortably in a government ambulance drawn by four mules—in fact it was Genl. Wilcox's own ambulance which he had fitted up for Father; they will be four days & a half on the way & as they go through a good game country they took rifles & shot guns with them & expect to have some good shooting. You should have seen their roll of blankets & comforters! for the nights are cold & they will have to do some sleeping out. When Thor saw the ambulance he insisted on going too & was cross & cranky all the day because he had been left behind, but he feels better tonight as I took him for a walk up the hill this evening & he saw two dead dogs which caused him to trot home with his tail proudly curled.

We have a right good market here, quite a decent lot of vegetables & in

The restored Frémont residence on the grounds of the Sharlot Hall Museum, Prescott. In the early 1900s, the house had been moved to Union Street from its original location at the corner of Gurley and Marina Streets. (Courtesy of the Sharlot Hall Museum/Library Archives, Prescott, Ariz., photo #SHM 213p.)

meats besides the usual muttons & beefs lots of good fat venison & wild turkey. Mr. Browne will tell you they are a combination of turkey & pheasant with a slight touch of guinea fowl; we think them very good & cranberries go with them quite as well as with the barn yard turkey—& we think wild grape jelly better with venison than currant jelly. . . .

Our household continues to work along smoothly—Mary has made quite a number of acquaintances, amongst them the four sisters of St. Joseph who have charge of the county hospital & the housekeeper of the hotel & she has the regular Sunday services of her church & a Wednesday lecture during Advent too—with the prospect of the present priest being changed for another who won't scold & dun quite as much as this one does. She is really quite contented here. Chung continues to be a treasure, getting along contentedly with an anything but complete batterie de cuisine & managing his department with intelligent economy. He likewise makes all sorts of handy contrivances out of old bits of iron & wood. This morning he made an excellent potato masher out of a most unpromising looking billet of wood. I think he would please Mr. Browne; I know his cooking would. We have very good fresh butter & fresh eggs brought to the door every Wednesday-Saturday by an Italian from the Southern slope of Mt. St. Gothard who has a farm a few miles out of town. Our vegetables are all raised by chinese who also bring them to the door in the regular paniers on a stick we are used to on the five cent fans. I find pigeon English the hardest to understand of any broken English I have yet had to do with, but the men are patient & by dint of repetitions & sign language I manage to understand. Chung speaks quite well as he has been so long with Betty & I often have to get him to act as interpreter. How pleased Mrs. Browne must have been to go to Europe. This will reach you along about Christmas. I can't get beyond loving good wishes for you & the babies this year but I begin to have hopes that before this time next year we can make up for arrears of Xmases & birthdays. In the meantime we have to take it out in good wishes & you know Nelly dear how hearty & thorough they are for you & yours. Yours lovingly,

Lily Frémont

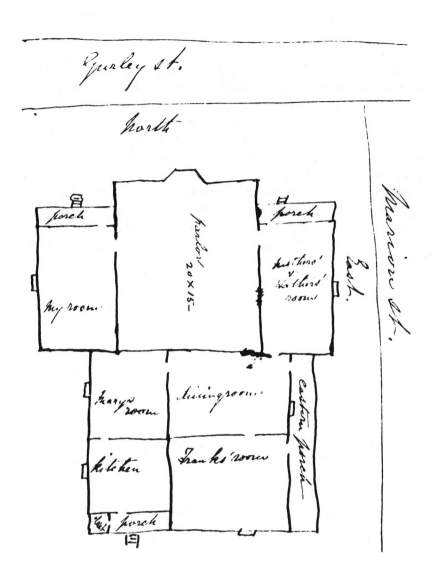

Floor plan of the Frémont residence in Prescott. (Courtesy of the Bancroft Library, University of California, Berkeley, in Frémont Family Papers, BANC MSS C-B 397.)

I have made Frank's room out of proportion—large—& Mother's & mine long & narrow whereas they are nearly square; & I forgot to leave places for the front door which opens from the parlor onto the northeastern porch; & for the door from parlor to the living room. The wriggle on the eastern wall of the parlor is meant for the open fireplace, which has one like itself in Mother's room. There is a good stove in the dining room & one in my room which has a place on it where I put a thing with water when I light the fire in the morning & by the time I get up to dress the water is very warm. Frank's room is warmed by a pipe from the kitchen stove. We only need the fires at night & in the early morning for the days are pleasantly warm. Frank's room has a window to the South & is flooded all day with sunshine. On Marina *[spelled Marion on floor plan]* street to the East of us there are no buildings as the block above us is reserved for the future capitol & other government buildings, so on that side we have an upward slope of hillside with some beautiful tall pine trees. Across the way on Gurley st. are two large cottages used as lodging for gentlemen who take their meals at restaurants down on the Plaza, a block below us.

~

Notes

Introduction

1. Officially called Whipple Barracks after April 5, 1879 (Frazer, *Forts of the West*, 15).
2. For the founding and early histories of Prescott and Fort Whipple, see Henson, *Founding a Wilderness Capital*, and Wallace, "Fort Whipple."
3. *Arizona Miner*, Apr. 18, 1879; *Weekly Arizona Citizen*, Mar. 5, 1880.
4. *Arizona Enterprise*, Oct. 30, 1878. See also Nov. 20, 1878.
5. San Francisco *Bulletin*, printed in *Arizona Miner*, Dec. 17, 1878.
6. Hinton, *Hand-Book to Arizona*, 253. However, the *Arizona Enterprise* (Sept. 21, 1878) lamented the lack of a woolen mill.
7. JCF to Charles Edwards Lester, New York, July 2, 1879, giving the contents of a letter from JBF, Allan Nevins Papers (copy from Waitt Papers), Columbia University.
8. Hamilton, *Resources of Arizona*, 1881 ed., 28.
9. *Arizona Miner*, Sept. 13, 1878.
10. The unnamed local paper was quoted in *Spirit of Missions* 44 (June 1879): 221.
11. EBF to NHB, Oct. 31, 1878, FP.
12. JBF to Spalding [ca. Mar. 1879], printed in Herr and Spence, *Letters*, 460–63.
13. *Arizona Miner*, Oct. 1, 1880. In appealing for donations, the Reverend R. A. Windes of the American Baptist Home Missionary Society announced that the Baptists had just dedicated a $2,500 chapel. In addition to the Catholics, the Methodists, the Baptists, and the Congregationalists, the Presbyterians also had a "handsome" church (Hamilton, *Resources of Arizona*, 1881 ed., 28).
14. For horse racing and cockfighting, see the *Arizona Enterprise*, Nov. 16 and 20, and *Arizona Miner*, Dec. 17, 1880. Arizona was the only place at the time in the United States where a lottery was authorized by law, the Louisiana lottery having been legislated out of existence (*Arizona Enterprise*, Mar. 1, 1879). For the authorization and quick demise of the Arizona lottery, see Wagoner, *Arizona Territory*, 172–73, and Smith, *Goldwaters*, 62–66.

15. *Arizona Enterprise,* Sept. 21 and Oct. 12, 1878.

16. EBF to NHB, May 11, [1880,] FP.

17. The *Arizona Miner* (Apr. 23, 1880) noted the sale of the Fitch home to Clark Churchill; Lily reported the gossip (EBF to NHB, May 11, 1880, FP).

18. JBF to William J. Morton, June 26, 1878, printed in Herr and Spence, *Letters,* 444; Fireman, "Frémont's Arizona Adventure," 14.

19. Wagoner, *Arizona Territory,* 164.

20. *Arizona Miner,* Aug. 29, 1879; JBF to NHB, Oct. 3, 1879, printed in Herr and Spence, *Letters,* 469–70.

21. *Arizona Miner,* Nov. 12, 1879.

22. These mines were the Black Warrior, Tuscumbia, and Tuscarora (JCF to W. K. Rogers, Mar. 10, 1880, RP).

23. JBF to W. K. Rogers, Nov. 9 and Dec. 2, 1879, RP.

24. JBF to W. K. Rogers, Dec. 7, 1879, RP.

25. JCF to W. K. Rogers, Mar. 10, 1880, RP.

26. *Arizona Miner,* May 27, 1881.

27. JBF to Hayes, undated letter, Rutherford B. Hayes Library.

28. See Lister and Lister, "Chinese Sojourners"; JBF to Geordie Browne, Nov. 14, 1878, FP.

29. EBF to NHB, Aug. 8, 1880, FP.

30. For expressions of anti-Chinese sentiment in Prescott, see *Arizona Miner,* Nov. 29, 1878, and Aug. 6, 1880. For treatment of the Chinese in territorial Arizona and Prescott, see Fong, "Sojourners," and Lister and Lister, "Chinese Sojourners."

31. JBF to Kit Carson, [May 1863,] Graff Collection, Newberry Library.

32. *Arizona Weekly Star,* Dec. 1, 1881.

33. EBF to NHB, Jan. 13, 1880, FP.

34. EBF to William J. Morton, Feb. 18, 1879, MP; EBF to NHB, Aug. 8, 1880, FP.

35. EBF to NHB, Easter Sunday 1880, FP.

36. EBF to NHB, Feb. 22, 1872, FP.

37. EBF to Sarah McDowell Preston, Aug. 1907, Preston Family Papers, University of Kentucky.

38. EBF to NHB, Jan. 26 and Sept. 7, 1879, FP.

39. JBF to Elizabeth Blair Lee, [Dec.] 14 [1855], printed in Herr and Spence, *Letters,* 82.

40. *Arizona Miner,* Mar. 17, 1881.

41. In an undated letter, JBF recounted to NHB Lily's description of the move (FP).

42. For a general discussion of JCF's interest in southern Arizona and Mexico, see Fireman, "Frémont's Arizona Adventure," 17. For major documents on these grandiose schemes, some involving the lawyer Santiago Ainsa in Tucson, see JCF to W. K. Rogers, incomplete and undated letter, RP; agreement between Edgar Conkling of Cincinnati and JCF, May 6, 1880, Ruther-

ford B. Hayes Library; Santiago Ainsa to JCF, Apr. 28, 1881, RP; and JCF to W. K. Rogers, [early June 1881,] RP. Ainsa noted that he had made one of the contracts in Silent's name to protect the governor from criticism.

43. Alexander Willard to JCF, Apr. 4 and June 3, 1882, FP; Alexander Willard to W. K. Rogers, Apr. 6, 1884, RP.

44. *Arizona Miner,* June 24, 1881.

45. *Weekly Arizona Citizen,* Mar. 27, 1881.

46. JBF to Julius E. Hilgard, Sept. 13, 1881, printed in Herr and Spence, *Letters,* 489–90.

47. JBF to Richard C. Drum, Sept. 13, 1881, and to William T. Sherman, Sept. 18, 1881, both letters printed in ibid., 490–92.

48. JBF to NHB, undated letter, FP.

49. Officer, "Frémont House." The *Arizona Weekly Star* (May 19, 1881) reported that the directory would be ready for delivery "about the last of June." When it did appear, it noted on page 27, "Governor Frémont resides one-half the year in Tucson, the other half at Prescott."

50. EBF to JBF, Apr. 10, 1881, FP.

51. JBF to NHB, Aug. 22, [1881,] FP.

52. EBF to NHB, March 1903, FP.

53. Letter of Jan. 5, 1903, Southwest Museum; *Out West,* Jan. 1903, pp. 93–94.

54. Charley, who had become a vice admiral, offered her a home. He died in 1911, eight years before Lily. Major Frank Frémont had serious problems, some of them financial. He was court-martialed and dismissed from the army in 1909.

55. Silent, who died five months before Lily, practiced law in Los Angeles and became a member of the park commission. He first developed Chester Place, an exclusive residential park in Los Angeles, before turning his attention to the Glendora area, where he transformed a mountainside into a place of beauty with palms, exotic trees, and shrubs alternating with beds of flowers. Because he often entertained, he constructed small palm-thatched guest houses on the grounds (Goff, *Arizona Biographical Dictionary;* Powell and Powell, "Chester Place"; Jackson, *Beautiful Glendora*).

56. EBF to Senator Thomas R. Bard, Dec. 31, 1902, and Feb. 8, 1903; Charles Silent to Bard, Jan. 25, 1904, all in Bard Papers, Huntington Library.

57. For an account of Lily's property at Long Beach, and her many moves, see Nichols, "Lily."

58. EBF to NHB, Mar. 10, 1912, FP.

59. EBF to chairman, Nov. 15, 1912; also a photograph of the groundbreaking, both in the Southwest Museum.

60. Frank to EBF, Mar. 5, 1917, FP.

61. Los Angeles *Times,* May 29, 1919.

62. Lummis journals, June 2, 1919, Southwest Museum.

63. Lummis, *Bronco Pegasus,* 11.

64. F. P. Frémont's memo for Allan Nevins, FP.

65. EBF to NHB, [ca. summer 1872,] FP.
66. Fiske and Lummis, *Charles F. Lummis,* 155.
67. Chambers-Schiller, *Liberty;* Vicinus, *Independent Women;* and Freeman and Klaus, "Blessed or Not?" have been helpful in analyzing EBF's single state.
68. Written at Pocaho, Oct. 24, no year, MP.

Chapter 1
West to Prescott

1. Twenty-eight-year-old Mary McGrath was the Frémonts' long-time and faithful maid. She became a member of one of the committees of the Irish Land League, which had a branch in Arizona, and was provoked at Lily's being entirely out of sympathy with its objectives (EBF to NHB, Jan. 25, 1881, FP).
2. Imprecise quotation from John Mason Neale's *Good King Wenceslas.*
3. Thumb Butte, west of town, was in the shape of a hand doubled with the thumb slightly up and was often referred to by JBF as "the sphinx." Its elevation was 6,514 feet, whereas Granite Mountain to the north and northwest had an elevation of 7,626 feet.
4. Pennsylvania-born Rebecca Evans Buffum, the wife of William M. Buffum, a wealthy businessman, was a social leader in the bustling capital. The *Sharlot Hall Gazette* (vol. 7, no. 2 [1980]) gave a biographical sketch of her and her four sisters, who also went to Prescott and married prominently. In 1889, William Buffum gave up his business interests in Arizona and returned to Los Angeles, where he became associated with two other former Prescottonians, Moses H. Sherman and Eli P. Clark, in the street railway system (McGroarty, *Los Angeles,* 2:54–56).
5. During the winter of 1877–78 the Frémonts were in desperate economic straits. Debt had forced them to a public auction of paintings, books, and furniture and into a cheap rental house on the Staten Island esplanade. They felt the shame of it all.
6. The daughter of Leonidas Haskell, Ella (referred to variously as "Nelly," "Nellie," or "Nell") had married George Browne in 1873. The close friendship with the Frémonts dated back to 1859, when the families were neighbors at Black Point in California.
7. William Jeremiah Morton (1845–1920) became a close friend of the Frémonts after treating the pulmonary problems of their son Frank. The nervous system was his specialty, and after 1878 he was a neurologist in New York City and editor of the *Journal of Nervous and Mental Disease* (1882–1885).
8. The Darts were members of the families of James Dart and William M. Dart, who in 1874–1875 were both living at 44 Park Avenue, New York City. The editor has been unable to sort out the relationship of Maggie, Eleanor,

and the "two Fannys" to the men, but one Fanny seems to have been a wife and another Fanny a daughter. Eleanor and Maggie appear to have been young women at the time. In September 1879, Mrs. Fanny Dart went to Smith College to serve as a matron of one of the dwelling houses.

9. Alice Cornell Barlow (1833–1889), daughter of Peter Townsend of Goshen, New York, had married Samuel Latham Mitchill Barlow in 1852. She was a long-term friend of JBF's. The "Carry" who was with her was probably her niece, Carrie Townsend, who later married Frank Frémont.

10. The nature of "the talk" is unknown. In 1870, the Frémonts had purchased a place on Bald Porcupine, an island near Mt. Desert, off the coast of Maine, with the idea of building a summer house. JBF described it as "splendidly wooded except on the sea face which is a cliff of nearly three hundred feet" (to William Carey Jones, Aug. 22, 1870, Huntington Library).

11. The Frémonts' staghound.

12. James M. Kitchen, who later invested in a mill and mine at Lynx Creek.

13. Charles James (1817–1901), a lawyer from Albion, New York, had been an aide in JCF's campaign for the presidency. He later worked for the Frémonts at Las Mariposas and served as collector of the port of San Francisco during the Civil War.

14. Charles M. K. Paulison, from Bergen, New Jersey, had a varied career in Arizona until his death in Tucson in December 1881. He established a mining bureau in Prescott, became an agent for the Associated Press, invested in mining property on Lynx Creek, and became registrar of the land office at Florence (*Arizona Enterprise,* Oct. 23, 1878, and Jan. 25, 1879; *Arizona Miner,* Oct. 22, 1880).

15. Cape Horn is a favorite name for a place where the going is tough. The Central Pacific station near Colfax, California, was named Cape Horn by the construction engineers in 1866 because of a difficult curve and grade.

16. The Frémonts had lived in Bear Valley in 1858–1860 while JCF was developing the mines of Las Mariposas.

17. The cousins were the children of Eliza Benton and her husband William Carey Jones. The latter had died in San Francisco in November 1867. Betty had married the army officer William Burton Hughes in 1870 or 1871. Young William Carey Jones was an instructor in Latin at the University of California, Berkeley.

18. Joseph C. Palmer (1819–1882), one of the principals in the San Francisco banking firm of Palmer, Cook & Co. until its failure in 1856, had lent money to JCF for the development of Las Mariposas and had received government contracts from him during the Civil War when JCF commanded the Western Department in St. Louis. He later visited the Frémonts in Arizona.

19. The owner of the Palace Hotel was U.S. senator William Sharon (1821–1885), who had made a fortune out of the Comstock Lode in Nevada.

20. Cynthia H. Shillaber and her husband, Theodore, later became investors in an Arizona mine promoted by JCF and JBF.

21. Overlooking Alcatraz Island, Black Point or Point San Jose (later Fort Mason) had been the Frémont residence in 1860 and early 1861. During the Civil War, it had been seized by the federal government, which alleged that the Frémonts were illegal squatters because the land was coastal property and reserved for defensive purposes. For many years, JBF tried unsuccessfully to obtain compensation for the property, which she once described as "more beautiful than any Sea Dream that Tennyson or any poet ever fancied" (JBF to Elizabeth Blair Lee, June 2, 1860, printed in Herr and Spence, *Letters,* 227–29). Many documents relating to the claim may be found in the National Archives, Record Group 77, Records of the Office of Chief of Engineers, Land Papers, Point San Jose. General Irvin McDowell, who was in charge of the area, was a distant cousin of JBF's and one of the family's "most irritating enemies," according to Frank (memorandum for Allan Nevins, n.d., FP).

22. William Booth had been one of the four trustees when the Silver King Mining Company was incorporated under the laws of California on May 5, 1877, to work the rich Silver King Mine, north of present-day Superior, Arizona.

23. William Bradford (1823–1892), artist and photographer, was best noted for his arctic scenes and marine views, with many of his paintings selling both domestically and abroad for high prices. Queen Victoria purchased "Steamer Panther among Icebergs and Field Ice in Melville Bay, under the Light of the Midnight Sun." Although identified primarily with the east, he traveled extensively in the western United States, painting Yosemite and the Sierra Nevada Mountains. Lily wrote Dr. Morton that at the time of their visit, his studio was in the Palace Hotel (microfiche, New York Public Library Artists File; EBF to Morton, Sept. 12, 1878, MP).

24. Betty's young daughter.

25. In the conquest of California in 1846, Carrillo had sided with the Americans and had been one of JCF's aides. He had since served in the California legislature.

26. Theodoric and Caroline Severance had moved to California in 1875 because of his incipient tuberculosis. She was a leader in the woman's rights movement and later became a staunch friend of the two Frémont women when they moved to Los Angeles in 1888.

27. Late in 1873, Frank had been sent to Nassau in the Bahamas to recover from latent tuberculosis. The next year, JBF and EBF were able to join him for a few months.

28. Former U.S. marshall of Arizona, George Tyng was the editor of the Yuma *Sentinel.*

29. A widower and a veteran of the Civil War, Orlando Bolivar Willcox (1823–1907) had become commander of the Department of Arizona in March 1878.

30. Woodruff was posted to New York for two years and was delighted to be leaving Arizona.

31. The hero of *Pilgrim's Progress,* who travels toward Jerusalem.

32. The common purslane *(Portulaca oleracea),* sometimes used as an herb. In sandy soils, it is a troublesome weed.

33. The Frémonts had sometimes summered at Bar Harbor. D. Appleton and Company had published various works by Thomas Hart Benton, including his *Thirty Years' View.*

34. Charles Culling (d. Aug. 4, 1878) had married fourteen-year-old Maria Valenzuela at Wickenburg on December 17, 1871. In 1882, Maria married Joseph Drew, who continued the stage stop (biographical file, SHM).

35. Paul-Gustave Doré (1832–1883) was a French illustrator and painter whose exuberant and bizarre fantasy created dreamlike scenes.

36. See chapter 1, note 10.

37. The territorial secretary, John J. Gosper, had coveted the governorship; he and JCF became bitter enemies. He acted as governor for long periods of time during JCF's visits to the east and used the Phoenix *Herald,* of which he was part-owner, to criticize JCF, whom he labeled a "carpet-bag" official responsible for the later lawlessness around Tombstone. Gosper had brought the first windmill into Arizona and had a cattle ranch on the Verde River (Goff, *Arizona Biographical Dictionary*).

38. Famous in his day as the "Silver Tongued Orator of the Pacific," Thomas Fitch (1838–1923) tried his luck at journalism, mining, land speculation, politics, law, and the theater and in many states and territories. In Prescott, he was associated with Clark Churchill in the practice of law, and in fall 1878, he was elected to the territorial legislature. For a biography, see Moody, *Western Carpetbagger;* for his contributions as an actor and theatrical impresario, see Gipson, "Tom Fitch's Other Side." Fitch's wife, Anna, became a good friend of JBF's. Both women were writers, with poetry, plays, and novels being credited to Anna (undated clipping, SHM). *The National Union Catalog, Pre-1956 Imprints* gives her name as Anna Mariska Fitch; Moody wrote that her name was Anna Shultz (*Western Carpetbagger,* p. 10). Anna died of cancer in Los Angeles.

39. Robert H. McLean had graduated from Annapolis with Charley Frémont in June 1872. He had been a frequent visitor in the Frémont home at Pocaho and corresponded with both Lily and Jessie. He resigned from the navy on Sept. 27, 1888.

40. Mr. and Mrs. John Dixon kept a station in Skull Valley (*Arizona Miner,* Dec. 13, 1878).

41. The two sons in the carriage were Charles W. and Orlando B., ages approximately eight and ten, respectively. Making up the escort into Prescott was a third son, Lieutenant Elon Farnsworth Willcox, a graduate of West Point and his father's aide.

42. Mrs. Hoyt, the former Lettie J. Lewis (1848–1916), was the governor's wife.

43. Mrs. Bean was Mary (May) Bean, wife of Curtis C. Bean and mother of three daughters. She had been born in Tennessee and did not like living on the frontier. Perhaps her attitude had been conditioned by the fact that she

had a long litigation over her interest in the Peck Mine. See Henderson, "Peck Mine."

44. Probably young Minnie Bowen, the wife of Charles E. Bowen, who had mining interests in Prescott and whose father, also named Charles E. Bowen, lived in Oakland, California.

45. The Fitch house had nine rooms and seven closets (EBF to NHB, May 11, 1880, FP).

46. Lily had met Dr. Jameson, who was a Britisher and a married man with a family, in Nassau in 1874.

47. Benjamin Morgan was associated with J. P. Hargrave in the practice of law.

48. Marie Willcox, who was twenty-four.

49. Curtis Coe Bean (1828–1904), a resident of Arizona since 1868, was a mining expert and railroad promoter. He had been a member of the just-concluded territorial council and in 1884 became a delegate to Congress.

50. Prussian-born Robert H. Burmister was a partner in the mercantile firm of L. Bashford & Co. along with his brother-in-law, William C. Bashford. Margaret F. Bashford and Robert Burmister had married in 1873. After the retirement of her uncle, Levi Bashford, in 1886, the store became known as the Bashford-Burmister Mercantile Company of Prescott. Burmister was a director of the Bank of Arizona in Prescott for a time in the 1880s and also served as mayor for the town. The Robert H. Burmister home was at the northeast corner of Gurley and Mt. Vernon. See Nelson, "Prescott."

51. Lily may be referring to Edward Payson Roe's *Gentle Woman Roused: A Story of the Temperance Movement in the West,* which had been published by the National Temperance Society in 1874. Roe (1838–1888) was a Presbyterian clergyman and popular novelist who often combined entertainment with moral purpose.

52. James Cooper McKee (1830–1897) had many years of service in the west before he became medical director of the army's Department of Arizona in 1877. His *Narrative of the Surrender of a Command of U.S. Forces at Fort Fillmore, New Mexico in July, A.D. 1861* was first printed at Prescott in 1878 and circulated among friends.

53. Charles Silent (1843–1918), a year younger than Lily, was a German-born lawyer who enjoyed a fine reputation as a promoter and railroad builder in California before his appointment as one of the three judges to the Arizona territorial bench. He had left his family in San Jose and resided alone in Prescott. He dined almost daily with the Frémonts and became JCF's "silent" business partner and a comfort to Lily when members of her family were out of town. He prospered and eventually moved back to California, where he also proved to be a kind and benevolent friend to the ex-governor and his family (Goff, *Arizona Territorial Officials*).

54. The *Arizona Enterprise* (Nov. 23, 1878) noted that Judge L. Archer of San Jose, California, had been examining mines in the Bradshaw Mountains but would soon be leaving for California.

55. The daughter of the general, Grace Willcox was about fourteen years old and a frequent caller at the Frémonts until she went "inside" to school.

56. Fanny Weeks was the teenage daughter of Colonel George Henry Weeks and his wife, Babbitt, of Fort Whipple.

57. Charles P. Eagan of Fort Whipple was the chief commissary officer. He was bitter about his assignment to Arizona and had feuded with the previous commanding general, Augustine Valentine Kautz. In time he became unfriendly toward the Frémonts and Judge Silent, especially with respect to judicial decisions concerning the Peck silver mine in the Bradshaw Mountains in which he had financial interests.

58. Mary Louise Evans Bashford was the wife of William C. Bashford, the son of Coles A. Bashford, who had moved to Arizona in 1864. Mary Louise and William purchased a simple two-story house in the heights overlooking Prescott in 1878, and over the next ten years the couple remodeled it into a beautiful home. In 1974 it was moved to the grounds of the Sharlot Hall Museum. William and his brother-in-law, Robert H. Burmister, were partners in the family's general mercantile business (see ch. 1, n. 50). JCF appointed William Bashford adjutant general in 1879.

59. Mrs. Goodfellow was the wife of Dr. George Emery Goodfellow (1855–1910), who was contract surgeon at Fort Whipple and had an unsuccessful private practice in Prescott. In 1880, he contracted for duty at Fort Lowell near Tucson, but he soon left the army and moved to Tombstone, where for twelve years he was the leading physician, surgeon, coroner, and self-taught expert on bullet punctures. He also perfected the perineal prostatectomy and was among the first to use spinal anesthesia using cocaine crystals and to advocate open-air treatment for tuberculosis. He became a prominent surgeon in San Francisco, but after the 1906 earthquake he went to Mexico as surgeon-in-chief for the Southern Pacific railroad of that country. See Quebbeman, *Medicine in Territorial Arizona.*

60. A newcomer to the territory, Lily had not yet sorted out all the personal relationships. Moses Hazeltine Sherman (1853–1932), the principal of the public school in Prescott, and later superintendent of education for all of Arizona, was not yet married. The woman with him was his sister, Lucy Sherman, who taught at the elementary level (see ch. 2, n. 41). Moses Sherman had a knack for finance as well as education and acquired various pieces of town property in Prescott; he also built a hostelry. In the early 1880s he transferred his operations to Phoenix, where he married and invested heavily in banks, the Phoenix Water Company, and the city rail lines. Eventually, he became convinced that the future lay with Los Angeles, moved there, and became involved in a multitude of projects, including land development and the electric street railway system. In the latter, he was associated with his brother-in-law. See Hendricks, *M. H. Sherman.*

61. A play by Bulwer.

62. Clark Churchill was Tom Fitch's law partner and in the 1880s served terms

as adjutant general and attorney general. His young wife's name was Margaretha. She had been born in Darmstadt, Germany, and died in Phoenix in 1890.

63. Probably Cotesworth P. Head, who lived on Gurley Street, although his brother, William S. Head, also lived in Prescott. The two were associated in a mercantile firm that specialized in grains, and both were active in territorial politics. C. P. Head was an investor in several mines, including the Accidental and the Senator, the latter in the Hassayampa district.

64. Their landlord was the bachelor contractor W. Z. Wilson. He and his partner, A. S. Haskell, had just completed the brick courthouse on the plaza. The house the Frémonts rented was at the corner of Gurley and Marina Streets. During the construction, the *Arizona Miner* (Apr. 23, 1875) noted that it was of the "Gothic style" with the bay window on the Gurley Street front. The 1880 census seems to indicate the entrance was on Marina Street. The parlor was fourteen by twenty feet but could be lengthened to twenty-eight feet by sliding open a door that separated it from a sitting room.

65. Both Mineral Park and Mohave Fort were in Mohave County. Mineral Park took its name from the surrounding parklike basin between mountains rich in minerals. Mohave Fort was at Beale's Crossing on the Colorado River.

66. The press and the public knew they also went to examine mining property (*Arizona Miner,* Dec. 13, 1878).

67. Charles A. Tweed (1813–1887) was JCF's age. He had married for the third time in San Francisco in March 1878. His bride, Maria Tweed, was in her late forties. After Tweed's term as associate justice expired in 1878, he practiced law in Mineral Park and then in Phoenix (Goff, *Arizona Territorial Officials*).

68. Lily wrote that John E. Anderson had been three years at Annapolis, part of the time in Charley's class; he had had to leave because of an accident to his eyes, but his sight was eventually restored by a Dr. Williams of Cincinnati (EBF to NHB, letter fragment, no date, FP). JCF, who wanted a postal agent appointed specially for New Mexico and Arizona, requested the place for Anderson (to Governor Lew Wallace of New Mexico Territory, Nov. 23, 1878, Indiana Historical Society).

69. Hannah Lawrence (1833–1898), born in Bayside Queens, was a long-term friend of the Frémonts and had visited them at Bear Valley in 1859. She was the sister of Effingham Lawrence, who had had a plantation on the Mississippi River near New Orleans, and of Joseph E. Lawrence, a San Francisco newspaperman.

70. Sometimes referred to as Estelle or Estill, the bachelor James R. Estell was a clerk in the Subsistence Department at Whipple Barracks. He was the brother of Joey Estell, Hannah Lawrence's friend (EBF to NHB, Nov. 24, 1878, FP). The *Arizona Enterprise* (Nov. 16, 1878) noted that he had entered a colt in the Prescott horse race.

71. Mrs. Cory was the mother of Ann Fitch. The *Arizona Enterprise* (Sept. 21, 1878) noted that she had worn "black and white grenadine" to the reception for General Sherman.

72. Canadian-born Crawly P. Dake was U.S. marshall for the Territory of Arizona. At this time, his wife, Catherine, was living in Oakland, California. Dake was the supervisor for the 1880 census in Arizona. A sketch of his life may be found in Ball, "Pioneer Lawman."

73. The nature of the controversy is unknown, but it must have involved Frederick Crayton Ainsworth, the surgeon at Fort Whipple, whose biographical sketch appears below.

74. JBF later wrote about her work in the Prescott Free Academy in "My Arizona Class."

75. The next year, at the age of sixty-seven, Alexander Gilmore (the chaplain at Whipple Barracks) established a school at Peeples Valley.

76. Frederick Crayton Ainsworth (1852–1934), an 1874 graduate of the University of New York and a favorite pupil of the Frémonts' old physician, William H. Van Buren, went to Arizona as assistant surgeon in 1878 after tours of duty in the northwestern states and Alaska. Ellen McGowan Biddle noted that he was a master in his profession and regretted that he gave it up for work in the Record and Pension Bureau; he eventually became adjutant general of the U.S. Army. He stretched the powers of his office in ways that brought him into conflict with Chief of Staff Leonard Wood and with Secretary of War Henry Stimson (Deutrich, *Struggle for Supremacy;* Biddle, *Reminiscences,* 183).

77. Lieutenant Harry Leland Haskell (1840–1908), born in Clinton, Maine, had seen service in the Civil War and was at the time chief of scouting operations on the southern border of Arizona and New Mexico. In June 1881, he married May, daughter of Dr. V. J. Fourgeaud of San Francisco. By 1899, he was a major and in 1904, when he was retired for disability, he was a brigadier general.

78. Maggie Townsend was the daughter of John D. and Caroline Townsend and sister to Carrie, Frank's future wife.

Chapter 2
Tenth Legislative Assembly

1. The Goldwaters who called were no doubt Michel and his son Morris, although another of Michel's sons, Samuel, was also in town, clerking in the family's mercantile firm of J. Goldwater & Bro. Michel and his brother, Joseph, both born in Poland, emigrated from England in 1852 and opened their first store in Arizona at La Paz on the Colorado River about 1860. The store was later moved to Ehrenberg, and Joseph was still operating the business in 1879. After a failure in Phoenix, Michel and Morris went to

Prescott and opened a store on the southeast corner of Cortez and Goodwin Streets. Shortly afterward, they built a fine new store at Union and Cortez. Morris soon began his long political career with a one-year term as Prescott's mayor. He was never out of political office for very long and altogether had the mayorship for more than twenty years. At times he also served in the territorial legislature and was vice president of the Arizona Constitutional Convention. Another of Michel's sons, Henry, moved to Prescott before the 1880 census was taken. For a history of this prominent Arizona family, see Smith, *Goldwaters*.

2. Edward Franklin Bowers (b. 1839) was one of the four Bowers brothers who moved to Arizona from New Hampshire via California. He was a proprietor of a hotel in Prescott, tax collector, and sheriff of Yavapai County.

3. The three Sisters—Mary Martha Dunne, Mary Rose Dorna (sometimes given as Doran), and M. John Berchmans Hartrich—had moved from Tucson in 1878 to open the hospital.

4. Alice Martin was the wife of Colonel James Porter Martin.

5. *Led Astray* was a famous five-act comedy that had been produced five years earlier in New York. Dion Boucicault had made a French love triangle over into an Irish love triangle.

6. J. D. Rumburg was a member of the house and introduced a bill to outlaw horse racing in Arizona after he lost a large sum of cash on the horses (Wagoner, *Arizona Territory,* 172).

7. Etta F. Parker, who often had parts in plays, married Coles A. Bashford on September 17, 1879.

8. One of the Pines was probably Carrie E. Pine, who had a role in the play *Helping Hands* and who married Louis B. St. James on May 14, 1879 (see ch. 3, n. 22).

9. A Mississippian whose older brothers had been killed fighting for the Confederacy, Lieutenant Robert Kennon Evans had known Frank at West Point, although he had been a class ahead of Frank. The two young men were often together, and because Evans was interested in learning French, he went to Lily and Jessie for instruction. His mother lived with him at the fort.

10. Probably Coles A. Bashford; at the time he was a clerk within his stepfather's general mercantile store.

11. In place of more costly costumes, guests to such a party would arrive in sheets and pillowcases, dance to music for a time, then lay aside their white robes, revealing their identities, and repair to the dining hall for a festive supper. Dancing might resume after the feasting. The Napa *County Reporter* (Sept. 15, 1882) described such a party in California; it had been held in a granary festooned with evergreens and Chinese lanterns. See Etter, *American Odyssey,* 187.

12. Arizona's territorial delegate to Congress, John G. Campbell (1827–1901), was a prominent stockraiser and merchant who had lived in Prescott since 1863 and who had served in the house of representatives. He was a staunch

Democrat but ran in the 1878 election as an "Independent." Technically, his service in Congress was illegal because he was still a citizen of Scotland, from which country he had emigrated at the age of fourteen. As Lily's diary later indicates, he became a bitter foe of Judge Silent and attempted to have the judge removed from the bench.

13. The play, by Tom Taylor, was a tearjerker about honest poverty, much suffering, and an eventual reward (Gipson, "Tom Fitch's Other Side," 200).

14. Walter Lennox Vail (d. 1906) was a member of the territorial assembly. While still in his twenties, Vail was one of the owners of a 160-acre ranch—the Empire Ranch—located southeast of Tucson, between the Whetstone and Santa Rita Mountains. Over the years, he added ranch after ranch until at its peak the Empire Ranch included one million acres and 40,000 head of cattle. He and partners also took $500,000 in silver out of the Total Wreck Mine in Empire Mountain. In challenges to his and his partners' ownership of the mine, the plaintiffs were represented by Tom Fitch; the defendants' attorney was Benjamin Morgan, who had made an eloquent speech welcoming JCF to Prescott and to Arizona (Park, "Walter Vail"; Dowell, "Total Wreck").

15. John Tabor Alsap (1830–1886) was said to have been granted a degree in medicine and law by a university in New York. He moved to Arizona from California, where he had practiced medicine, and he did give medical assistance to a few Arizonans wounded by Indians in 1864, but he soon abandoned that profession and concentrated on law and politics. He served as treasurer of the territory, speaker of the house, and president of the council. He also enjoyed the distinction of being a joint owner of the first saloon in Prescott and was a member of the committee that selected the Phoenix townsite in 1870 (Quebbeman, *Medicine,* 62, 94; Goff, *Arizona Biographical Dictionary*).

16. Charles G. W. French, born in Massachusetts, was chief justice of the territory.

17. The daughter of Enos Thompson Throop Martin, Mary Martin (d. 1884) lived at "Willowbrook" near Auburn, New York (New-York Historical Society—Willowbrooke scrapbook). After her family's sudden impoverishment in the early 1870s, she began a jam and preserves business, running it as a women's cooperative with profit sharing among the employees. Making Mary the subject of her "Play and Work" article in *Wide Awake,* JBF admiringly noted that the work "remains as a proof of what a woman's mind and will can do to make a way out of hard business care."

18. Lieutenant Timothy A. Touey of the Sixth Cavalry was acting engineer officer for the Department of Arizona and was engaged in making maps of the country (Altshuler, *Cavalry Yellow*).

19. Annie Kethroe had charge of the primary department of the Prescott Free Academy. Her brother, Henry H. Kethroe (d. Aug. 1879), was proprietor of the Turkey Creek station and overseer of Road District No. 1 (Prescott to

Bradshaw), and her sister, Nellie, was teacher at the Skull Valley School. Later, in Los Angeles, Annie married a Reverend Curtis, who for a time had been minister of the Methodist Church in Prescott (*Arizona Enterprise,* Aug. 31, 1878, Apr. 12 and July 3, 1879; Prescott *Weekly Arizona Democrat,* Jan. 30, 1880).

20. Sarah Blake was the wife of Francis W. Blake, assayer in Prescott, agent for Wells Fargo & Co., and an ex-mayor. "Mrs. Rush" was probably Sarah M. Rush, wife of John A. Rush, who was an attorney and former judge (although their son, Charles B. Rush, was also married and living in Prescott). Isabella Lewis, whose parents had been born in Bavaria, was the wife of Sol Lewis, president of the Bank of Arizona in Prescott. The Lewises were close neighbors of the Frémonts and frequent visitors. Martina Kelly was the wife of William N. Kelly, a general merchant. Miss Stephens was probably Martina Kelly's sister, Josephine. Both Martina and Josephine were daughters of Varney A. Stephens, who was associated with his son-in-law in the merchandise business. Josephine Stephens married M. Warren Potts on Feb. 7, 1883.

21. Both Fred G. Hughes and J. M. Kirkpatrick represented Pima County in the council.

22. Samuel J. Purdy, who had been a soldier stationed in Prescott in the mid 1860s, was Democratic representative from Yuma County. In 1881, he took up the editorial mantle of the Yuma *Sentinel,* but the newspaper owner, a dedicated Republican, fired him when he struck out at JCF. Purdy then resurrected the *Free Press;* when it folded, he left Yuma to edit the Tombstone *Epitaph.* Lily seems to have known his sister, Gin, and his brother "Sparrow." W. Carpenter was the sergeant of arms. A. E. Fay, the Democratic editor of the *Arizona Star,* was representing Pima County. He also went to Tombstone to edit the *Nugget.* See Lyon, *Those Old Yellow Dog Days,* 8, 31, 75, 109, 134–35; Wagoner, *Arizona Territory,* 90, 199, 514; EBF to NHB, Jan. 26, 1879, FP.

23. A number of Fosters lived in Prescott. The most likely candidates for Lily's "Mr. Foster" were two single men. One was thirty-four-year-old C. Burton Foster, a civil engineer who had been born in New York. He had been a member of the legislative assembly of 1877 and had a profitable mining business in the Agua Fria district. A second was William C. Foster, secretary of the Prescott Dramatic Society and deputy county recorder.

24. This had been the address of a home of the Frémonts in New York City.

25. Probably Delia Ellis, wife of Nathan Ellis, a prominent grocer and politician who had been born in Poland.

26. Charles the Great, king of the Franks and emperor of the West, died on Jan. 28, 814.

27. Ellen McGowan Biddle—wife of Colonel James Biddle, who was at Fort Whipple as inspector general of the Department of Arizona—wrote about Prescott in her *Reminiscences of a Soldier's Wife* (1907) but did not mention

the Frémonts. Mrs. Biddle, who was thirty-three at the time, had been born in Maryland. She left two sons in the east when she went west and had two children born in Arizona—Nicholas in the winter of 1879 and Alice in February 1880.

28. Wilhelmine Smith was the wife of Lieutenant Frederick Appleton Smith, regimental adjutant of the Twelfth Infantry. The couple often called to give Lily rides into the country.

29. Adonde, in Yuma County, was an old stage station before the Southern Pacific Railroad went through on January 8, 1879. The railroad company used the wells there to water its engines.

30. Between March 8 and December 13, 1879, the San Francisco *Mining and Scientific Press* published six of W. H. Seamans's letters or notes on Arizona, the contents of which were primarily devoted to mining. After his initial visit, he seems to have returned to Arizona to live, for he was JCF's host in Tucson in November 1880 and is listed in the Tombstone directory of 1883–84 as clerk of the federal court in the First Judicial District.

31. Thomas Cordis was the internal revenue collector.

32. Probably P. Thomas, a member of the council from Pinal County.

33. From 1876 to 1883, Charles W. Beach was the owner and editor of the *Arizona Miner,* which published daily and weekly editions. Beach treated JCF favorably in 1878 but ambivalently in 1879 and turned on him in 1881 when the prospect of moving the capital to Tucson surfaced. When Beach left newspaper work, he engaged in the stock business and in contracting; he enjoyed the reputation of being the principal builder of the Prescott and Arizona Central Railroad. His wife, Cora, was the daughter of widowed Clarissa Kelsey. Mrs. Kelsey, whose ranch received water from Kirkland Creek, became involved in a legal battle with Patrick McAteer over water rights, which brought a bloody court scene before Judge French with Clark Churchill and Charles B. Rush being opposing attorneys. McAteer stabbed Beach in the neck, and in return Beach shot him in the back. In 1889, Beach was killed by an irate husband. Two of Beach's wives showed up to claim his extensive property holdings. See Lyon, *Those Old Yellow Dog Days,* 24–25, 54–55, 134; Wagoner, *Arizona Territory,* 183–84.

Seventeen-year-old Carrie Wilkins was Beach's ward and lived in his household. She is often mentioned by Lily as being an organist and participating in musicals and plays. After the performance of *Damon and Pythias,* Clark Churchill stepped up to the stage and presented her with a lovely set of gold earrings, which had been donated by her friends in appreciation of her many services in Prescott (*Arizona Miner,* Nov. 5, 1880). Two weeks later, the *Daily Arizona Citizen,* Nov. 19, 1880, noticed that she and her good friend Minnie Atkinson were candidates for clerkships in the territorial council.

34. The child was Ernestine, familiarly called Ernie or Erny, daughter of Louis and Fannie Wollenberg. The surname was often written "Wollenburg."

Louis Wollenberg had been born in 1842 in that part of Poland then occupied by Prussia and had come to Arizona from California. With stores in Prescott and Camp Verde, he had contracts with the army to furnish food, flour, and grain to soldiers and to the Apaches on the Verde River. In order to fulfill his contracts, he established a freighting firm and at one time had about 400 mules and horses carrying supplies from the Colorado River and Santa Fe to Prescott (Wollenberg, "Recollections").

35. For some time federal officials in Arizona, including army officers, had been concerned about the dire straits of the Pimas and Maricopas, who had lived along the Gila River in central Arizona when the first whites arrived. Over the years, whites upstream on the Gila had withdrawn so much water that the Pimas and Maricopas, primarily agriculturalists, faced starvation; about half of them migrated to the Salt River Valley, where there was considerably more water. At first some white settlers welcomed them because they provided protection from the Apaches, but as time wore on, the relationship became strained: some whites surveyed and claimed existing Pima and Maricopa farms on the grounds that they had not been reserved for the Indians. In November 1878, the commander of Fort McDowell reported that the Pimas were using about 1,520 acres in the Salt River Valley. He proposed that they be given this land as well as another 1,000 to 1,500 acres of "fair" land onto which they could expand. Indian Agent J. H. Stout urged the establishment of a reservation on the Salt River, and General Willcox recommended that all public lands on the Salt River be temporarily withheld from entry, sale, preemption, and homestead location. President Hayes's executive order of January 10, 1879, went far beyond the recommendations of army officers and Indian Agent Stout: it removed from sale all public lands in the Salt River Valley and for two miles on each side of the Salt River between the valley and the White Mountain Apache Reservation. The setting aside of this huge block of land caused much excitement because within its bounds were 78,000 acres already filed upon, many other farms that were occupied but not yet registered, and the towns mentioned by Lily. Comeaux, "Creating Indian Lands," provides maps of the original and proposed reservation and gives a history of the controversy. The *Arizona Miner* (Feb. 3, 1879) headlined an article: "Five Thousand People Homeless! One Million Dollars Taken from Settlers. Agent Stout Triumphant. Pima Scavengers Rich." In a letter to Morton (Feb. 18, 1879, MP), Lily wrote that 300 "paying farms" would be affected. On June 14, 1879, President Hayes canceled the previous executive order and followed with another that created an Indian reserve of about 46,000 acres, but this reserve did not include the land the Pimas and Maricopas had been farming and which the whites had coveted (Comeaux, "Creating Indian Lands"). As early as mid April, JCF claimed credit for influencing the federal government to reduce the size of the reservation (e.g., diary entry for Easter Sunday, 1879).

36. W. K. Meade was representing Pinal County in the house of representatives. In 1885, President Grover Cleveland appointed him U.S. marshall for Arizona.

37. Anson P. K. Safford had been governor of Arizona Territory from 1869 to 1877. After leaving the governorship, he became interested in the Tombstone mines and was able to enlist eastern capital for their development. Later, he turned his attention to real estate development in Florida.

38. Marie S. Parker, born in Illinois, was the wife of Frank G. Parker, a young Prescott architect and builder.

39. Carl Schurz (1829–1906), the secretary of the interior. During the Civil War he had served in the Mountain Department, which JCF had commanded for a short time.

40. The Omnibus Divorce Act had divorced fifteen couples, including John J. Gosper from his wife, Watie, who was then living in Lincoln, Nebraska, and William F. Smith from his wife, Eudora, in California. The criticism of the "Smith divorce" was especially sharp for two reasons: Smith had taken up residence in Yuma for the purpose of obtaining the divorce, and his "lady love" was Annie Carpenter, the niece of the wife of Thomas Fitch, who had assisted in the passage of the bill. The San Francisco *Post* (Feb. 5, 1879) alleged that it was Fitch who slipped Smith's name into the divorce bill, but Samuel Purdy, the representative from Yuma, took the responsibility for having done so; Fitch had placed Gosper's name in the bill. Fitch admitted that the relations between Miss Carpenter and Dr. Smith were unfortunate and deplorable, but he believed they were not criminal and protested that it was "a lie" that he and Anna had assented to them. Mrs. Smith brought suit in the Fourth District Court of California to compel her husband to maintain her without divorce (*Arizona Miner,* Feb. 14, 1879). Annie Carpenter and Smith seem to have married (the marriage would have been legal if performed in Arizona). The *Miner* (Nov. 3, 1879) later noted the arrival of young Frank Fitch with Mrs. W. F. Smith, who intended to take up her residence in Prescott. Lily wrote that "Miss" Carpenter, whom the Catholic Sisters had at first refused to call upon, had the roll of Josephine in *Pinafore,* a charitable benefit for the school the Sisters planned to open (see ch. 6, n. 7; EBF to NHB, Jan. 13, 1880, FP).

41. Eli P. Clark was a lumber merchant and the territorial auditor. He married Lucy Sherman the next year (see ch. 1, n. 60) and in 1891 joined his brother-in-law in Los Angeles in organizing the Los Angeles Consolidated Electric Railway Company. Sherman was the president; Clark the vice president and active manager (McGroarty, *Los Angeles,* 2:189–91).

42. Although the editor has been unable to establish a direct connection, the brother of Lieutenant Haskell may have been Abram S. Haskell, the partner of William Z. Wilson, the builder of the house the Frémonts were renting. Both Haskell men had been born in Maine. Abram's wife died when she was quite young, and their daughter was reared by the maternal grand-

parents, James and Johanna Miles, residents of Prescott (Elva Haskell Carroll manuscript, Arizona Historical Society, Tucson).

Chapter 3
Lily Gives French Lessons, Jessie Teaches History

1. Paul-Weber, publisher of the *Arizona Enterprise*.
2. The tenth legislature had created Apache County out of the eastern part of Yavapai County.
3. See chapter 2, note 40.
4. Fitch and JCF were rumored to be very much behind the lottery. The bill establishing it would make the governor lottery commissioner and entitle him to receive $100 for each drawing.
5. Martha Field, daughter of Edward Field of Providence, Rhode Island, who had married Joseph C. Palmer on June 18, 1844, at Nantucket. Lily wrote Nell that she was threatened with blindness (EBF to NHB, Feb. 24, 1879, FP).
6. The wife of Colonel Robert C. Wood, an ex-Confederate officer, who had a ranch near Tucson (*Arizona Enterprise,* Mar. 1, 1879; Heitman, *Historical Register*).
7. Named for its first keeper, Patrick Burke, Burkes Station had been established on the Butterfield Overland Stage Route in September 1858.
8. Sir Nathaniel William Wraxall (1751–1831) was an English writer of historical memoirs.
9. Taylor's Comedy and Concert Company billed "Little Mattie" as the "most wonderful of all actresses." The company toured the west.
10. Anderson's hand had come in contact with a buzz saw at the planing mills of Wilson & Haskell. He seems to have lost at least one finger.
11. Asa M. Buffum was thirteen at the time. He was building a fine career in the U.S. Postal Service in Los Angeles when he was killed in a hunting accident in 1904 (McGroarty, *Los Angeles,* 2:56–47).
12. Ohio-born William King Rogers (1828–1893) was President Hayes's private secretary. He was to have financial interests in the eastern mining syndicate that the Frémonts formulated, and he used his influence in the government to promote their interests and to protect JCF from criticism.
13. JCF believed that the climate and vegetation of Arizona could be improved if a vast inland sea could be created by tapping the northern end of the Gulf of California and letting its waters run into and fill up the Colorado Desert (Frémont, "Annual Report").
14. The Woodruff expedition was to be a scientific and educational voyage around the world on the Clyde-built steamship *General Werder,* officered by men from the U.S. Navy. It was canceled for lack of patronage (*New York Times,* Mar. 27, 28, Apr. 3, 4, and May 9, 1879).

15. Mary Thibodo was the wife of Augustus J. Thibodo, a Prescott physician who was a graduate of Trinity University, Canada.
16. This may have been A. T. McMillan, who had pianos for sale in Prescott.
17. The callers would have been Mrs. Frank G. Parker and Miss Etta Parker (see ch. 2, nn. 7, 38).
18. Fitch left San Francisco with C. C. Bean to promote mining interests in New York.
19. Murat and Florence Masterson had moved from San Diego to Prescott in 1876. An attorney, Masterson had spent his boyhood at sea, had been a blockade runner during the Civil War, and had studied law in Kentucky, where he no doubt met his wife. He was elected to the council in 1880 (Wagoner, *Arizona Territory,* 176–77).
20. The *Arizona Enterprise* (May 10, 1879) reported that Gideon Tucker had been secretary of state in New York. For a few months, he was associated with the Fitch and Churchill law practice, and then in the summer of 1880 he assumed the editorial management of the *Arizona Democrat* (*Arizona Enterprise,* June 21, 1879; *Daily Arizona Citizen,* July 13, 1880).
21. Dubbed "young silver tongue" by the newspapers, nineteen-year-old Frank Fitch, just out of a Michigan law college, had arrived in Prescott on May 5. He was reputed to be a Latin scholar and to have control of three languages; he performed nicely on the piano but excelled on the flute. He was "writing" in the law office of his father and Clark Churchill (*Arizona Miner,* May 9 and 16, 1879).
22. Carrie E. Pine and Louis B. St. James were married by Reverend Gilmore, chaplain at Whipple Barracks, in the Marina Street Methodist Episcopal Church.
23. The Peck was a rich silver mine in the Bradshaw Mountains. Named after its discoverer, Edmund G. Peck, the mine was at first owned by him and his prospecting partners: T. M. Alexander, Curtis C. Bean, and William Cole. See Henderson, "Peck Mine," for the early legal wrangles among the owners. By the time Lily wrote of the "imbroglio," Cole had died, Peck had incorporated the company in both Arizona and California, and Bean had sold out his holding to California investors. Among the major California investors were William S. Hobart and Alvinza Hayward, to whom Eagan had close ties. (Eagan may have been an investor also.) Hobart and Hayward maneuvered to acquire Peck's shares but retained him as a figurehead director and sent their superintendent, William Hardy, to operate the mine. Between May and December 1878, Hardy gutted the lode and milled the entire ore reserve, producing $400,000 in silver—with $235,000 of it mysteriously ending up in the coffers of Hayward and Hobart, according to Peck. Peck sued the Peck Mining Company for a share in the profits and for a restoration of his stock (Spude, "Land of Sunshine and Silver," 44–46, 55). Violence at the mine became a genuine possibility (*Arizona Miner,* May 22 and 23, 1879). One of the incorporators of the Arizona company, Catharine

Alexander, wife of T. M. Alexander and mother-in-law of Peck, also sued to recover the value of her stock in the company (*Arizona Miner,* Jan. 9, July 9, Nov. 12, and Dec. 3, 1880). Peck and Mrs. Alexander did regain their stock in 1880, but by then it was of little value. The glory days of the Peck Mine had ended.

24. There were two lieutenants with the name of Kingsbury in Arizona. The one mentioned here seems to be George Washington Kingsbury, who had been regimental quartermaster with the Twelfth Infantry at Fort Whipple since July 1878. When relieved from staff duty on July 1, 1879, he joined Company C at Camp Apache and commanded scouts from that post. Henry Peoble Kingsbury of the Sixth Cavalry had been at Fort Whipple during the summer of 1876, but at this time he was assigned to Camp Verde (Altshuler, *Cavalry Yellow*).

25. The nautical comic opera by William S. Gilbert and Arthur S. Sullivan was extremely popular.

26. James Gordon Bennett, proprietor of the *New York Herald,* sent Sir Henry Morton Stanley (1841–1904) to find David Livingstone, who was possessed with the idea of finding the source of the Nile River. He did locate Livingstone but failed to persuade him to return to England. Livingstone died in 1873, and Stanley then took up the exploration of Africa. His arduous journey to trace the Congo was described in *Through the Dark Continent* (1878).

27. The address is of interest to Lily because in 1877 the Frémonts had lived at 924 Madison Avenue.

28. S. T. Bitting advertised as having the "most elegantly fitted up saloon in the Territory" and noted that he was an agent for genuine J. H. Cutter Whiskey. In addition to operating a faro and gambling saloon, Daniel Thorne was the owner of the Silver Belt Mine. Eight months after the visit to Lily, his wife, Mary, died of puerperal septicemia following the birth of a daughter (see diary entry for February 2, 1880).

29. For a second fire, see diary entry, July 29, 1880.

30. These two women were Emma M. Noyes, wife of Albert M. Noyes, and Mary Brooks, wife of Hezekiah Brooks. Because Noyes had been a local justice, he was sometimes referred to as "Judge Noyes." Born in Maine, he was a machinist and had overseen the erection of Fred Williams's Grand Central Hotel in Prescott. Brooks had been one of the surveyors for the townsite of Prescott (*Arizona Enterprise,* Aug. 31 and Sept. 4, 1878).

31. Silas Wright (1795–1847) had been a powerful political figure in New York, serving as U.S. senator and as governor.

32. It is unclear whether Lily had talked with Sister Mary Martha Dunne or Sister Mary Rose Dorna. The ill Mother Superior was M. John Berchmans Hartrich.

33. Delia Ellis, wife of Nathan Ellis, a grocer who was also active in politics.

34. Reginald and Harriet Fowler and their son and daughter.

35. Occasionally, the Frémonts hid identities with code names. This was probably being done here.
36. Mother Mary Basil Morris had taken her vows in 1861 in Moutiers, France, the year she came to America. She was provincial superior at Tucson when St. Mary's Hospital opened but was transferred in 1881 to Georgetown, Colorado, where she became superior at St. Joseph Hospital (archivist Sister Patricia J. Kelly, CSJ, of St. Joseph Carondelet, St. Louis, May 4, 1988, to Mary Lee Spence).
37. Ellen Brannen was the wife of Peter B. Brannen, the post trader at Whipple Barracks. By this time he had probably gone to California in a futile attempt to recover his health. After his death, P. B. Brannen & Co. rented the store adjoining the Bank of Arizona in Prescott and had it fixed up for a liquor and grocery establishment (*Arizona Miner,* Nov. 7, 1879). Undoubtedly, the brother, Patrick B. Brannen, had an interest in the "new" store.
38. Former army officer William A. Hancock (1831–1902) had been a pioneer settler in the Salt River Valley and principal founder of Phoenix. For several years he was the law partner of Justice Charles A. Tweed; after the judge's death, he practiced alone. For his special interest in irrigation projects and other activities, see Goff, *Arizona Biographical Dictionary.*
39. Victoria Behan was the divorced wife of John H. Behan, who had represented Mohave County in the 1879 legislative assembly. He became sheriff of Cochise County when it was organized in 1881 and soon became embroiled in the lawlessness that accompanied the Earp-Holliday faction in Tombstone. Victoria and the Behans' son, Albert, lived with her mother, Harriet A. Bourke.
40. Mrs. Charles A. Luke later joined her husband in Phoenix. She died on April 6, 1880, following surgery in San Francisco.
41. Johanna Rodenburg, wife of Julius N. Rodenburg, a brewer in Prescott.
42. The Right Reverend Jean Baptiste Salpointe (1825–1898) was Bishop of Arizona.
43. Both Joseph W. Griswold and Edward P. Griswold of Chicago were interested in Big Bug mines. Lily does not specify which Griswold went to the governor's house with D. M. Caldwell and Gosper. The mining community of Big Bug took its name from the creek on which it was located; the creek had been named for the large, dark brown, shiny flying beetles in the area. The mines in the area, including the Silver Belt, were numerous and productive.
44. *Lucile* was a long romance authored by E.R.B. Lytton (1831–1891).
45. Known as "the Prince Imperial," Eugene Louis Jean Joseph Napoleon (1856–1879) was the only son of Napoleon III and his wife, the Spanish countess Eugénie de Montijo. He had joined the English expedition against the Zulus of South Africa and was killed in an ambush on June 1, 1879.
46. Under the auspices of the French army, Ferdinand Maximilian Joseph (1832–1867), the archduke of Austria, had become emperor of Mexico dur-

ing the Civil War in the United States. After the war was over, the United States demanded the withdrawal of French troops. Consequently, the Mexican army under Benito Pablo Juárez was able to triumph and shot Maximilian at Queretaro.

47. Lily wrote to Nell, "Mrs. Fitch has brought back many fine gowns & a toy black & tan terrier that wears an amber necklace & which she carries round in her arms. She did not bring her niece up here with her, fortunately—so we are spared having to refuse calling on her" (EBF to NHB, June 29, [1879,] FP).

48. Daughter of Colonel James and Ellen McGowan Biddle.

49. Probably Mary Martin's mother, Mrs. Enos Thompson Throop Martin.

50. Elizabeth Meagher was the sister of Mrs. Samuel Latham Mitchill Barlow and of John D. Townsend and the widow of the swashbuckling Thomas Francis Meagher, secretary and former acting governor of the Territory of Montana, who in 1867 fell from the deck of a steamer on the Missouri River and drowned (Athearn, *Thomas Francis Meagher,* 49–50, 166–67).

51. The *Weekly Arizona Miner* (Nov. 19, 1880) reported that the young schoolteacher had become a candidate for enrolling clerk in the house of representatives.

52. Maine-born Pamela L. Otis was the wife of Theodore Weld Otis, who was the postmaster of Prescott as well as a general merchant. She was a "mother advisor" to young lady teachers, such as Lucy Sherman, and was active in the temperance and woman's suffrage movements. Her husband organized classes to instruct the Chinese in English, using the Bible and a hymnal as texts (B. Sacks files, Arizona Historical Foundation, Tempe; Fong, "Sojourners," 252–53).

53. Since serving in the Civil War as an aide-de-camp on JCF's West Virginia staff, Rossiter Worthington Raymond (1840–1918) had built a distinguished career as a mining engineer and consultant. He had been U.S. commissioner of mining statistics and president of the Institute of Mining Engineers and later became editor of the *Mining and Engineering Journal.*

54. Edwin Babbitt Weeks (1863–1890) graduated from the U.S. Naval Academy in June 1883 but resigned the next year and entered the U.S. Army as a second lieutenant in the Fifth Infantry (*Army and Navy Journal,* May 24, 1890).

55. Silent, Frémont, and perhaps others had a bond on the Black Warrior Mine, which was in the Peck district adjacent to the Silver Prince.

56. In the 1870s, civilian clubs, state militias, and the army all became interested in better marksmanship, and the National Rifle Association (NRA) was formed. Engineer officers helped NRA members lay out a model range at Creedmoor on Long Island, and competitions in marksmanship began. In 1879, General Philip H. Sheridan ordered each of his four subordinate department commanders to select men to participate in the competitions at various levels (Coffman, *Old Army,* 280). The *Arizona Daily Star* (Aug. 15,

1880) reported the results of a match at Creedmoor between Canada and the United States. In an hour of rapid firing at the 100-yard range, the score for the Americans was 439, for the Canadians, 427.

57. The two men accompanying Louisa Powers and her husband, Ridgley C. Powers (former governor of Mississippi), to Arizona were J. W. Robbins, special correspondent to the Chicago *Inter-Ocean,* and Captain Shawhan, who had an investment in the Arnold lode (*Arizona Miner,* July 25, 1879).

58. Elizabeth Aram, wife of attorney Eugene W. Aram. The couple moved to Tombstone and then to Tucson. In 1885, Eugene W. Aram represented Pima County in the legislative assembly (*Arizona Miner,* May 23, 1879, and Dec. 2, 1881; Wagoner, *Arizona Territory,* 517).

59. Sara Y. Abbott, wife of Nathan Abbott, a physician in Chicago.

60. Mr. and Mrs. Amos M. Smith had just arrived from Chicago; he was general manager of the Golden Era Mining Company, which had its operations in the Cherry Creek Mining District, about thirty miles northeast of Prescott. They later established residence in a little community called Smithville.

61. Theresa Crist Bowers, wife of Nathan B. Bowers (whose brother Edward had died early in 1879). Theresa and Nathan had a home in Prescott as well as one at Agua Fria, where he farmed. Edward Bowers's widow, Olive Ehle Bowers, stayed with her four children at the stage station in Peeples Valley until she married Herbert B. Crouch (information from Dawn Dollard, Dewey, Arizona).

62. Probably Mrs. Orlando Allen, whose husband was the keeper of a butcher shop in Prescott in fall 1878.

63. Probably Asher C. Baker, who graduated from Annapolis a year ahead of Charley Frémont. He was serving aboard the *Alliance* with the European squadron and returned to Boston in December 1879.

64. Gosper's proclamation had authorized the payment of $500 out of the territorial treasury to any individual who should kill the highway person who was in the act of robbing the mail, express, or passengers (*Arizona Miner,* Aug. 15, 1879).

65. Mr. and Mrs. J. D. Cook lived at Willow Creek.

Chapter 4
The Arrival of the Mining Experts

1. The two men who were murdered were John LeBarr, a saloonkeeper, and Luke Monihon, a rancher. The two who were hanged were John Keller and a man by the name of McCloskey (*Arizona Miner,* Aug. 22, 1879).

2. Probably John A. Walsh, proprietor of the Santa Fe Star Route Line, which carried both the mails and passengers. The *Arizona Miner* (Sept. 5, 1879) noted that he had been in Prescott attending to the affairs of his business.

3. Probably young Frank M. Murphy, who clerked in a store and prospected for mines over many years. He showed an interest in the Silver Trail Mine ten miles south of Prescott at the headwaters of the Hassayampa, bonded the Model Mine, and in spring 1880 visited the Santa Maria copper area. By 1887 he was a partner in Frank Murphy & Company, land and mine promoters.

4. Giant powder is a stable form of dynamite consisting of a mixture of nitroglycerin and a passive base of diatomaceous earth.

5. The new arrivals were Sister Theresa and Sister Monica (*Arizona Miner,* Sept. 6, 1879). The latter had been born in Canada in 1843 as Anna Taggert. After the death of her husband, a Mr. Corrigan, and her two children, she entered the Sisters of St. Joseph of Carondelet in 1867. Her account of the journey from St. Louis to Tucson in 1870 is printed in Ames, *The St. Mary's I Knew.*

6. George W. Maynard was an experienced mining engineer who had received his training at Freiburg, near Dresden. He was a good friend and nearby neighbor in Brooklyn of John Raymond Howard and Rossiter Raymond, both of whom had been on JCF's Civil War staff.

7. In Uzbekistan on the lower Amu Darya, which once flowed into the Caspian Sea. The town was formerly the center of a flourishing kingdom of great antiquity.

8. M. & S. Sternberger had sent out R. Einhorn, educated at Freiburg, to advise them on the value of the property that JCF, Silent, and the syndicate had for sale.

9. George H. Adams had come from Colorado. He soon began publishing the Arizona *Methodist,* which was scheduled to appear every three months.

10. Perhaps with tongue in cheek, the *Arizona Miner* (Sept. 26, 1879) noted, "J. W. Benjamin, correspondent to the Globe Democrat, took the back track this afternoon for home. He saw sufficient in Arizona to induce him to return to Little Rock and lead 200 good Republicans to the Territory. The whole party will bring their wealth with them, which will be in the shape of cattle and horses. Mr. Benjamin alone will bring 1000 head of fine cows and two hundred head of fine brood mares. It strikes us that if he hurries up a little with friends they may be able to vote at the next election for Delegate, at which time the lines have got to be drawn."

11. The *Arizona Miner* (Sept. 26, 1879) noted that the experts were examining the Mono Mine at the head of Maple Gulch for Nathaniel Ross. By April 1880 Ross was located in Phoenix.

12. Probably Hugo Richards, who in the 1880 census gave his occupation as "a miner" and his marital state as "single." He had represented Yavapai County in the territorial legislature in 1875 and 1877.

13. "Nob Hill" seems to have been Gurley Street between Cortez and Mt. Vernon. A Prescott resident wrote, "City Hall on 'Nob Hill' begun July 10, 1884" (Angie M. Brown's "Notes," Box 37, Diary 21, SHM).

14. Probably John Tasker Howard (d. 1888), JCF's long-time political and business associate and father of John Raymond Howard, who had been JCF's private secretary during the Civil War (Howard, *Remembrance of Things Past*).

15. The editor has been unable to ascertain the specific location of Charley Frémont's old lots, but at one time all the Frémonts had held considerable land in California besides Las Mariposas and Black Point. For specific references to their holdings, see Spence, *Expeditions,* lxx–lxxiii; for vague references to children's properties and the alienation of these properties, see Herr and Spence, *Letters,* 412 and 420.

16. Lieutenant Colonel Robert Smith La Motte and his wife, Ellen, had been at Fort Whipple since September 12, 1879. He was the commander of the post.

17. The mine, touted as being very rich in silver, was situated about one-half mile south of the Peck Mine. On August 2, 1875, it had been located by the Irish-born bachelor Andrew Curtin, who quickly deeded Dorr K. Houghtelin a one-third interest. The two men obtained a U.S. patent on November 9, 1878, and JCF, Silent, and their syndicate obtained options to buy the mine (Yavapai County, Ariz., Recorder's Office, Book C, pp. 339–40; Book 7 of Deeds, p. 15; Book 11 of Deeds, pp. 254–59).

18. Jenny Hargrave, wife of Joseph P. Hargrave, an attorney.

19. Dorr K. Houghtelin, who had a one-third interest in the Silver Prince. See note 17 above.

20. Extensive research and many inquiries have failed to reveal beyond question the identity or meaning of "Z. E. K.," which also appears after the entry for October 20, 1880, but the editor suspects it refers to Károly Zágonyi. He was the flamboyant cavalry officer who organized the Frémont Bodyguard in 1861 and who commanded its successful recapture of Springfield on October 25. Note that Lily follows her entry for October 25, 1880, with "(Springfield)," indicating that events of many years past are still in her memory. The day for the birth of Károly Zágonyi, the date of his first meeting with Lily, and his middle name, if he had one, have not been determined. Because Hungarians put the family name first, and assuming that Zágonyi's middle initial was "E," these would be the initials of his name written in the Hungarian fashion: Zágonyi E. Károly.

    Zágonyi was a married man sixteen years older than Lily. He may have captured the heart of the young woman; if so, it was a secret to be buried. Zágonyi was much with the Frémonts in the 1860s. He was the hero of JBF's book, *The Story of the Guard,* and helped read its proof; he rode with Lily "every day" for a time and visited the Frémonts in their summer cottage at Nahant, going with JBF and Lily to visit the poet John Greenleaf Whittier (JBF to James T. Fields, Oct. 26, 1862; JBF to T. S. King, early 1863; JBF to J. G. Whittier, Oct. 17, 1863, all printed in Herr and Spence, *Letters,* 334–35, 338–41, 356–59).

Chapter 5
Selling the Silver Prince

1. No doubt a reference to Andrew Curtin and the Silver Prince.
2. By the selection of the title, German Egyptologist and novelist George Moritz Ebers (1837–1898) wished to convey the meaning "I am a man and feel that I am above all else a man." The romance dealt with the anchorites of the Sinaitic peninsula in 430 A.D.
3. Presumably this ore was worth $1,000 a ton.
4. George Rodney Smith was a second lieutenant in the Twelfth Infantry. In the 1880 census, his wife's name appears to be Carissa.
5. William Greenleaf Eliot (1811–1887), a Unitarian minister and founder of Washington University in St. Louis, had worked with JBF to establish the Western Sanitary Commission during the Civil War.
6. Young Georgie H. McClintock was the telegraph operator and the sister of Charles E. McClintock, who had founded the *Salt River Herald,* and of James Harvey McClintock, who later wrote a history of Arizona. She boarded in the Francis W. Blake household.
7. More than two years later, McMillanville, a mining town in Gila County, was included in the series of attacks by Nan-tia-tish and his band of Apaches, but the inhabitants were saved.
8. Mrs. Ogier was visiting Rebecca Buffum.
9. "The Belt" was the Silver Belt Mine in the Goodwin district, about twelve miles east of Prescott. The *Arizona Miner* reported May 9, 1879, that its owners were Daniel C. Thorne and W. W. Hutchisson. In 1880, it was reported sold a dozen times, but as far as the *Miner* was able to determine, on November 12, 1880, it was still in the hands of Thorne and Hutchisson.
10. Frances Adams Bashford was the widow of Coles Bashford, who had been governor of Wisconsin (1856–1858) and secretary of Arizona Territory and delegate to Congress. The home he built a year before his death in 1878 is considered to be the oldest private residence still standing in Prescott. The daughter accompanying Mrs. Bashford was either Lillian (Lilly) or Elizabeth (Lizzie). The latter remained in the territory and lived with her sister, Margaret Burmister.
11. Frank Staples was post trader at Fort Apache, located south of the Mogollon Plateau on the south bank of the east fork of the White River.
12. Emma Lewis was celebrating her ninth birthday.
13. The *Arizona Miner* (July 25, 1879) had observed that the Eureka was probably the most extensive deposit of copper in Arizona Territory. It was situated on the east slope of the Black Hill range, about four miles west of the Verde River and about twenty-eight miles northeast of Prescott. At this time it was owned by Hugo Richards and C. P. Head.
14. The petroglyph is located in a subdivision called Forest Trails in 1995, on property owned by Prescott College. A large piece has been chiseled out,

and no "Colorado canoe" is visible (information from Norm Tessman, curator of collections, SHM).

15. Lily does not mention the Wyoming project again. There were two Wyoming Mines in Arizona: one in the Oro Blanco district of Pima County, the other in the Silver King district of Pinal County (Hinton, *Hand-Book to Arizona,* 135 and 153). Lily probably was referring to the latter.

16. DeForest Porter was a federal judge in the Second Judicial District from 1873 to 1882 and later mayor of Phoenix.

17. Oscar Lincoln advertised as a "druggist and dentist," but no medical diploma is recorded. He became one of the first of three directors of the insane asylum built in Phoenix in 1886 (Quebbeman, *Medicine,* 200, 354).

18. After he purchased the Vulture Ledge claims, James Seymour of New York put G. W. Shipman in charge of the mining work. Shipman put in a larger stamp mill and arranged for the ore to be hauled sixteen miles to Wickenburg.

19. The Catholic priest was Jules Deraches.

20. In 1856 the Californian Tiburcio Vásquez (1835–1875) began a career of cattle and horse stealing, stagecoach robbery, murder, and pillaging, and because it was largely directed against Anglos, he came to be viewed by Mexicans as a champion of the poor. In the 1870s he organized a gang and stepped up activities. The governor of California offered a reward for his capture, and Sheriff John H. Adams of Santa Clara County was one of his active pursuers. Vásquez was captured in Los Angeles in 1874 by a posse headed by Sheriff Rowland and hanged the next year in San Jose (May, "Tiburcio Vásquez").

21. Before having commands at Fort Wingate and Fort Bayard in New Mexico, William Redwood Price had seen extensive service in Arizona and had suggested using Hualapais as scouts against the Yavapais. Promoted to lieutenant colonel in the Sixth Cavalry in April 1879, he had returned to Arizona and was stationed at Camp Verde.

22. Carl F. Palfrey was a first lieutenant of engineers at Whipple Barracks.

23. Elizabeth (Lizzie) Bashford, who lived in the home of her sister, Margaret Burmister. She married Gustavus Spercher in 1883.

24. Correspondent of the Bank of Arizona, Messrs. Laidlaw & Co. was a banking firm at 33 Pine Street, New York City.

25. The Frémonts were trying to interest Charles A. LaMont of New York City in acquiring mining claims in Arizona, and ultimately they were successful. On February 20, 1880, the Frémonts' young friend Lieutenant Robert K. Evans and William H. Ferguson deeded interests in the Walker Mining District to LaMont. These included claims on the Bonnie Bell and Santa Cruz ledges and to the Zella, the Mark Twain, the Vanderbilt, and the Silver Chief Mines (Yavapai County, Ariz., Recorder's Office, Book 13 of Deeds, pp. 322–35).

26. The bill of Senator James T. Farley (1829–1886), a Democrat from Califor-

nia, would reestablish a federal district court for southern California. It was never reported out of the Committee on the Judiciary to which it was referred, and it was not until 1886 that Congress gave back to southern California its district court (*Congressional Record,* 46th Cong., 2d sess., vol. 10:135; Cosgrave, *Early California Justice,* 63–64).

27. James Hickey was suing the Tiger Mining Company for $50,000 for injuries he had sustained in an accident.

28. James Miles, the son of Johanna and James H. Miles, a cabinetmaker, had been indicted for the murder of J. T. Shannon at Tip Top on December 7, 1879.

29. The jury decided in favor of Hickey, setting the damages at $10,000 (*Arizona Miner,* Jan. 2, 1880).

Chapter 6
Mineral Wealth on Every Hand

1. When members of the jury convicted Bernhard Vogt of manslaughter in the death of Jean Harbrau at the Oro Benito Mine, they had recommended that the court impose the lightest sentence possible. Acting Governor Gosper commuted the original sentence of one year's imprisonment in the territorial jail at Yuma to one year in the county jail (*Arizona Miner,* July 4 and 8, 1879). JCF pardoned him.

2. Possibly L. F. Rowell, assistant superintendent of Wells, Fargo & Co., which operated in the express field. The *Arizona Miner* (Apr. 16, 1880) noted another visit of his in April.

3. The new baby was a daughter, Eva.

4. Eveline Wainwright was visiting her brother, Lieutenant William W. Wotherspoon. She was married to Captain Richard Wainwright of the U.S. Navy.

5. Cerilda Cartter, wife of Harley H. Cartter, attorney-at-law and former probate judge and justice of the peace.

6. Cynthia H. Shillaber and her husband Theodore ceded their interests in the Silver Prince to New Yorker Abram S. Hewitt (1802–1903), the first American manufacturer of steel and a former president of the American Institute of Mining Engineers. Active in the establishment and management of Cooper Union, Hewitt had just completed a service of four years in the U.S. House of Representatives. For the cession, see Yavapai County, Ariz., Recorder's Office, Book 12 of Deeds, pp. 230–34.

7. Annie Carpenter, the wayward niece of Anna Fitch (see ch. 2, n. 40, and ch. 3, n. 47).

8. Anna Curtis, wife of George W. Curtis, a lumber merchant.

9. Jeanette Levy, wife of Polish-born David Levy, a general merchant.

10. The Gray Eagle (sometimes spelled "Grey") was in the Bradshaw Moun-

tains. The *Arizona Miner* (Jan. 23, 1880) noted that Philip Richardson, "who knows just about as much in regard to what constitutes good mining property as any man in Arizona," had disposed of it to a Mr. LaMont, through Frémont and Silent, "for the nice sum of $30,000." For LaMont's acquisitions of other mining claims, see note 25, chapter 5.

11. John S. Alexander, a Philadelphian, who was interested in acquiring mining property.

12. F. M. Larkin had been one of the representatives from Pima County in the territorial house in 1873. He lived four miles west of Florence at the little community of Adamsville.

13. Kathryn Dunning (1846–1921), born in Plattesburg, New York, had taken the place of Annie Kethroe at the Prescott Free Academy. She was boarding with the Theodore Otises on Gurley Street and later married Amos D. Adams, a local business man.

14. "Yonkers" was probably a code name for a mine, in all likelihood a silver mine in the Trigo Mountains in Yuma County. Maynard had been examining mines in Yuma County in late October 1879, and Silent was coming from Yuma to meet JCF in Maricopa. The camp of "Silent" is shown on the map accompanying Hamilton's *Resources of Arizona* (1884) in the "Silver District" of Yuma County (about forty miles north of Yuma); between November 8, 1880, and 1884 this camp became the post office of "Silent." The Red Cloud Mine in the district came to be known as the Silent Mine (Love, *Mining Camps,* 90–93). It was sold to the Iron Cap Mining Company, who were reputed to have sold it to New Yorkers in May 1880. Lily's entry for June 15, 1880, however, indicates that Frémont and Silent still had an interest in "Yonkers." Perhaps the sale fell through, or perhaps "Yonkers" refers to the New York lode in the same district (Hamilton, *Resources of Arizona,* 1884 ed., 238–41). With Silent's and the Frémonts' concern about conflict of interest and breach of confidentiality, the use of a code name is logical.

15. Maggie, who had been born in Ireland, married Fred, who had been born in France and who farmed at Agua Fria. The *Arizona Enterprise* (Sept. 4, 1878) gave his surname as Hilderbrand, the *Arizona Miner* (Aug. 15, 1879) as Hilterbrandt, and the 1880 census taker as Hildebrandt.

16. This was a reference to David Neahr's operations. Formerly an engineer on a Colorado steamboat, Neahr had become a merchant in Yuma when he erected a five-stamp mill to crush gold ore from the Picacho mines six miles back from the Colorado River (Love, *Mining Camps,* 57–74). On September 11, 1879, the *Arizona Enterprise* reported a rumor that he had been offered $15,000 for his Picacho mines in 1878.

17. Biddle's copper mine has not been identified. As early as November 10, 1879, Biddle and JCF had filed a claim on the Copper King Mine in the Verde district (Yavapai County, Ariz., Recorder's Office, Book H. 8. of Mines, pp. 244–45). Two weeks earlier, Biddle and Frank Frémont had

recorded a claim to the nearly Green Crystal (ibid., pp. 303–4; Fireman, "Frémont's Arizona Adventure," 15). The Copper King bordered the south boundary of the Eureka Mine, which later became prosperous (see ch. 5, n. 13).

18. Abram S. Hewitt had sent out twenty-five-year-old Francis Morris Rutherford of New Jersey to look after his interest in the Silver Prince Mine.

19. The charges were actually brought by Arizona's territorial delegate to Congress, John G. Campbell, but Eagan was prominently involved in the scheme to discredit Silent and force his removal from the bench. They set forth in substance that Silent should not be allowed to continue in office as judge because he was "notoriously" engaged in buying, selling, and bonding mines within his judicial district, which often had mining litigation. Furthermore, they noted his business partnership with the governor, who, after a decision by Silent against the Peck Mining Company, offered to bond the mine "at an absurdly low price, accompanied by an offer that he, Fremont, would settle the litigation." It was further charged that Silent was in receipt of three salaries, one of them from the counties of Yavapai and Mohave, which were required to pay it by an act of the territorial legislature: one of Silent's intimate friends, Thomas Fitch of the law firm of Fitch & Churchill, was alleged to have been responsible for the passage of the compensation act. Fitch & Churchill had undertaken suits against the Peck Mining Company upon contingent interest of one-half of whatever might be recovered from the company. Silent was presumed to have favored Fitch & Churchill as a pay-off for his compensation (undated clipping from *Daily Democrat* in the EBF diary, Apr. 5, 1880).

20. The Havasupai lived in the Grand Canyon and along the South Rim and also ranged into north-central Arizona, particularly the San Francisco Mountains.

21. Caroline E. Weaver, wife of Benjamin H. Weaver (1837–1920), a general merchant, who had been one of the co-owners of the *Arizona Miner* when John Huguenot Marion purchased it in 1867 (see note 23 below).

22. Both a former editor of the *Weekly Arizonian* (see note 23 below) and mayor of Tucson, Sidney R. DeLong (1828–1914) was a partner in the large mercantile firm of Tully, Ochoa and DeLong. When it went bankrupt in 1880, he continued as post trader at Fort Bowie, located in the Chiricahua Mountains of southeastern Arizona. Lily may be referring to DeLong's schoolteaching at Drytown, Amador County, California, before 1861; Silent may have been one of his pupils (Kane, "Honorable and Upright Man").

23. Praised by some as the "most talented and vigorous of pioneer editors" and disparaged by others as a "slandering reptile," John Huguenot Marion had been owner and editor of the *Arizona Miner,* and then of the *Arizona Enterprise,* which name he changed to the *Arizonian.* When JCF sought him out, he seemed to have been out of journalism and devoting his time to developing a ranch at the mouth of Granite Creek. In January 1882, he founded the

Prescott *Morning Courier,* and he edited it until his death in 1891 (Abbott, "John Huguenot Marion").

24. The Hassayampa River was the scene of an early gold rush, whence a legend arose that whoever drank its waters could never tell the truth again.

25. Dr. Frank Lightfoot's diploma from Rush Medical College was not recorded in Yavapai County until September 12, 1883. He later, for a short time, became a physician for the Ayer Lumber Company at Flagstaff (Quebbeman, *Medicine*).

Chapter 7
Judge Silent's Vindication

1. Emmy, Minnie, and Addie.

2. After Lucy Sherman's marriage to E. P. Clark in April, Miss Ella Gulliver began teaching the primary class in Prescott. She had been born in Maine, but her teaching credentials were from Missouri and California (*Arizona Miner,* Apr. 2, 1880).

3. Thomas Jonathan Jeffords (1832–1914) had been a friend of Cochise's (although he confessed in later life that he had never turned his back to the Indian chief) and the agent to the Chiricahuas during the four years they had a reservation in southeastern Arizona. Cochise's death and the removal of the Chiricahuas in 1876 to the reserve of San Carlos brought additional turmoil; and it had been Jeffords's and Haskell's daring visit to Juh and 100 of the hostiles in the Guadalupe Mountains which had persuaded them to surrender in 1879 (Thrapp, *Conquest of Apacheria;* Cramer, "Tom Jeffords").

4. Crawley P. Dake, along with Charles M. K. Paulison, had interests in the Accidental Mine, located in the Walker district near Lynx Creek (Richard E. Elliott and A. G. Elliott to Charles M. K. Paulison and Crawley P. Dake, Nov. 16, 1878, Yavapai County, Ariz., Recorder's Office, Book 11 of Deeds, pp. 190–92). The *Arizona Miner* (July 18, 1879) reported that it had been bonded in the sum of $50,000 to capitalists from San Francisco and the east. Perhaps this was a result of some of JCF's and Silent's operations.

5. The twenty-nine-year-old milliner, Sarah L. Watson, married John J. Gosper on January 26, 1881.

6. Lily must mean feathers from the duck *Aythya ferina.*

7. "Piano" was a code name for Joseph Hale of New York City, a piano manufacturer to whom Charles Silent sold a one-eighth undivided interest in the Silver Prince on March 26, 1881 (Yavapai County, Ariz., Recorder's Office, Book 13 of Deeds, pp. 636–38).

8. The Comtesse de Rémusat (Claire Elisabeth Gravier de Vergennes [1780–1821]) had been a lady in waiting to the Empress Josephine, the wife of Napoleon Bonaparte. The *Memoirs* were available in English translation by 1879, but Lily may have read them in French.

9. In late April or early May, Lily and Mrs. A. M. Smith helped Margaret Churchill cut and sew carpets for the house which the Churchills had purchased from the Fitches (EBF to NHB, May 11, 1880, FP).

10. Emma Carpenter was the wife of John H. Carpenter, a clerk. The baby died before she could be taken east (*Arizona Miner,* July 30, 1880).

11. Rosiland Wells, wife of Edmund W. Wells (d. 1929), and Nellie Banghart were sisters. Wells had been a member of the council and became an associate justice of the territory in 1891 and gubernatorial candidate in 1911, at which time he was believed to be the wealthiest man in Arizona.

12. Buffum and Edward L. Gobin had interests in the Tuscumbia and Black Warrior Mines. The *Arizona Miner* (Aug. 6, 1880) reported that the two mines had been under bond for several months, pending sale for $45,000 each. The newspaper thought they would soon be transferred to a New York syndicate, that is, JCF's syndicate.

13. The *Arizona Miner* (May 21, 1880) reported that James William Gough (1848–1880), who had been born in Bristol, England, died suddenly in his room at the residence of Murat Masterson. He had been in the employ of the quartermaster's and internal revenue's offices and suffered from epilepsy.

14. Sarah M. Rush and her daughter-in-law, Mary.

15. Wilhelmina Raible, wife of John Raible, a brewer. She had been born in Baden; he in Würtemburg.

16. The young, single attorney John W. Stephenson had been born in Arkansas.

17. Alonzo E. Davis was quite active in territorial politics, having been a member of the house in 1866, a member of the council in 1875, and a candidate for delegate to Congress in 1878. His twin brother, E. A. Davis, was active in California politics.

18. "Jacques" may have been the name of the Lewises' dog; the family had no sons in 1880. When the Frémonts arrived in Prescott, the Lewis girls were three, five, and seven and had a French nurse and a "very quiet old horse and two donkeys." Sometimes all three girls rode the old horse at the same time.

19. Charles Devens, the U.S. attorney general.

20. Ellen Smith, wife of the army surgeon Andrew K. W. Smith.

21. The mining community of Alexandra was named after Catherine Alexander (1828–1898), the mother-in-law of Edmund G. Peck, wife of T. M. Alexander, and one of the incorporators of the Peck Mining Company (see ch. 3, n. 23).

22. Wife of Dorr K. Houghtelin, who had sold his interest in the Silver Prince Mine to Cynthia H. Shillaber.

23. Frank M. Murphy's brother was Nathan Oakes Murphy, likewise born in Maine. He did not settle in Prescott until April 1883, although he was on the western frontier earlier. His terms as governor of Arizona Territory

(1892–94, 1898–1902) were broken by service as a representative in the U.S. Congress.

24. Philip Richardson, an engineer, owned part of the Gray Eagle, a quartz mine located in the Tiger Mining District in the Bradshaw Mountains.

25. A supply that, although it appears to be meager, is, or seems to be, inexhaustible.

26. *Drappie* is the Scottish form of *drop*. Lily implies that the crowd is mildly intoxicated.

27. Walter Scott Hobart (dead by 1892) was a San Francisco millionaire with large mining and real estate interests (Spude, "Land of Sunshine and Silver"). He had visited the Peck Mine in February 1878 and with Alvinza Hayward, another giant financier, came to have controlling interests in it.

Chapter 8
Territorial Politics

1. The Democratic Party nominated Winfield S. Hancock for the presidency; the Republicans, James A. Garfield.

2. Eagan had sought the assistance of Nevada senator John Percival Jones (1829–1912), a Comstock millionaire, in his attempts to discredit Silent.

3. Granville H. Oury (1825–1891) had gone to Tucson in 1856 and early became active in territorial politics. He had given his support to the Confederacy, but after the war was over, he took the oath of allegiance to the United States.

4. Lily does not indicate the variety of Silent's dysentery. It was probably not malarial dysentery, for which quinine was the most successful remedy. See "Dysentery" and Quebbeman, *Medicine,* 76, 173. The editor was unable to find in the medical literature of the 1870s any remedy called "East Indian."

5. Joseph F. Long, the jailer.

6. This was a reference to the classical myth of Danaë in which Zeus visited her in the guise of a shower of gold [i.e., as a rain god] and fathered Perseus by her.

7. The new brick Goldwater store was located at the corner of Cortez and Union Streets (see ch. 2, n. 1). Within a few weeks of the fire, work was begun to dig four additional wells (with pumps) on the public plaza, one at each corner (C. E. Yount, "Notes on the History of Prescott's Water Supply," typescript, p. 3, Arizona Historical Society, Tucson). In the summer of 1900, a fire burned four and a half blocks of buildings in the center of town, almost destroying Prescott. The plaza wells had been covered because the city had built a new reservoir, but because of the drought the reservoir was nearly dry (Nelson, "Prescott").

8. First published in 1879, *A Fool's Errand* was written by Albion Winegar Tourgée, a Civil War veteran from Ohio, who regarded himself as a fool for

having gone into the postwar South believing that he could have a happy and constructive life there.

9.   Thomas J. Butler, a former owner of the *Arizona Miner,* was treasurer of the territory.

10.   Sarah McClintock, a widow, was the mother of Georgie, the telegraph operator in Prescott; of Charles, the editor of the Phoenix *Salt River Herald;* and of James, a young printer, who later wrote a three-volume history of Arizona and a book on Mormon settlement in Arizona.

11.   The *Arizona Miner* (Oct. 1, 1880) reported that James H. Warren had "successfully organized a Congregational Church in Prescott" and had left for California.

12.   Nellie Young Egbert was the wife of Brevet Major Harry Clay Egbert, who had moved to Fort Whipple with his company in August 1880. He had commanded at Camp Verde, and before the year was over, he became judge advocate of the Department of Arizona.

13.   Bean eulogized the railroad as the "King of Speed" and noted that in his recent return home from the east, he had been able to take the Atchison, Topeka and Santa Fe as far as Albuquerque. The road was completed for another twenty-nine miles toward Prescott, and grading parties were working as far west as Fort Wingate (*Arizona Miner,* Sept. 24, 1880).

14.   Probably Adelaide E. Hamilton, wife of Samuel Hamilton, an attorney.

15.   Anna Cline was a married washerwoman with several small children, but no husband was present. The subscription was for her relief (*Weekly Arizona Miner,* Oct. 1, 1880). She was later adjudged insane, and the children were to be given to responsible persons for adoption.

16.   Louise Stahl was the wife of Edward Stahl, a furniture dealer and assayer.

17.   The Eureka Mine (see ch. 5, n. 13).

18.   On March 5, 1880, the *Arizona Miner* reported that the Silver Prince Mining Company had just concluded the purchase of the Black Warrior, Tuscumbia, and Tuscarora mines at "prices which have not been made public." On April 27, 1880, the Silver Prince Mining Company was incorporated in the state of New York with a nominal capital of $2 million divided into 200,000 shares of $10 each (Bert Fireman Papers, Box 3, Arizona Historical Foundation, Tempe). Because the company was not able to make arrangements for treatment of the ores at the Peck mill, it entered into a contract whereby the owners of the Bradshaw Basin Mill and Mining Company worked the ores. Mule trains were employed to pack the ores from the mine to the mill for treatment. Legal complications arose almost immediately. The *Arizona Miner* (Dec. 24, 1880) reported that the Bradshaw Basin Mill and Mining Company, through its attorneys, Messrs. Churchill and Masterson, commenced suit against the New York syndicate for refusing to deliver ore to the pack train. Next the operator refused to deliver the bullion until the costs of treatment were paid for (*Arizona Miner,* Aug. 12, 1881; Abram S. Hewitt and John Alexander v. F. W. Blake, May 21, 1881,

Case No. 949, and Abram S. Hewitt v. C. P. Dake, John J. Gosper, et al., Sept. 23, 1882, Case No. 1055, 3rd Judicial District, Yavapai County Courthouse, Prescott, Ariz.).

19. Kate McCandless was the wife of the physician James Newton McCandless (1837–1904), who attended citizens of Prescott and surrounding communities from 1868 until the end of the century.

20. Charles was seven at the time and moved with his family to San Francisco in 1891. He became a pharmacist and ultimately director of the San Francisco Board of Public Health. For recollections of his boyhood in Prescott, see Wollenberg, "Recollections."

21. Probably a reference to Mrs. Cline (see n. 15 above).

22. JCF may have been trying to sell this mine in the east. It was rumored to have been sold a dozen times, but the *Arizona Miner* (Nov. 12, 1880) reported that the editor had investigated, and as far as he was able to determine, it was still in the hands of W. W. Hutchisson and Thorne.

23. Lily was reading *Bismarck in the Franco-German War, 1870–1871,* by Moritz Busch (1821–1899). An English translation was available in 1879, but she may have read it in German.

24. Mark Tapley was the humble but indomitably cheerful companion who visited America with Martin in Charles Dickens's *Martin Chuzzlewit.*

25. The Frémont Bodyguard, commanded by Károly Zágonyi, recaptured Springfield, Missouri, on October 25, 1861.

26. The public reception was at Levin's Hall on the evening of October 27 (*Arizona Daily Star,* Oct. 28, 1880). The next evening there was a special, private reception for JCF and General Willcox at the home of C. H. Lord, with nearly 200 guests (*Daily Arizona Citizen,* Oct. 29, 1880); and on October 29, a large reception was given by JCF, General Willcox, Mr. and Mrs. T. Brown, and Mr. and Mrs. E. B. Pomroy at the residence of the Browns (*Arizona Daily Star,* Oct. 30, 1880).

27. One of the four Bowers brothers. The Great Register (1879) of Yavapai County lists him as a rancher; the 1880 census as a miner. He was single at the time. An undated clipping giving information about his will may be found in Angeline Mitchell Brown's scrapbook (Doc. Box 87, p. 7, SHM).

28. A committee of the Tucson bar had telegraphed President Hayes requesting that he take no action with respect to the resignation of Silent because the members hoped to induce Silent to reconsider (*Arizona Miner,* Nov. 12, 1880).

Postscript

1. On the night of June 27, thirty thousand pounds of tonite and vulcan powder exploded in William Zeckendorf's powder magazine, located more than a mile from the main part of town. The cause of the explosion was

unknown, but the most plausible theory was that it was from spontaneous combustion (Phoenix *Herald,* June 29, 1881, citing Tucson *Citizen,* June 28, 1881).

2. The president was shot by Charles J. Guiteau on July 3, 1881; he did not die until September 19.

3. The heavy rains came in late July and the first half of August (*Arizona Weekly Star,* July 21, 28 and Aug. 4, 18. The story of August 4 reported the effects on the town and how washouts on the Southern Pacific had delayed trains up to seventy-two hours. Under the heading of "Furious Floods," the article of August 18 noted that Tucson had received just under two and a half inches between 1:00 p.m. and 1:10 p.m.

4. The snakebite seems to have occurred early in July before the rains began. The young boy was treated by Dr. Charles Holbrook (*Arizona Weekly Star,* July 7, 1881; Quebbeman, *Medicine,* 348).

5. Back in the east, JBF wrote, Lily "has had some fever which made me very really miserable. I had to work hard for health myself I grew so homesick and yearning to get to her. But she is well—entirely. And has good friends there who drive her out often and make it as much homelike as possible. . . . It is lonesome for her. But she is in her own places. And there come times when one cannot choose but must just go day by day through their lives" (letter fragment, JBF to NHB, Aug. 22, 1881, FP).

6. After her return to the East, Lily wrote that her illness had caused her to lose hair and muscle strength (EBF to NHB, Nov. 30 and Christmas [1881]; New Year's Day, 1882, FP).

7. This was a reference to Biddle's and JCF's claim to the Copper King Mine in the Verde district, filed on November 10, 1879 (Yavapai County, Recorder's Office, H. 8. of Mines, pp. 244–45). The mine bordered the southern boundary of the Eureka Mine, which proved to be extremely rich in copper. Frederick Tritle, who succeeded JCF as territorial governor, interested a group of men, including Eugene Jerome of New York City, in developing the deposits. This became the great Jerome operation, subsequently acquired by Clark. Still later it was purchased by the Phelps Dodge Corporation, in which the family of former ambassador Lewis S. Douglas had large interests (Fireman, "Frémont's Arizona Adventure").

8. By his preaching, Noch-ay-del-klinne, a medicine man, had caused unrest on the San Carlos and Fort Apache Indian Reservations. General Willcox ordered Colonel Eugene Asa Carr of Fort Apache to arrest the disrupter. With 117 men, including 23 Indian scouts, the colonel took Noch-ay-del-klinne into custody on August 30 at the prophet's lodge near Cibicue Creek. Shortly after, the Apaches launched an attack in which some of the scouts joined. One captain and 3 or 4 privates were killed; 3 more privates were wounded, and 2 of them soon died. The prophet and more than 18 Apaches were killed. Lily's account is quite different from those given by Altshuler (*Cavalry Yellow,* 60) and Thrapp (*Conquest of Apacheria,* 217–30).

Before Carr could reach the fort, the word had already been telegraphed that his entire command had been massacred.

9. Morrell's warehouse burned on the night of October 10, about six weeks after the affair at Cibicue. Many prominent New Yorkers sustained substantial losses (*New York Times,* Oct. 11–16, 18, 25, 1881).

10. In JCF's *Memoirs,* xvi, JBF recounts how the Frémont family lost many treasures in the fire, but that the materials for her husband's book had been placed in "safes below the pavement" and the fire had left them unharmed. The *New York Times* (Oct. 25, 1881) reported the unearthing of the vault on the previous day with most of its contents saved.

11. Lily returned to New York sometime in November after her father had resigned the governorship.

Bibliography

The manuscript returns of the tenth census of the United States (1880) for Arizona were used extensively: Reel 37, containing the returns for Yavapai County, was especially helpful. Sources are not cited for information to be found in standard bibliographical dictionaries or guides to literature.

Major Manuscript Collections

Bancroft Library, University of California, Berkeley: Frémont Papers (FP), William J. Morton Papers (MP), William King Rogers Papers (RP)
Sharlot Hall Museum, Prescott Historical Society (SHM)
Yavapai County, Prescott, Records of the County Recorder

Books and Articles

Abbott, Mary H. "John Huguenot Marion: Frontier Journalist." *Journal of Arizona History* 21 (summer 1980): 127–46.
Altshuler, Constance W. *Cavalry Yellow and Infantry Blue: Army Officers in Arizona between 1851 and 1886.* Tucson: Arizona Historical Society, 1991.
Ames, Aloysia, C.S.J. *The St. Mary's I Knew.* Tucson, Ariz.: privately printed, 1970.
Athearn, Robert G. *Thomas Francis Meagher: An Irish Revolutionary in America.* University of Colorado Studies, Series in History No. 1. Boulder: University of Colorado Press, 1949.
Ball, Larry D. "Pioneer Lawman: Crawley P. Dake and Law Enforcement on the Southwestern Frontier." *Journal of Arizona History* 14 (autumn 1973): 243–56.
Barter, G. W., comp. *Directory of the City of Tucson for the Year 1881.* . . . San Francisco: H. S. Crocker & Co., Printers, 1881.
Biddle, Ellen McGowan. *Reminiscences of a Soldier's Wife.* Philadelphia: J. B. Lippincott Company, 1907.
Callahan, Edward W., ed. *List of Officers of the Navy of the United States and of the Marine Corps from 1775 to 1900.* New York: L. R. Hammersly, 1901.

Chambers-Schiller, Lee Virginia. *Liberty, a Better Husband.* New Haven: Yale University Press, 1984.

Coffman, Edward M. *The Old Army: A Portrait of the American Army in Peacetime, 1784–1898.* New York: Oxford University Press, 1986.

Comeaux, Malcolm. "Creating Indian Lands: The Boundary of the Salt River Indian Community." *Journal of Historical Geography* 17 (July 1991): 241–56.

Cosgrave, George. *Early California Justice: The History of the United States District Court for the Southern District of California, 1849–1944.* Ed. Roy Vernon Sowers. San Francisco: Grabhorn Press, 1948.

Cramer, Harry G., III. "Tom Jeffords, Indian Agent." *Journal of Arizona History* 17 (autumn 1976): 285–300.

Deutrich, Mabel. *Struggle for Supremacy: The Career of General Fred C. Ainsworth.* Washington, D.C.: Public Affairs Press, 1962.

Dowell, Gregory P. "The Total Wreck: Arizona's Forgotten Bonanza Mine." *Arizona and the West* 20 (summer 1978): 141–54.

"Dysentery." *Encyclopaedia Britannica.* 9th ed. [American reprint]. Philadelphia: J. M. Stoddart & Co., 1878.

Etter, Patricia A., ed. *An American Odyssey.* Fayetteville: University of Arkansas Press, 1986.

Fireman, Bert. "Frémont's Arizona Adventure." *The American West* 1 (winter 1964): 9–19.

Fiske, Turbesé Lummis, and Keith Lummis. *Charles F. Lummis: The Man and His West.* Norman: University of Oklahoma Press, 1975.

Fong, Laurence. "Sojourners and Settlers: The Chinese Experience in Arizona." *Journal of Arizona History* 21 (autumn 1980): 227–56.

Frazer, Robert W. *Forts of the West: Military Forts and Presidios and Posts Commonly Called Forts West of the Mississippi River to 1898.* Norman: University of Oklahoma Press, 1965.

Freeman, Ruth, and Patricia Klaus. "Blessed or Not? The New Spinster in England and the United States in the Late Nineteenth and Early Twentieth Centuries." *Journal of Family History* 9 (winter 1984): 394–414.

Frémont, Elizabeth Benton. *Recollections of Elizabeth Benton Frémont.* Compiled by I. T. Martin. New York: F. H. Hitchcock, 1912.

Frémont, Jessie B. "My Arizona Class," in *How to Learn and Earn,* pp. 444–79. Boston: D. Lathrop & Co., 1884.

——. "Play and Work." *Wide Awake* 30 (April 1890): 336–39.

——. *The Story of the Guard.* Boston: Ticknor and Fields, 1863.

Frémont, John C. "Annual Report of the Governor of Arizona, 1879, to the Secretary of the Interior." House Ex. Doc. 1, 46th Cong., 2nd sess., Serial 911, pp. 383–400.

Gipson, Rosemary. "Tom Fitch's Other Side." *Journal of Arizona History* 16 (autumn 1975): 287–300.

Goff, John S. *Arizona Biographical Dictionary.* Cave Creek, Ariz.: Black Mountain Press, 1983.

——. *Arizona Territorial Officials: The Supreme Court Justices, 1863–1912.* Cave Creek, Ariz.: Black Mountain Press, 1975.

Granger, Byrd H. *Will C. Barnes' Arizona Place Names.* Tucson: University of Arizona Press, 1960.

Hamilton, Patrick. *The Resources of Arizona.* Prescott, Ariz., 1881. Reprint, San Francisco: A. L. Bancroft, 1884.

Heitman, Francis B. *Historical Register and Dictionary of the United States Army, 1789–1903.* 2 vols. Reprint, Urbana: University of Illinois Press, 1965.

Henderson, Patrick C. "The Peck Mine: Silver Bonanza in the Bradshaw Mountains." *Arizona and the West* 4 (autumn 1962): 227–36.

Hendricks, William D. *M. H. Sherman: A Pioneer Developer of the Pacific Southwest.* Corona del Mar, Calif.: Sherman Foundation, 1973.

Henson, Pauline. *Founding a Wilderness Capital: Prescott, A.T., 1864.* Flagstaff: Northland Press, 1965.

Herr, Pamela, and Mary Lee Spence. *The Letters of Jessie Benton Frémont.* Urbana: University of Illinois Press, 1993.

Hinton, Richard J. *The Hand-Book to Arizona: Its Resources, History, Towns, Mines, Ruins and Scenery.* San Francisco, 1878. Reprint, Glorieta, N.Mex.: Rio Grande Press, 1970.

Howard, John Raymond. *Remembrance of Things Past.* New York: Thomas Y. Crowell Company, 1925.

Jackson, Sheldon G. *Beautiful Glendora.* Azusa, Calif.: Azusa Pacific University Press, 1982.

Kane, Randy. "'An Honorable and Upright Man,' Sidney R. DeLong as Post Trader at Fort Bowie." *Journal of Arizona History* 19 (autumn 1978): 297–314.

Lister, Florence C., and Robert M. Lister. "Chinese Sojourners in Territorial Prescott." *Journal of the Southwest* 31 (spring 1989): 1–111.

Love, Frank. *Mining Camps and Ghost Towns: A History of Mining in Arizona and California along the Lower Colorado.* Los Angeles: Westernlore Press, 1974.

Lummis, Charles F. *A Bronco Pegasus.* Boston: Houghton Mifflin, 1928.

Lyon, William Henry. *Those Old Yellow Dog Days: Frontier Journalism in Arizona, 1859–1912.* Tucson: Arizona Historical Society, 1994.

May, Ernst R. "Tiburcio Vásquez." *Historical Society of Southern California* 29 (Sept.–Dec. 1947): 123–35.

McGroarty, John Steven. *Los Angeles: From the Mountains to the Sea.* 3 vols. Chicago: American Historical Society, 1921.

Moody, Eric N., ed. *Western Carpetbagger: The Extraordinary Memoirs of "Senator" Thomas Fitch: Western Carpetbagger.* Reno: University of Nevada Press, 1978.

Nelson, Kitty Jo Parker. "Prescott: Sketch of a Frontier Capital, 1863–1900" [with map of the town]. *Arizoniana* 4 (winter 1963): 17–38.

Nichols, Roberta. "Lily." *Los Fierros* 13, no. 3. Long Beach, Calif.: Docents of Rancho Los Cerritos and the Long Beach Public Library, 1976.

Officer, James E. "The Frémont House." Unpublished ms., 1993.

Park, Charles S. "Walter Vail and the Empire Ranch." *True West* 42 (March 1995): 36–41.

Powell, Ruth, and Chuck Powell. "Chester Place." Pamphlet. Los Angeles: Historical Society of Southern California and the Southern California Chapter of the American Institute of Architects, 1964.

Quebbeman, Francis E. *Medicine in Territorial Arizona.* Phoenix: Arizona Historical Foundation, 1966.

Smith, Dean. *The Goldwaters of Arizona.* Flagstaff, Ariz.: Northland Press, 1986.

Spence, Mary Lee, ed. *The Expeditions of John Charles Frémont.* Vol. 3, *Travels from 1848 to 1854.* Urbana: University of Illinois Press, 1984.

Spude, Robert L. "A Land of Sunshine and Silver: Silver Mining in Central Arizona, 1871–1885." *Journal of Arizona History* 16 (spring 1975): 30–76.

Thrapp, Don L. *The Conquest of Apacheria.* Norman: University of Oklahoma Press, 1967.

Vicinus, Martha. *Independent Women: Work and Community for Single Women.* Chicago: University of Chicago Press, 1985.

Wagoner, Jay J. *Arizona Territory, 1863–1912: A Political History.* Tucson: University of Arizona Press, 1970.

Wallace, Andrew. "Fort Whipple in the Days of the Empire." *The Smoke Signal* [Tucson Corral of the Westerners] (fall 1972): 114–40.

Wollenberg, Charles M. "Recollections of Arizona, 1876–1891." *Western States Jewish Historical Quarterly* 15 (Oct. 1982): 31–39.

Newspapers and Periodicals

Arizona Citizen (Tucson), 1879–1881. Title varies: *Weekly Arizona Citizen, Daily Arizona Citizen.*

Arizona Enterprise (Prescott), Sept. 1, 1878–July 5, 1879.

Arizona Miner (Prescott), 1878–1881. Title varies: *Weekly Arizona Miner, Daily Arizona Miner,* etc.

Arizona Star (Tucson), 1879–1881. Title varies: *Arizona Weekly Star, Arizona Daily Star.*

Arizona Weekly Democrat (Prescott), 1880–1882. Title varies: *Weekly Arizona Democrat* or simply *Arizona Democrat.*

Army and Navy Journal (New York), 1890.

Herald (Phoenix), 1881.

New York Times, 1878–1881.

Out West (Los Angeles).

Sharlot Hall Gazette (Prescott), 1980.

Spirit of Missions (New York), 1879.

Times (Los Angeles).

Index

Fitch, Thomas, 9, 37, 42, 47, 102, 233n; discourses of, 42, 49; goes east, 71, 75–76, 245n; and lottery, 61; returns to Arizona, 85; and Smith divorce, 243n; and theater, 46, 111

Foster, Mr., 53, 63, 64, 65, 66, 69, 156, 213, 240n

Fowler, Reginald, 69, 80, 246n; wife of, 98

Frémont, Elizabeth Benton (Lily), 13–21; alienated from Willcox, 177, 185, 212; attends weddings, 108, 163–64; celebrates Silent's vindication, 183; comments on preacher, 106; defends Silent, 162; depends on Silent, 151, 196; describes journey to Prescott, 25–39; describes petroglyph, 122–23, 252n; dislikes small politics, 207; distributes trees, 175; experiences in Tucson, 215–20; feels invitation slight, 177; fondness for Silent, 20; gives Evans French lessons, 80, 81, 84, 94, 96; headaches of, 43, 65, 72, 116, 150; loneliness of, 20–21, 214; reacts to chimney fire, 156; reading material of, 65, 66, 70, 74, 75, 97, 117, 143, 166, 190, 197, 206; receives flowers, 99, 169, 173, 189; receives fruit, 166, 173, 185, 190, 202, 203; receives mirror, 91; returns to New York, 220, 263n; rides horseback, 43; serves as father's secretary, 57, 75, 78, 115, 124; sews, 45, 66, 72, 113; spends Thanksgiving alone, 124; visits a poor woman, 205–6; walks and picnics of, 75, 98, 119–20, 173; worries over Silent's dysentery, 191–95; writes to Mrs. Silent, 164

Frémont, Francis Preston (Frank), 3, 24, 25, 31; as actor, 40, 48, 54, 71; army appointment of, 85, 93, 94, 96, 97, 99, 100, 108; as father's aide, 44, 46, 57, 61, 75, 78; Fort Whipple assignment of, 114, 115; friendship with officers, 48, 85, 94; goes to Camp Verde, 75, 77–78; looks at mines and ranches, 40, 41, 107–8; ordered to Montana, 119, 120; plays organ and piano, 23, 42, 70–71, 72, 73; plays violin, 57, 68; visits San Francisco, 61, 64, 66; writes to EBF, 18–19, 126, 137, 139, 148

Frémont, Jessie Benton, 3, 5, 7, 24, 31, 33, 37, 50; considers Thibodo house, 103; consults Rogers on Silent affair, 159; goes east on mining business, 11, 114, 115, 116, 119; illness of, 23, 42, 47, 48, 137; possessions burn, 220, 263n; receives fruit, 64, 93; rents house in east, 145, 147; reports on business, 125, 127, 129, 130, 153, 155, 170; sends flowers for Gosper, 78; sewing and needlework of, 54, 65, 66, 68, 70, 71, 72, 80, 90; teaches history class, 41, 42, 67, 70, 73, 75, 78, 84; urges transfers for sons, 16; visits Morton, 122; writes for JCF, 53, 57, 61, 86

Frémont, John Charles: appointed governor, 5, 23; checkered career of, 3–5; considers Weber place, 138; examines mining property, 41, 107–8, 145–47, 236n; fears undercutting by Bean, 129; goes east, 16, 62, 156, 213; goes to Yuma on business, 124–25; and Indians, 40, 104; issues Thanksgiving proclamations, 40, 213; meets with mining experts, 105, 106; message to legislature, 46–47; mining business of, 81, 84, 94, 101, 141; mining syndicate of, 104, 109, 112; plans move to Tucson, 203, 213; plans to meet Hayes, 207; possible loss of mines, 111, 112; proposes inland sea, 68, 244n; reacts to Indian unrest, 117–18, 120, 127; reacts to news of Salt River reservation, 55–56, 242n; receptions for, 39, 40, 210; recommends Silent for judgeship, 13; relations with legislature, 59; resigns governorship, 17, 263n; returns to Prescott, 15, 101, 212–13; takes oath of office, 37; writes and speaks on schools, 47, 50–51

La Motte, Mrs. Robert Smith, 114, 122, 127, 209, 251n

Lawrence, Hannah, 41, 236n

Lewis, Sol, 68, 89, 122, 165, 175, 198, 240n

Lewis, Mrs. Sol, 51, 83, 91, 93, 183, 240n; daughters of, 122, 158, 214, 257n

Lightfoot, Frank, 156, 159, 257n

Lincoln, Oscar, 123, 191, 192, 253n

Long, Joseph, 192, 193, 204, 259n

Lord, James Henry, 31, 32, 39

Luke, Mrs. Charles A., 83, 99, 118, 247n

Lummis, Charles F., 17, 18, 19, 20, 21

Magrath (driver), 31, 39

Marion, John Huguenot, 151, 256n–57n

Markham, Pauline, 139, 141

Martin, Alice, 151, 170, 238n; as actress, 46, 71; baby of, 70

Martin, James Porter, 105, 121, 129, 105, 177, 238n; as actor, 41, 71

Martin, Mary, 49, 239n

Masonic Order: cemetery of, 45; holds ball, 131; holds installation ceremonies, 42

Masterson, Murat, 71, 245n; wife of, 203

Maynard, George W., 105, 106, 250n; examines mining property, 107–8, 109, 110, 115; telegraphs about hydraulic property, 121

McCandless, Kate, 205, 261n

McClintock, Georgie H., 120, 153–54, 178, 181, 203, 252n; mother of, 201, 260

McDowell, Irvin, 30, 232n

McGrath, Mary (maid), 23, 25, 31, 50, 82, 230n; assists Catholic Sisters, 80, 82, 223; assists during Silent's illness, 191, 192; attends ice cream social, 199; attends July 4 picnic, 190; attends wedding, 147; growling fits of, 42, 43, 133–34; in Tucson, 216; moves into FPF's vacant room, 116

McKee, James Cooper, 40, 71, 79, 94, 107, 177, 234n; gives dinner party, 172

McLean, Robert H., 37, 233n; news of, 49–50, 68, 69, 99, 106, 244n

McMillan, A. T., 71, 72, 73, 86, 87, 245n

Meade, W. K., 56, 243n

mines: Accidental, 163; Big Bug, 84, 89, 108, 247n; Black Warrier, 88, 122, 130, 152, 154, 155, 177, 179, 190, 197, 210, 248n; Castle Dome, 32; Copper King, 220, 262n; Eureka (in Black Hills), 110, 122, 144, 147, 220, 262n; General Crook, 92; Gray Eagle, 142, 254n–55n; Jerome (Copper King and Eureka); Neahr, 147, 181, 255n; Peck, 75, 149, 245n–46n; Silver Belt, 121, 126, 127, 145, 206, 252n; Tiger, 125; Tonto Basin, 99, 129, 130, 145; Tuscumbia, 149, 152, 154, 167, 168, 173, 190, 197, 210; "Yonkers," 146–47, 149, 153, 181, 189, 255n. See also Silver Prince

Mont. See LaMont, Charles A.

Morgan, Benjamin, 39, 156, 234n; wife of, 56

Morris, Mother Mary Basil, 82, 83, 87, 159, 247n

Morton, William Jeremiah, 24, 25, 26, 31, 35, 39, 41, 230n; engagement and marriage of, 64, 176, 185, 188

Murphy, Frank M., 104, 199, 250n; brother of, 181, 258n

Noch-ay-del-klinne, 262n–63n

Noyes, Emma M., 79, 100, 135, 246n

Ogier, Mrs., 121, 156, 161, 164, 252n

Otis, Pamela L., 87, 88, 169, 248n

Otis, Theodore W., 99, 133, 248n

Oury, Granville H., 190, 259n

Palfrey, Carl F., 126, 172, 253n

Palmer, Joseph C., 29, 30, 137, 231n; in Arizona, 54, 55, 56, 57; pushes gravel mine, 112–14, 123, 127, 231n; wife of, 62, 244n

Palmer, Potter, 25

About the Author

Mary Lee Spence was born and reared in Texas. She has B.A. and M.A. degrees from the University of Texas and a Ph.D. from the University of Minnesota and had taught at Southwest Texas State University, San Marcos, and at Pennsylvania State University before becoming a member of the faculty in history at the University of Illinois, Urbana-Champaign, in 1973. She began her work on the Frémonts as coeditor and then editor of the multivolume set *The Expeditions of John Charles Frémont* (1970, 1973, 1984). With Pamela Herr, she edited *The Letters of Jessie Benton Frémont* (1993) and with Clark Spence, Fanny Kelly's *Narrative of My Captivity among the Sioux Indians* (1990). She is a past president of the Western History Association and professor emerita at the University of Illinois.